WITH

HEART,

MIND

&

STRENGTH

THE BEST OF
CRUX - 1979 - 1989
VOLUME ONE
EDITED BY DONALD M. LEWIS

CREDO
PUBLISHING CORPORATION

In memory of Klaus Bockmuehl (1931-1989)

Canadian Cataloguing in Publication Data

With heart, mind and strength

ISBN 0-920479-30-8

1. Bible - Criticism, interpretation, etc.
I. Lewis, Donald Munro, 1950-
B8540.W57 1990   220.6   C90-091213-8

Published by CREDO Publishing Corporation

ISBN 0-920479-30-8
(Paperback)

Cover design by Dal Schindell / A. Ison Design

CREDO Publishing Corporation
P.O. Box 3175
Langley, British Columbia V3A 4R5

Printed in the United States of America

Table of Contents

Section Four: History

Section Five: Inter-disciplinary Studies

Preface

The task of an editor is not an enviable one, especially when one is called upon to evaluate the writings of colleagues and friends. The limitations of space and finance constrain one's choice, as does the need to balance articles in different disciplines. Excellent material has been omitted; room has not been found for poetry.

This volume seeks to offer readers a balanced diet of Regent's best fare: articles in biblical studies, theology, spirituality, history and inter-disciplinary studies. These five areas are the foci of theological education at Regent College; the final category represents our special concern with the integration of Christian thought with all areas of learning and culture; hence articles under this rubric constitute the largest section of the book.

No apology need be offered for the fact that this collection includes four articles by Klaus Bockmuehl. In themselves they would justify the publication of this volume. Indeed, his contribution "The Greatest Commandment" has deliberately been chosen as the lead article inasmuch as its insights are so profound and challenging. It is this article which has suggested the title of this work.

Dr. Bockmuehl believed strongly in the value of the printed word and did much to promote and advance the publication of *Crux*, both as a supportive faculty member and as its editor over a period of four years. It is to his memory that this volume is dedicated.

My appreciation needs to be expressed to a number of people who made this volume possible: to Dal Schindell, the Managing Editor of *Crux* who handled the art direction of the work, proof-read the volume and who has been so helpful in putting this book together; to A. Ison Design for the cover artwork; to Wayne and Jocelyn Cameron of Credo Publishing for their assistance and advice in the production of the book; to Barbara McTier who has been such a patient and accurate typesetter; to J. I. Packer for his advice and for suggesting the title and writing the introduction; and to Hugh Steven for his involvement in the initial stages of the project. A final word needs to be expressed to the anonymous donor who has underwritten the cost of this volume: thank you.

Donald M. Lewis
Regent College
April, 1990

Introduction

Regent College has been fortunate in its names. *Regent,* lifted in 1969 from a development company, suggests both the dignity and the responsibility of man's cultural role under God as steward of creation. *Crux,* the already-established name of the quarterly that Regent took over in 1979, is Latin for *cross*: it suggests that here is a forum for matters of debate (*cruces*), and also that enquiries will be irradiated by the cross of Christ, from which alone the light of true wisdom flows. In no way are these suggestions misleading; handling God's creation for his glory is one of Regent's main concerns, and *Crux* has hewed to this twofold line throughout.

Regent College, now twenty years old, has always pursued the large vision of equipping the people of God, as such, for all the theologically informed activities that make up the worship and service of God, as such. Regent has a wider range than the conventional seminary or Bible college; Regent seeks to give wisdom and direction for all the relational and vocational responses to God in Christ that there are. This explains Regent's many interdisciplinary programmes, and also Regent's stress on the need for Christians to integrate all their living and thinking into that unity of vision, adoration, affection and endeavour which from an objective standpoint is one's worldview and from a subjective standpoint one's godliness. When Regent identifies lay vocation as its focus of concern, "lay" bears not its secular sense of "non-clerical," but its theological sense, whereby it includes all who belong to God's *laos,* the "laity" who are his people. Every concept, trend, and phenomenon that bears on Christian existence today thus becomes Regent's academic business, while the Regent community, though not itself a church, stands committed to practise Christian togetherness, cooperation, and support in all appropriate forms.

In pursuit of its vision and agenda, Regent College has been fortunate in both its teachers and its students, as also in the high-powered battalion of adjunct professors that it has built up over the years. Regent's unique sense of purpose has attracted an unusually gifted and enterprising cross-section of Christians, and the contents of *Crux*—mainstream evangelical yet not stereotypical; whether opening up the offbeat or reinforcing the conventional, always fresh and interesting—have constantly reflected this.

With Heart, Mind, and Strength: The Best of Crux 1979-89 seeks to cream off especially memorable material in a way that shows what essentially for the past decade Regent College, and *Crux* as its organ of expression, have been about: namely, the many modes of loving work for our God and our neighbour. The need to secure a proper coverage of disciplines and themes and a balanced parade of contributors, plus limitations of space that no form of entrepreneurial horse-trading could overcome, obliged the editor to omit much that he had at first hoped to print. The prominence given to superb articles by the late Klaus Bockmuehl, who edited *Crux* for some years and died in harness in 1989, needs no justification. Academically and spiritually he was a quiet giant, and Regent is poorer for his passing. In token of our gratitude to God for Klaus, this volume is dedicated to his memory.

J.I. Packer

The Great Commandment

Klaus Bockmuehl

Vol. XXII, No. 3 (September 1987):10-20

"But when the Pharisees heard that he had put the Sadducees to silence, they gathered together. Then one of them who was a lawyer, asked him a question, testing him, and saying, 'Teacher, which is the great commandment in the Law?' Jesus said to him, 'You shall love the Lord your God with all your heart, with all your soul and with all your mind. This is the first and great commandment. And the second is like it: You shall love your neighbour as yourself. On these two commandments hang all the Law and the Prophets' " (Matthew 22:34-40).

Jesus is under investigation. A scribe and Pharisee gives him an examination in ethics. He tries to catch him teaching some moral heresy.

But his question concerning which commandment was to be looked at as the highest of them all is at the same time an honest question. Pharisaism reckoned with roughly six hundred commandments, none of which was to be neglected. But could somebody really respect them all alike and to the same extent? Should one not be permitted to assume some order or rank of the commandments? This man, then, addresses to Jesus (the apparent innovator in ethics) a question which he had been discussing long and fruitlessly with his own colleagues.

The scribe here touches on a problem which we also constantly encounter today, even if we do not presuppose six hundred commandments: What is the heart of that large body of timeless and time-conditioned moral postulates? Which of the innumerable possibilities of human existence are we to realize first of all? As human beings, insecure and unfinished by nature, we can never get rid of the question of ethical preference as long as we have to choose, decide and act, to shape our own lives and to respond to our environment. Therefore, what are we to do above all? That is the honest question of the Pharisee, and it is our constant question, too. Let us try to understand Jesus' answer step by step.

I. "You should love the Lord your God with all your heart, with all your soul, and with all your mind."

I.a. "...love the Lord your God"

To start with, we need to recognize that Jesus' answer to this basic ethical question was thoroughly traditional, an answer which came from the very heart of the Old Testament. On the one hand, the commandment to love God was part of that fundamental Jewish formula of faith, "Hear, O Israel," (Deuteronomy 6:4). On the other, the commandment to love one's neighbour, found in the so- called Holiness Code (Leviticus 19:18), had long been understood as the summary of the second table of the Ten Commandments, i.e., those commands which cover the relationships between man and fellow man. Jesus, then, gives a totally traditional, non-revolutionary, unsensational, and unproblematic answer.

Unproblematic? According to Luke's report this Pharisee had immediate problems with the concept of neighbour. In Protestantism we do not even get that far. Our first problem arises with the very concept of love of God: Must we, may we, can we even love God? It is an open secret that concerning love of God the Protestant has to go and search for wisdom either in Roman Catholic spirituality, or perhaps with a few mysterious figures in the history of Protestantism who, however, clearly do not represent its mainstream.

Jesus says we are to love God, which is a harrowing postulate, especially today. We live in a climate of atheism, often enough unconsciously practise atheism ourselves, and find ourselves confronted with conscious and theoretical atheism. "We don't need God as a hypothesis" is the tenor of our time. God is no longer the presupposition of human thought, neither in the humanities, nor the social and natural sciences. Even in theology it has become fashionable to call for an understanding of human existence *quasi Deus non daretur*, as if God did not exist. Occasionally, like a voice in the wilderness some poet may cry "It is time to think of God," or a philosopher finds God an object still worthy of study. But to *love* God?—too much seems to speak against that.

In antiquity Aristotle thought it inappropriate to speak of love of God; the leading philosopher of modern times, Kant, resumed this attitude reasoning that we can only love something that is an object of our senses. Even more influential was the repudiation of love of God by Martin Luther the Reformer. He taught: we cannot love God in his majesty; we must love God in his creatures. God wants to be loved in our afflictions, and in the person of our neighbour, but not directly, without intermediary. Rather, we must love God where we know that he is, i.e., in the preaching of his Word, in our parents and in those in authority over us.

The Protestant Reformation developed this doctrine in reaction to a medieval theory which supposed religious works and love of God to be meritorious and thus had corrupted the doctrine of justification by grace alone. However, as happens so frequently, Protestants have absolutized this Reformational response which made more sense in its relative, immediate historical situation. Modern Protestant theology, adding philosophical and theological arguments, seems to be united in declaring: God can only be loved in the person of our neighbour. Only Karl Barth in his later years, through constant study of Scripture and especially of the Gospel of John, was led to a correction of this position which earlier had also been his own, acknowledging that there is indeed such a thing as love of God and love of Jesus.

We have to put these traditions of our own scribes and elders on the side and recover and preserve the biblical teaching. "You shall love the Lord your God" dominates some of the most important passages of the Old Testament. It is the centerpiece not only of the "Hear, O Israel" but also of the preface to the Ten Commandments (Deuteronomy 5), and returns in a weighty summary at the end of the book of Deuteronomy: "I call heaven and earth to witness against you this day, that I have set before you, life and death, blessing and curse; therefore choose life, that you and your descendants may live, *loving the Lord your God*, obeying his voice, and cleaving to him; for that means life to you and length of days . . . "

In the fundamental passage, "Hear, O Israel," the commandment of love of God is the logical consequence of the oneness of God: "Hear, O Israel: the Lord our God is one Lord," *therefore* "you shall love the Lord your God." The oneness of God can only be matched by the wholehearted commitment which we describe with the word "love."

This correlation continues in the New Testament. Jesus blames his Jewish adversaries because of their lack of love: "If God were your Father you would love me" (John 8:42). And Paul even calls love of Jesus, God's Son and Messiah, the sign of membership in the

Christian church: "If anyone does not love the Lord Jesus Christ, let him be *anathema*," i.e., excluded from the church (1 Corinthians 16:22), since those who are called because of divine election would love God. Therefore, too, all things must work together for good to them. God's grace remains unchanged over all who love the Lord Jesus Christ. Moreover, the Apostle Peter, preempting Kant's dictum, expressly praises those believers as blessed, who love the Lord Jesus without having seen him (1 Peter 1:8). Finally, the passage "the Lord may direct our hearts into the love of God" remains important all the time as it demonstrates that Paul makes love of God the object of his blessing for churches.

However, in spite of all these biblical testimonies, the commandment to love God strikes us as alien, even beyond our inherited philosophical and theological prejudices. It meets human nature like a message from another planet. Is it not utterly strange to our way of thinking that on the one hand we should understand God as Lord, i.e., acknowledge him as the authority above us, and on the other hand love this Lord, love the authority over us? The mind of the twentieth century does not expect to love authorities.

Today, even where the existence of the divine is taken for granted, do we not rather hear the voice of Prometheus, the ancient mythical rebel: "I hate all gods?" Or, if not hate, is it not rather fear of the gods and their unpredictability that dominates the history of religions? Closer to home, in our own time, are not many simply ignorant of God? They don't know what has become of him, and they don't want to know. They don't care. They observe strict neutrality with regard to God. Others again, in their God relationship, resemble marriage partners living in separation: they continue their legal status but are no longer on speaking terms.

Again others in this sequence of attitudes are willing to respect the God and father of Jesus Christ, but they demand that religion be kept in its proper place and don't want to see faith take over direction of a person's life. Some do take trouble with God and strive beyond this well tempered God relationship. But even they seem to be miles away from actually loving God. But the commandment demands nothing less than that. What we thus understand as a pinnacle of piety rarely ever attained, Holy Scripture seems to describe as a normal state of affairs.

The Bible defines loving God making use of three additional qualifications: "with all your heart, with all your soul, and with all your mind." We quickly tend to think that Scripture here speaks a bit plerophorically, and what is really meant is just generally a commitment of the whole person. However, the three qualifications given, point so precisely to three different aspects of the mental and spiritual organization of man that it seems appropriate to look at them individually.

I.b. "... with all your heart"
This phrase envisages the inward center representing the totality of human life, i.e., the commandment to love God addresses the whole content of our life. The heart stands for the person him- or herself: no merely exterior service, only the free self-giving of our will counts. As Calvin put it: love of God is the beginning of all religion for God does not want human obedience that is merely enforced. In biblical thought the heart connotes the will of a person. The commandment therefore aims at conscious, intentional commitment to God. Charles de Foucauld, the saint of the Sahara, frequently emphasized: love must be willed. Under this perspective, love of God turns to obedience. Affective love becomes effective love. We are to love God, like our brethren, not only in word or in tongue, but in deed and in truth (1 John 3:18).

In this way love develops both persistence and faithful service, right in the conditions of every day life. The rapture of passion is converted into sustained work. This is true for human love. The lover builds a dwelling place for the loved one, tries to help the other one, makes the concerns of the beloved his own. It is the same with the love of God: whoever loves God, will take a passionate interest in the state of God's affairs in the whole world, and attempt to further their progress in every field, as best as he can. Love "with all your heart" is active and at work. But it also allows itself to be directed and guided by God. For stubborn love would be a contradiction in itself.

I.c. "... with all your soul"
Soul emphasizes the emotional side, desire, longing, the sentiments.

In this sense, love expresses itself firstly in joy over the beloved. It can be a secret inner glow, but also an enthusiasm shining in the world. Its dedication comes to the fore in a verse like "A day in your courts is better than a thousand. I would rather be a doorkeeper in the house of my God than dwell in the tents of wickedness" (Psalm 84:10). Yet the loving soul feels not only joy and admiration, it has a real passion for its object. To love God with all one's soul—the psalmist gave expression to this when he wrote, "As the deer pants for the water brooks so pants my soul for you, O God. My soul thirsts for God, for the living God. When shall I come and appear before God?" (Psalm 42:1f). To "love God with all your soul" means to think of him at night and in the morning (Psalm 63:6).

Can a person be so captured by God, so exclusively filled by and concerned with him? Do we know God as such a comprehensive and engaging reality? Hebrew poetry says, "Love is strong as death, jealousy is cruel as the grave. Its flashes are flashes of fire, a most vehement flame" (Song of Solomon 8:6). Is that our concept of love of God? Do we rejoice with God or suffer with him when his honour, the validity of his commandments, or the advance of his Gospel is at stake? Or do we remain cool with regard to the course of God's concerns in this world? Then we would not love God with all our soul.

Lovers are people of a single topic. To love means to, as it were, move to an "eccentric position," that is to move out of oneself and find one's centre and one's meaning in the other one, in God, no longer within oneself. To love means to put oneself at risk; it has an affinity with the passion of the gambler. Love never settles for mediocrity.

Where passion and the will to act meet we see men of God like the prophet Elijah. Also the martyrs of the church at all times are witnesses of this love, true lovers who would rather be separated from their body than from the One they loved. We should not be surprised to see the half-committed reject those who are fully committed. Are we still able to love, or has our sophistication taken away that ability?

The lover, especially when he has been strengthened by his decision, now dwells somewhere else with his whole heart and soul. But he does not become mindless and inattentive about what he has to do. Rather, even in the tasks of the normal working day he is motivated by the thought of the Beloved, and with the eagerness of love seeks to shape the world for him and for the common future. Whoever loves God, has it as his goal that God's will be done in all his creatures, in his whole creation. He strives to make of each of his works a ministration and "something beautiful for God."

I.d. "... with all your mind"

Love is a sentiment—that we know. It also claims a person's will—that we have heard. But what of the mind, the faculty of thought? Can we love with our thought? Is it not the virtue of the mind and of reason to be without passion? Does it not rather look at the eagerness of love with a hidden smile and a hint of skepticism?

Unfortunately, the history of Christian piety seems to confirm this division. Pietism and other early forms of Evangelicalism reclaimed the love of Jesus which seemed to have been abandoned by the

Reformation. Pietists understood this love primarily as sentiment and also, in some places —we think of their dedication to missions and evangelism—as the surrender of the will, the practical stance which gladly serves Jesus and his commission. But "to love God with all our mind"? For many Evangelicals the world of thought is a remote part of their view of the universe and not easily reached by the transforming power of the gospel.

However, it is quite unacceptable that our minds should be excluded from the rule of God. Reason needs to be put at God's disposal just as much as our other faculties. All the traditional "fear of thought" and the mistrust that piety has often felt towards philosophy, does not justify abstinence from reason and thought. At this point a distinction becomes absolutely necessary, a distinction which Paul already made when he wrote: Our weapons in God's service are strong enough to destroy all "arguments and every high thing that exalts itself against the knowledge of God." Arguments are being liquidated but the faculty of thinking, the mind, is brought "into captivity to the obedience of Christ" (2 Corinthians 10:5).

To love God "with all your mind"—with its choice of expression the Old Testament describes more precisely that type of thought which can become serviceable to the love of God. We could translate the concept appropriately as "practical reason." It denotes the ability to distinguish and the exclusively human faculty to plan and project. The Old Testament uses the very same term in characterizing the "skilled designer" and "every able man in whom the Lord has put ability and intelligence to know how to do any work," i.e., in accordance with the instructions of the Lord, regarding the construction of the sanctuary (Exodus 36:1). In another pertinent passage the term is used of King Solomon in whom was the wisdom of the Lord which enabled him to pronounce righteous judgment.

It is that quality of mind or type of thought that one needs to make the right decisions with a view to one's actions. It is the quick eye of love. Correspondingly, Paul prays for his churches that they might attain precisely this gift, so that their love would "abound still more and more in knowledge and in all discernment" and explicitly in the direction of the "fruit of righteousness" with which they must be adorned for the day of Christ's return (Philippians 1:9-11).

If we are to love God "with all your mind" then this type of love, although passionate, clearly is not blind but circumspect and discerning in the pursuit of its aims.

In summing up: God seeks our counter-love with all the abilities that he has been furnished us with, namely will, feeling, and thought. Our love is determined, joyful, passionate and circumspect, all at the same time.

We recognize such a comprehensive love in Jesus. He put his whole life at God's disposal; "the life that he lives, he lives to God" (Romans 6:10). He fully observed and implemented the first commandment, passionately serving the one God and no one else beside him. He loved God with all his heart, his soul, and his mind. Such love existed on earth.

Acknowledging this, we arrive at a climax that looks like the final act of the story. Have we described a state of perfection and a way of life that for us must resemble the dream vacation proposed by a colourful brochure, which nevertheless remains financially quite unattainable to us? Is loving God an "impossible possibility"? And yet we are dealing with a divine commandment. So we find ourselves on the horns of a dilemma. With good reason, some theologians therefore immediately interpret this commandment merely in terms of accusation. To love God so completely is impossible to realize. It can only show us what we are lacking. And at this point we need honesty about ourselves before God in order to learn the truth about ourselves: our lack of love for God and our remarkably small willingness and ability to give God more of ourselves. In short, we do love God, yes, but with what strength?

Scripture has a simple and straightforward answer to this question. It observes, "We love him because he first loved us" (1 John 4:19). Similarly, in the Old Testament, the fact of God's love is the presupposition of the commandment to love him. Although "heaven and the heaven of heavens, the earth and all that is in it" belong to God, "yet the Lord set his heart in love upon your fathers and...descendents..." a small, insignificant nation (Deuteronomy 10:14f.). The commandment to love God meets man as the invitation of him who has said: "My heart yearns for him. I will surely have mercy on him" (Jeremiah 31:20).

Thus our love for God is to be the response to God's love for us. That is what Jesus teaches in his parable of the Two Debtors with the conclusion: He who loves much does so because his many sins have been forgiven (Luke 7:47). Love of God is nothing that we can or should mount from our own resources. Love of God stems from gratitude for forgiveness experienced.

This is supported by another observation: a peculiarity of the text of our passage in the Old Testament Hebrew original points to a parallel in the creation story. It reminds us that the One who gives this commandment is none other than the One who has created the world. "You shall love God" therefore is also to be understood as:

It shall come to pass that you love God. The commandment of the creator contains a promise. This promise is being fulfilled by the Holy Spirit through whom the love of God has been poured out into our hearts (Romans 5:5). Love is a gift of God himself, a piece of the new world. It is a beginning, certainly beyond our own possibilities, but a beginning for which we can pray just as for all the other gifts of the Spirit.

II. "And the second is like it"

If we found the commandment to love God a controversial topic, this statement of Jesus challenges us once more. The commandment to love God is being called the first and great commandment; but now paradoxically, the second commandment, the command to love our neighbour is to be just as great and important as the first: "This is the first and the great commandment and the second is like it: You shall love your neighbour as yourself." We are faced with the fact that Christian love has *two* objects: God *and* our neighbour.

At this point human reason goes on strike. Ludwig Feuerbach, the great nineteenth century critic of Christianity raised his voice in protest claiming the seemingly obvious objection of logic: You cannot at the same time look at heaven and at the earth unless you are cross-eyed. In the same vein, others in our own time have declared: Love for God is love stolen from one's neighbour.

Martin Luther struggled with this twofold perspective: "Both seem to be against each other. There are two looks in the one word." If you do love God with your whole heart, you no longer have room in your heart, even less your whole heart free for your neighbour. Luther solved the problem by interpreting the *equality* of the two commandments, in the sense taught by Jesus, as an *identity* or sameness: "Jesus melts the two commandments into one and makes them the same work." Perhaps this is a logical consequence of his discounting of the love of God which we mentioned earlier. In reaction against the opposite onesidedness with which people in the Middle Ages, at the expense of neighbourly love put all their energy into works dedicated to God, Luther now demands ministry to the neighbour to such an extent that he turns love of God into love of neighbour. He quotes the proverbial ancient desert saint who had said: "If I spoke with people I could not speak with angels," and replies: "Love your neighbour! With these angels we are to speak!" So the Reformer reflects antithetically the earlier onesidedness which had reduced the double commandment to the commandment to love God.

At this point, we feel some more caution is in place. Certainly, the bond between the two commandments can be cut and one of the two be lost. But if we pursued Luther's argument further we might also have to replace prayer with dialogue with other people, just as it has recently been suggested by some secularist theologians. That is, however, not the intention of the Bible, neither concerning prayer nor regarding love. Unmoved by the objections of reason and human logic the Apostle writes: "And this commandment we have from him: that he who loves God love his brother *also*" (l John 4:2l). That is not a bad rendering of the double commandment of the Master himself.

The Pharisee and lawyer had (just like ourselves) asked for *one* highest commandment. Jesus answered with two: there is not only one, but *two greatest* commandments. Although this contradicts our common garden logic and our tendency to reduce everything to a single principle, we simply must learn and hold fast: Christian love, like the ellipse, has two foci. Truth in the New Testament often comprises two apparently competing (if not seeming irreconcilable) concepts. It is like the formula of "two times one hundred percent": one hundred percent justification by grace and one hundred percent sanctification in good works; one hundred percent love of God and one hundred percent love of neighbour. These things cannot be exhausted by our limited and antithetical categories of thought.

Yet even so, a question remains: Is that which seems to be theoretically impossible to the human mind practically possible? The answer is: In the history of Christianity, those who loved God with all their heart, and all their strength also became great benefactors of people. One could mention a number of names but Jesus himself is the best example of the realization of this love; he is the incorporated image of the implementation of the double commandment. He loyally served people *because* he remained faithful to God's commission.

III. "You shall love your neighbour as yourself"

III.a. Love of neighbour, not "self-fulfillment"

Even if the commandment to love God was met with different objections one should think that the commandment to love one's neighbour would receive the undivided applause of everyone. That is not the case, however. A good part of our natural practical behaviour is already adverse to this commandment. "Charity begins at home," we say, and mean: the Ego, "Number One" comes first. On an international level it was revealing to see how the oil crisis quickly undermined existing alliances. It demonstrated that in moments of decision egoism tends to determine our actions.

But our theories are not much better than that. Some are convinced that, anyway, "Everybody is an island." Others consciously cultivate "splendid isolation" and favour an exclusive life-style. The commandment to love one's neighbour conflicts with the fashionable and pervasive programme of "self-fulfillment." It is being proclaimed and accepted as a great discovery but in truth, it is as old as the mountains: already the ancient philosophy of the Stoa taught that one's conduct of life must foremost serve the development of one's self. Life was to be compared to the expressive action of an artist, as contrasted to that of a physician attending others. Here, the prudent person seeks perfection in himself.

Biblical ethics, on the contrary, points us not to a cultivation of ourselves but to our neighbour. The Creator "commended to each one his neighbour" (Ecclesiastes 17:12). Self-fulfillment of individuals must create havoc in inter-personal relationships, just as national self-fulfillment has created oppression and destruction on an international level. Again, we are to serve our fellow man concretely and not abstract ideals like justice, prudence or general philanthropy. Even Christian activism can fail to meet this commandment as is shown in the following little anecdote: One of my senior friends, a pastor now deceased, once dreamt that he was led into a churchyard and before a tomb. There on the stone he could make out read his name and birthday; the day of his death remained unclear. Below ran the caption: "He was too busy to care for people." From that day on my friend changed his life completely. In order to safeguard us from the mistake of loveless activism Jesus instructed his disciples: "A new commandment I give to you that you love one another; as I have loved you, that you also love one another" (John 13:34).

III.b. Who is my neighbour?

Once we have established the basic commandment we seem to run immediately into the next problem, i.e., how to define the term neighbour. What does it include or exclude, to what extent will it go, and where are its limits? Again, it is almost natural that the concept of neighbour should be problematic. The ancient Greeks (not much different from ourselves!) thought of social life and loyalties in terms of concentric circles around the ego. Friendships, e.g., would work out best with someone from one's own family or relations, and beyond that perhaps with a person of the same age and the same social standing. The Jews thought similarly. They, too, raised the

question: "Who is my neighbour?" Pharisaism enquired into the
limits of love of neighbour and came up with the answer: "You must
love your fellow countryman but you may hate your enemy."
Indeed, in the Old Testament the neighbour often is the nearest
relative, a close friend, the farming neighbour, in short: the
members of one's people. Therefore, e.g., it was forbidden to take
interest from a fellow Israelite, but not from the stranger.

Many prominent Christian teachers interpret the commandment
to love one's neighbour quite in the same fashion. One's neighbours
are father, mother, brother, sister, husband, wife, and children.
Especially in the tradition of the Protestant Reformation, love of
neighbour is primarily *pietas domestica*, the ethics of the family and
the house. True enough! We are to love the people close to us, the
younger ones and the older ones that have been committed to our
care. To honour our parents with personal attention and interest,
granting them fellowship in their old age when they easily become
lonely—this understanding of the commandment to love our
neighbour is certainly correct and may already prove a tough test of
our practical Christianity. But there is still more to it.

We have an authentic interpretation of the concept of neighbour
in Jesus' parable of the Good Samaritan. To begin with, Jesus
replaces the ego with the neighbour as the centre of our worldview.
More over, he explodes the limitations of our natural concept of
neighbour. Intentionally, it seems, Jesus chooses for his parable a
situation not in the city, or in the house and family but *on the road*. He
forces us beyond our homestead horizon. In his parable the
neighbour is a stranger. In addition, he is the weak who cannot help
himself. Our attention and our help is to be focussed especially on
the sick and burdened, on all those whose life is reduced. There is
enough misfortune in the world, and people who suffer from it.
They need our assistance first. In the intention of Jesus, they are our
neighbours. Finally, Christian love of neighbour must necessarily
turn to exercising mercy everywhere in actions that aim at sustaining
life as were those of the Good Samaritan. Jesus returns to this theme
emphatically with his list of the so- called six bodily works of mercy
(Matthew 25:31-36): to give food to the hungry, drink to the thirsty,
shelter to the stranger, clothes to the naked, and the fellowship of
visiting to those sick and in prison. Jesus is convinced: "You have
the poor with you always" (Matthew 26:11); there will always be
occasion for acts of mercy. "Whoever has this world's goods, and
sees his brother in need, and shuts up his heart from him, how does
the love of God dwell in him?" (1 John 3:17).

The parable of the Good Samaritan teaches us, as we have said, to love the stranger, the foreigner, the one who does not belong to our own in-group, to our own tribe and nation. That reminds us of the remarkable instruction already found in the Old Testament: "Love the sojourner" (Deuteronomy 19:19). It establishes that love is not a "respecter of persons" in the sense of assessing their worth. Christian love differs from its ancient counter- image in that it does not only love the good, beautiful, dignified, useful, or that of related stock; it simply does not first make up an account of values, but then it also does not change when the neighbour changes. It serves everybody who needs our help, without partiality (James 2:1). As the parable of the Good Samaritan indicates and Jesus teaches on another occasion, Christian love even applies to the enemy and the persecutor. The Christian is to become a neighbour in a way which exceeds the limited ideals of Jews and Greeks.

The parable of the Good Samaritan also assumes the object of love's concern, the neighbour, is an individual human being and not a situation. The Good Samaritan does not first inaugurate a survey to analyse the situation; he does not rush back to Jerusalem in order to call for a thorough purging of the area of all bandits. He tends to the wounded before him. He does not think in terms of "the greatest happiness of the greatest number." The individuality of his love is obvious. In the eyes of Jesus love is not in the first place concerned with changing structures but with relief for the concretely suffering neighbour.

III.c. What does it mean to *love* one's neighbour?

If we continue to follow the parable of Jesus, love begins with seeing, with perception of persons, with attention for the need of a neighbour. Parallel to the qualities of love for God, love of neighbour combines affective compassion, determined action, and circumspection in the situation and beyond it. Love of neighbour is service. The Good Samaritan characteristically already fulfills Paul's rule, "Bear one another's burden, and so fulfill the law of Christ" (Galatians 6:2). In doing so, he generously puts his possessions at the disposal of his neighbour: his own donkey, wine and oil are immediately made available; money plays a role, too, not to speak of the time the benefactor loses. Love of neighbour means: to go out of one's way and to make the other's concern and need one's own. Here, indeed, is a man who not only looks towards his own interest, but also towards the interest of the other one, according to the example of Jesus (Philippians 2:4f).

The parable of the Good Samaritan teaches us, as we have seen, that love of neighbour according to Jesus is primarily concerned with the sustaining of life, with concern for the essentials of our neighbour's existence. We are to look after his fundamental needs. The parable clearly points to the needs of the body and to material provisions. No one who has listened to Jesus' parable will bypass and ignore this basic level.

However, the ministry of love cannot be limited to material assistance alone. Our neighbour has been entrusted to us at the same time with regard to the sustenance and growth of his spiritual life, his participation in the Kingdom of God, and his ongoing assimilation to Jesus Christ. The overall intention is that God's will may be done in the life of our neighbour just as in our own lives. Jesus looked after both the spiritual and physical needs of people. To love means to take responsibility for people, responsibility for their complete restoration.

Finally, love must be realized as we go. Let us not think that we shall do the good deeds once we have reached a certain goal or a higher level of spirituality in our own lives. It is a temptation to think like that. For the Christian, any time, any place, including the road, the secular locale, presents the location for love and service.

In order to open our eyes for our opportunities, Martin Luther insisted that we should serve our neighbour with the special gifts with which God has equipped us. He wrote: "If there is anything in us, it is God's gift and not our own. We owe it to the service of love and the law of Christ. I must use it to serve others and not myself. Thus my knowledge is not mine but belongs to those who are ignorant; I am their debtor. Similarly, whatever wisdom I have belongs to the unwise, whatever power, to the oppressed, whatever riches I have, to the poor, and my righteousness to the sinners, in order to sustain them all."

Love begins with the prayer of intercession. It opens our eyes to that which is necessary. It almost goes without saying that the merciful ministry of Christian love does not represent either a masochistic self-abasement and servility, as the anti-Christian philosopher Nietzsche branded it, or an act of patronizing condescension, as Kant saw it. Both interpretations would not apply to the action, e.g., of a physician either. Christian ministry is essentially comparable to medical action. It is an act freely undertaken by which we participate both in God's work of preservation and in Christ's work of salvation.

III.d. "...as yourself"

Again, the little phrase calls for precise attention as it represents a further stumbling block. We usually pick this sentence up with a slight reinterpretation as if it read: You shall love your neighbour *and* yourself. Many even say that one must first learn to love oneself before one can love others, and psychologists and counselors recommend "self-acceptance." It seems to be natural that in this respect everybody look after himself first. The debate over the interpretation of "as yourself" also had a prominent place in the history of theology. Did it mean that both were commanded, to love our neighbour *and* ourselves, or that we were told to love our neighbour according to the love that we have for ourselves?

Clearly, the latter is what the text says. "As yourself" defines the mode and not a second object of love. It states an exact parallelism to Christ's Golden Rule which says that we are to love our neighbour according to the example of love that we already have for ourselves. "Whatever you want men to do you, you also do to them" (Matthew 7:12). That is the proper interpretation of "as yourself."

It is only through the Protestant Reformation that this understanding came to prominence again. In his expositions of Romans, Galatians, and the parable of the Good Samaritan, Martin Luther again and again argued in this direction: "What do you do for yourself? Well, whatever you do for yourself, you should also do for your neighbour. You certainly don't let yourself go hungry, but look after your body with garment, food, and rest, in illness you look after your health, you pray for yourself and ask for grace and that you may understand God's Word. Do all this also for your neighbour!"

In ourselves we possess the most instructive example and an ever present monitor; our own experience testifies to what we owe our neighbour at any given moment. Love of neighbour does not need books and experts. Whoever follows this commandment knows from his own life what is necessary. He makes his neighbour equal to himself in his needs exactly as Paul demands in his exhortations for the collection taken for Jerusalem (2 Corinthians 8 and 9). This interpretation seems to be confirmed also by the original Hebrew text of the Old Testament passage (Leviticus 19:18). An exact translation would run as follows: "Love your neighbour according to what or how you [are]." That is why Martin Buber, the famous Jewish philosopher rendered this text with the unforgettable words: "Love your neighbour. He is like you."

We have heard the clear, uncompromising divine command: "You shall love your neighbour." But even if we are agreed on its theoretical understanding, we are still a long way from actually practising it. With a view to the commandment the question once more arrives: but how, by what strength? Again here, we easily find ourselves on a level below neighbourly love, whether we hate our neighbour or think little of him or don't register him at all, or just tolerate him one way or other. All that is less than love. Honest people will admit that sometimes it requires them to make an effort to go beyond tolerance and neutrality to a positive, living relationship even with the people nearest to them. But if it already takes an effort in the family, what about the sick, the stranger and the enemy? Our forefathers said: look at the Ten Commandments and you will see that you have sinned against love.

What is to be done? Our gracious God knows that at this point we are in need of a motivation which we cannot generate ourselves. Therefore already the Old Testament points to God's steadfast love and mercy, by which he saved Israel from Egypt, from the house of bondage, as the foundation of love of neighbour. Jesus seems to indicate the same in his parable of the master of the merciless servant: "I forgave you all your debt. Should you not also have had compassion on your fellow servant?" (Matthew 18:32f.). That is God speaking. He lets us understand: Love of neighbour, too, arises from gratitude for forgiveness experienced. This also settles the frequent objection that one has to struggle to become a self first before one can love one's neighbour, because this commandment rests on the presupposition that God loves us, that we are already being loved, that we are already somebody, that we have dignity because of God's gift. That is why one no longer needs to battle to establish oneself but can forget oneself and begin to make the other one great.

IV. "On these two commandments hang all the Law and Prophets"

Jesus concludes his answer to the question of the Pharisee with an additional proposition. It deals with the relationship of law and love. It challenges another common contemporary prejudice. It describes the Double Commandment of Love as the focus of concentration of the law, and the law as the unfolding of love.

Our own time finds it difficult to accept a positive relationship between love and law. We tend to think that legalism necessarily is lovelessness, that the law is against love and love against law. At best we are willing to compare law and love with cocoon and butterfly or with dregs and wine. The Old and New Testaments have it—he who has ears to hear, let him hear—*differently*. The whole law, Jesus says, hangs on love like a door on its hinges. Correspondingly Paul writes: "Owe no one anything but to love one another, for he who loves another has fulfilled the law," and continues "And for this, 'you shall not bear false witness, you shall not covet,' and if there is any other commandment, it is *summed up* in this saying, namely, you shall love your neighbour as yourself" (Romans 13:8-10).

Love has a precise *organic* relationship to the law: it "recapitulates" the law, comprises its ordinances as in a summary. Love is the head, the commandments are the body and its members, just like according to Ephesians 1:10, all things in heaven and on earth are gathered together in one, i.e., Christ.

The Double Commandment of Love relates to the individual commandments, e.g. the Ten Commandments, like the source of the river. Love remains the ground and rule of the law. All individual commandments must be understood and interpreted from the commandment of love. We see this in the way Christ handles the Sabbath commandment. Love is the "royal law" (James 2:8).

Love relates to the individual commandments like the revealed formula of a curve which previously was only known by a number of mathematical points. Similarly, one could describe love's relationship to the commandments using the image of a circle surrounded by tangents. The commandments are so many descriptions of places of love, limitations of a rigid kind, "definitions," approximations, auxiliary devices, attempts to, for the time being, comprehend the living thing using lifeless concepts. The commandments can only "circumscribe" the perfection of love. The law is the framework of love. It describes the terrain in which love will be active.

For the coordination of law and love, then, the following two statements are valid and in order:

First, love unfolds into the commandments. They serve it. The commandments are the shoes of love in which it walks through the working day. Luther, as always, has a stringent little example: the mother demands of her daughter that she love her, nothing else. But then, practically, the daughter shall help with the cooking and milk the cow. Will she also do that or grumble when love becomes concrete? "Thus God posits commandments manifold, but he only wants to test our love and give us opportunities to implement it." The works of the commandments are the outflow of love. That does away with *antinomianism,* the imagination that love stands for lawlessness.

Second, conversely, all commandments aim at love as their perfection (1 Timothy 1:5). That does away with *legalism,* the idea that biblical ethics consist of a mere observation of the commandments.

Love never goes hand in hand with lawlessness. It is in alliance with the law and the prophets. According to a memorable word of Jesus (Matthew 24:12), love will grow cold when (and because) lawlessness will abound. This establishes that love cannot coexist with lawlessness.

"If you love me, keep my commandments," says Jesus (John 14:15). The law is to the activity of love what canvas is to needlework. From the education by the commandments grows the discipline which is necessary for the ministry of love in service and missions, just as abstinence and prayer correspond with each other. Thus, the law is no longer a purpose in itself. It names the norms of preparation for the service of love in the discipleship of Jesus. Whosoever loves him, will keep his commandments.

The Ten Commandments: Are They Still Valid?

Klaus Bockmuehl

Vol. XV, No. 4 (December 1979):20-25

A re the ten commandments still valid for us today? Are they valid only for Christians, or for all people? Or are they perhaps only for Jews and pagans, but not for Christians? And is it merely piety or the inertia of conservatism that keeps them in our catechism, in the doctrinal strong-room of the church? Are they still with us simply because no one has dared to question the ancient moral habits of the church? Wouldn't a business, eager to rationalize for the sake of success, have long ago cleared them out and relegated them to a museum of the ancient Near East?

Some prominent speakers in the church have come to just this conclusion and caught the headlines with it. One, a German church president, stated that it was impossible to prescribe a catalogue of eternal norms of conduct; rather, the Christian was to decide in the given situation what love would command him or her to do. Therefore, when it came to personal ethics, the decalogue was out of the question. On another occasion this same man said that it was equally impossible in a pluralistic society to accept the ten commandments as the basis for social morality and the law of the state—something most countries took for granted until very recently.

Another Protestant ethicist, with earned doctorates in theology and sociology, brought his sociological thinking to bear on the decalogue. Calling the ten commandments "those ancient norms" and "a nomad law," he relativized them historically and sociologically. The civilized world of the industrial age was too far removed from the world of the ten commandments: they could hardly help us, let alone be authoritative. They were, rather, a hindrance to modern life.

According to at least two theologians, then—to put it in terms used during the Reformation—the decalogue belongs neither to the pulpit nor to the town hall. Where then does it belong? Merely to the history of Israel? How shall we answer these two suggestions? Should we agree with one or the other, and if not, why not? Why does the church continue to preach the ten commandments? To whom are the ten commandments given?

I shall try to answer these questions with three theses: 1) the ten commandments obligate the people of God to whom they are given; 2) the ten commandments recommend themselves to every person as an approproiate definition of the good; 3) the ten commandments are the framework of Christian ethics; they need to be filled with love, by the guidance of God's Spirit.

Is the decalogue valid today, and for whom? It is indeed still necessary to ask·these questions. While studying the Bible, it is of primary importance to take notice of the circumstances and context of the text. For example, consider this introduction to the ten commandments:

> And now, O Israel, give heed to the statutes and the ordinances which I teach you, and do them; that you may live, and go in and take possession of the land which the LORD, the God of your fathers, gives you. You shall not add to the word which I command you, nor take from it; that you may keep the commandments of the LORD your God which I command you (Deuteronomy 4:1-2).

To whom is this appeal of Moses directed? To "Israel," of course, and more exactly to a certain generation in the history of the people of Israel—those who came out of Egypt. The Exodus is the original historical setting of the ten commandments.

But is that single generation the only one to whom the decalogue is addressed? Already at Mt. Sinai, questions about the general and timeless applicability of these words were raised—the first precedent for similar questions asked today:

> When your son asks you in time to come, "What is the meaning of the testimonies and the statutes and the ordinances which the LORD our God has commanded you? (Deuteronomy 6:20).

"The Lord *our* God"—that the Lord of the decalogue is our God is accepted. But as to the commandments, we hear the little note of dissociation, as verses 21-25 go on to say, "which the Lord has commanded *you.*" This second generation was already being told that the commandments were binding on all generations of Israel, every living generation, because they all belong together as a "corporate personality."

The decalogue, then, is addressed to Israel, meaning this distinctive *nation* which has come from Egypt. The introduction to the actual text of the decalogue makes this point:

I am the LORD your God, who brought you out of the land of Egypt, out of the house of bondage (Exodus 20:2).

And in Deuteronomy, the peculiar and unique character of Israel is unmistakably expressed:

Or has any god ever attempted to go and take a nation for himself from the midst of another nation, by trials, by signs, by wonders, and by war, by a mighty hand and an outstretched arm, and by great terrors, according to all that the LORD your God did for you in Egypt before your eyes? (Deuteronomy 4:34).

Therefore, the answer must clearly be "No, the decalogue is not just addressed to a single generation." Israel is a special case. They are God's covenant people, and the ten commandments, as has been shown by Old Testament scholars, are the basic law and constitution of this covenant.

In his teaching on the decalogue and in general, Martin Luther stressed the importance of discerning to whom a biblical text is addressed, and especially "whether it means you." Concerning the ten commandments, he said: "From the text we clearly see that the Ten Commandments (as such) do not concern us. Because God has not brought us from Egypt, but only the Jews"(mentioned in his sermon of August 27, 1525, "Instruction on how Christians are to apply Moses"). Consequently, the law of Moses does not bind the Gentiles—it has no authority for non-Jews.

Such startling conclusions raise a number of questions: How then does the decalogue get into Luther's small and large catechism, and so into the confessional writings of the Lutheran Church? And why would Luther himself have expounded the decalogue, through preaching and print, more than a dozen times during his lifetime? How then does the decalogue get into the Christian church and pulpit? There are several answers to these questions.

First, although Christians do not belong to Israel in a biological sense, yet from the perspective of the history of salvation Christians are included in the "new covenant," are members of the one people of God:

That in Christ Jesus the blessing of Abraham might come upon the Gentiles (Galatians 3:14).

In another place, Paul makes the same point with an illustration which must have been as much a paradox to him as it still is to us:

> But if some of the branches were broken off, and you, a wild
> olive shoot, were grafted in their place to share the richness
> of the olive tree (Romans ll:l7).

If this is true, then we should ask not whether the ten
commandments are valid for us today, but rather how could the
Christian church ever legitimately drop them? One of the former
generation of Swiss Reformed theologians, one-time Professor of
Ethics in the University of Berne, Alfred de Quervain, therefore
concluded rightly: "As we for Christ's sake and through the gift of
the Holy Spirit have become members of this people, and as these
commandments make known God's will for all sanctified—they also
bind us. Christ has not come to abolish the commandments, but to
fulfill them" (*Die Heiligung*, 1946, p.248).

Second, it is by the authority of Christ that the ten
commandments are valid for all who follow him. Moses is an
authority for Christians insofar as Jesus took up his teaching. Jesus
took the ten commandments seriously, unconditionally. In his
meeting with the rich young ruler (Matthew 19:18), he quoted them
as the basic instruction for the way to eternal life. He submitted to
the decalogue when he contrasted God's commandments to the
traditions of the elders (Matthew 15:2). Part of his Sermon on the
Mount is based on commandments from the decalogue; his own new
teaching is a heightening, an intensification of the decalogue's
commandments and not, as is often said, an antithesis to them. (The
wording of the Sermon on the Mount—"you have heard that it was
said...But I tell you..."—is antithetical, but there is radicalization of
the commandments, not antithesis, in the *contents* of what Jesus
says.)

Jesus warned his listeners not to misconstrue what he intended,
something which could easily happen when no distinction is made
between God's commandments and human moral traditions.
"Think not that I have come to abolish the law and the prophets,"
Jesus said, "*I have come not to abolish them but to fulfill them*" (Matthew
5:17).

In his actions, too, Jesus is true to the commandments. His
much-debated actions on the sabbath are no exception. If there is to
be no contradiction between Jesus' words and his actions, then his
deeds on the sabbath have to be understood not as the abolition, but
as the fulfilment of the sabbath commandment. For Jesus said:

> For truly, I say to you, till heaven and earth pass away, not
> an iota, not a dot, will pass from the law until all is
> accomplished. Whoever then relaxes one of the least of
> these commandments and teaches men so, shall be called

least in the kingdom of heaven: but he who does them and
teaches them shall be called great in the kingdom of heaven.
For I tell you, unless your righteousness exceeds that of the
scribes and Pharisees, you will never enter the kingdom of
heaven (Matthew 5:18-20).

This righteousness that exceeds that of the Pharisees is the
righteousness given to us freely by God. Jesus makes this clear
when he rebukes the scribes and Pharisees for teaching harsh laws
but never living up to them themselves (Matthew 23:1-4). This
righteousness, though freely given by God, must be realized in the
sentiments of our heart as well as in our actual deeds—keeping the
commandments and doing the things the Spirit teaches us which by
far surpass the law. For those, then, who according to the "great
commission" have been taught to obey everything he commanded
his apostles, the ten commandments remain in force "till heaven and
earth pass away."

That the apostles repeated the commandments in the letters of the
early church, and that the church as a matter of course continued to
single out a special day of the week, witness to the validity of the
decalogue for the Christian church. The Lord God of Israel is the
Father of Jesus Christ. His character, his sanctity and righteousness
will not change. By reason of the authority of Christ, the ten
commandments are valid for the people of God, today as much as
when they were first given. They are the framework, the basis for
God's communion with his people. Observing them spells blessing,
transgressing them brings the curse of the Eternal.

Concerning the ten commandments, Karl Barth wrote:

The Decalogue...is...in fact the basic event in the story of
Israel—it unfolds the programme of the whole history of this
people...and therefore by implication of His elect
community...the Church. It was not, therefore, without
justification that the Decalogue was adopted as the basis of
the Christian catechism. It is the foundation-statute of the
divine covenant of grace and valid for all ages. Everything
that the true God, the Founder and Lord of this covenant,
has commanded and forbidden, or will command and
forbid, is to be found within the framework of the
programme of all His decisions and purposes as contained in
the Decalogue (*Church Dogmatics*, vol. II/2, p.685).

The third reason for retaining the decalogue in the teaching of the
church is that it is the best comprehensive description of the natural
law concept which binds all people. This is the theme of my second
thesis.

If, as we have seen, the decalogue is given particularly to the people of God, what does it say to people in general? We find an answer in Deuteronomy 4:6:

> Keep them and do them; for that will be your wisdom and your understanding in the sight of the peoples, who, when they hear all these statutes, will say, "Surely this great nation is a wise and understanding people."

The decalogue is described as the special property and privilege of Israel, something which they will contribute to the family of nations. It is assessed as being especially wise and worthy of praise by all nations. This verse indicates that these commandments will be considered astonishingly judicious and sensible by every nation; everyone will reckon them to be a standard definition of the good. Throughout history their value has been discovered and rediscovered again and again. Something has been revealed to the people of Israel with which all nations agree. For all people strive after justice, and the ten commandments have proved to be an apt definition of it.

The apostle Paul expressed the same insight and experience in a more doctrinal manner:

> When Gentiles who have not the law do by nature what the law requires, they are a law to themselves, even though they do not have the law. They show that what the law requires is written on their hearts, while their conscience also bears witness and their conflicting thoughts accuse or perhaps excuse them (Romans 2:14-15).

To every person the consciousness of good and evil is given so as to make them realize and acknowledge the ten commandments as the definition of the good.

Precisely from Romans 2:14-15, therefore, Luther argued for the validity of the decalogue for non-Christians as well as for Christians: "For what God has given to the Jews through Moses, he has also written into the hearts of all men: Moses is consonant with nature" (Luther, in his afore-mentioned sermon). The mute moral consciousness within every person finds its proper expression in (at least) the so-called second tablet of the Mosaic decalogue.

Romans 2:14-15, thus, is the source of the acceptance within the Christian tradition of the idea of natural law. This concept, central to the exposition of Christian ethics for centuries, has come under strong attack only in the last two generations. Karl Barth's *Gospel and Law* (1935) is a milestone on the route to the rejection of natural law as a category of ethics. Even in Roman Catholic moral theology which, unlike Protestant ethics, is built thoroughly on the notion of natural law, the concept is being disputed. But while Catholic theologians are moving away from the concept of natural law, due at least in part to the demand for situation ethics (the very opposite to an eternal, natural law), within Protestant ethics there are traces today of a reconsideration of the concept. It may be recovered as an indispensable ethical category, for there surely must be something, some basic and indisputable morality, consisting of the norms which make possible the mere conservation of life.

The ecology debate, too, leads us to suspect that there must be certain fundamental rules in our relations with creation. It is this fundamentally life-preserving quality of the decalogue which links it with natural law. Dietrich Bonhoeffer, in his *Ethics*, therefore called the decalogue the "Law of Life," for "failure to observe the second table (of the decalogue) destroys life. The task of protecting life will itself lead to observance of the second table" (i.e., the commandments which rule inter-human relationships) (*Ethics*, E.T. 1955, Fontana 1964, p.341). Goodness or righteousness is what is right and fit for creation; the good is what will correspond to the laws in creation and so will preserve and promote life.

The life-sustaining quality of the natural law expressed in the decalogue brings us full circle, for this is exactly what was said of the ten commandments when they were originally revealed: keep them, so that you may live. The commandments are God's principles for sustaining his creation. With these commandments, God articulates the law of life of his creatures. Because they define what will promote life, the commandments are an extraordinary blessing for every living creature. They lay out, as it were, the space in which human life will blossom. Whatever action is taken beyond these borders will—sooner or later—destroy life.

So the sabbath commandment, for instance, is a great gift: you may rest on the seventh day. "Remember the Sabbath day, to keep it holy," is at the same time liberation from the burden of the working day, freedom from urge and anxiety. After liberation from the ceaseless toil in Egypt, after the liberation from foreign rule, Israel (and we all) shall not again fall prey to our own or others' wrong and destructive desires and ambitions.

Every other commandment similarly represents liberation from a dangerous and destructive temptation: in each instance I learn that I no longer need to search for the truth and fulfillment of my life. The fullness of life will certainly not be found in theft or with the wife or husband of someone else.

The ten commandments, then, are to the field of ethics what an area-code is to telephoning: They spare us the trouble and anguish of experimenting endlessly among the whole "keyboard" of human possibilities, most of which do not promote life and community at all.

Sociologists seem to confirm the "wisdom" (Deuteronomy 4:6) of this pre- or advanced-ordering of morality by God. Individuals would be overwhelmed by the effort to decide their actions each time from scratch, from the full range of what is conceivable or physically possible. The field or "area code" defined by the commandments is the place where life will prosper. That is why he who has received the commandments can be so joyful about them (Psalm 119), why he can sing "he maketh me lie down in green pastures" (Psalm 23:2).

What, after all, is the aim of those who declare the decalogue out of date? Do they wish to give freedom to gossip and theft? Do they expect by this to serve progress and further life? Is adultery ever good? for whom? also for the deceived party? Of course, those who consider the decalogue out of date do not wish to promote evil. But where the decalogue is not, there also the other good things bestowed by God are not. This goes both for creation and for redemption, and is true for all people—not just for Christians or Jews. This is how Luther is said to have put it: "He who breaks one of the commandments is like a man who bows too far out of a fourth floor window: he'll fall down and surely break his neck, be he Turk, Jew, Gentile or Christian."

For all humankind, then, the commandments are the proper ground where the house must be built and nowhere else. This the Creator has decided. And this lot will prove to be a sound place. There is no morass beneath it which cannot be fathomed, and no shifting sands, only firm ground and solid rock. A house built on these foundations will weather the crises of history. From other foundations one will have to move again and again, for they will not stand firm indefinitely.

God's commandments, then, promote life. This is what Deuteronomy says and experience confirms. However, we must not think of this truth as an impersonal law which functions independently of God. Rather, we should understand that it is the Lord who *makes* you live. You cannot grasp life with your own hands. It is in the hands of the living God. Godless, immanent ethical solutions, however well-intentioned, are always prey to the will of humans which can quickly change from good to bad. Independent of God's commandments, people may—even tomorrow—act and argue quite differently from today.

This means, moreover, that God's commandments must determine what is beneficial. The argument often heard today that we ought to keep the decalogue not as commandments from God but as rules pertaining to the benefit of man, opens the door to the corruption of ethics. It is God's authority which says "this is good." Human insight in the end will come to the same conclusion but often, before the final result of an action is evident, great damage has been done. Therefore, we must reject the fashionable demand today for an experimental ethics ("inductive approach," as J.A.T. Robinson calls it in *Christian Freedom in a Permissive Society,* 1970, p.31) which claims the right of everyone to discover his own ethics by trial and error. Against this it has to be remembered that often it is the other person who suffers the damage brought about by my deviation from the decalogue. Consequently, *I* may learn nothing, unless the other person, the victim of my experiment in ethics, takes revenge. In this way I may come to learn painfully what God's commandments sought to teach me without the rod, namely the contents of the "golden rule": "All things whatsoever you would that men should do to you, do you even so to them" (Matthew 7:12). The decalogue is nothing other than an exposition of the golden rule. As such, it belongs as much to the town hall as the pulpit.

We have stated before that the ten commandments are being surpassed by *Christian* ethics on the road to righteousness. The ten commandments are like the guard-rails of a road through a swamp or along a precipice. The rail itself is not the aim of the journey. And no one would wish to approach his destination with steering wheel locked, directed only by the painful scraping of the car along the rail. What you need instead is inside control—a steering wheel. The ten commandments are standards, but they are not the aim. They are the framework, but by no means the realization of God's plan in the world.

God's aim and our calling and destiny is the perfection of man according to the image of Christ. The aim is a kingdom of justice in the world where God's will is being done, for the benefit of his Creation. The decalogue is the framework for the accomplishment of this. But in a given situation, who or what will tell us what is the right thing to do out of a half of dozen good and permitted possibilities? If the decalogue resembled the area codes what, as it were, decides the individual number? Because the ten commandments as *law* only describe the scene of life negatively ("Thou shalt not..."), it still needs to be filled—we must get the particular number elsewhere. Romans 13:10 needs to be understood in this way ("Love is the fulfillment of the law") as does Romans 8:4, which is a fascinating and very comprehensive description of the process of Christian ethics: Christ came "in order that the righteous requirements of the law might be fully met in us who do not live according to our sinful nature but according to the Spirit."

Here we touch on that large chapter of Christian ethics which goes beyond the mere observance of the commandments. Here, too, it is legitimate to demand a *situation ethics*, because the decalogue will never tell you positively what is to be done in a given situation. Indeed, we may constantly expect—from the Holy Spirit—a Christian "new morality," to use the notorious phrase coined by Joseph Fletcher and Bishop J.A.T. Robinson. However, these authors used the demand for an ethics which is relevant to the situation in order to oust the decalogue from Christian ethics. That is why Robinson in his *Honest to God* (London: SCM, 1963) argued that nothing was wrong in itself; all depends on the situation; nothing was prescribed except love. The decalogue was removed from ethics because of its absolute and eternally-valid demands. The so-called "new morality" of the sixties maneuvered itself into an antithesis of law and love which certainly does not represent the spirit and substance or the wording of the New Testament.

The "new morality's" replacing of the stiff commandments with a flexible ethics of the situation is a reaction against much of traditional church morality which reduced the instruction of the living God to the ten commandments and perhaps a few ordinances for masters and servants, husband and wives, parents and children. Does God still speak and guide today? "No" seems to be the answer of traditional ethics. Traditional dogmatics rightly rejected a view of God as in Deism, which patterned him after a watchmaker who has made a clock and set it in motion, and then has left it to run by itself. But in ethics, these same theologians seem to confess a God who, after having pronounced the commandments, left the scene and is now silent. Hence, there is a certain historic justification for the rebellion of the new morality.

In the New Testament, however, the ten commandments are not abolished, they are surpassed, and thus fulfilled. Christians must reject Fletcher's and Robinson's antithesis of law and love, and their consequent dismissal of the law. This is not compatible with Paul's phrase, "love fulfills the law." Instead, they read Paul as if he had said, "love bypasses the law." We must not succumb to a dichotomy of law and love. Christian ethics involves not the alternative of law or freedom, but the synthesis of law and spirit.

The same idea lies behind Luther's much-quoted statement: "A Christian will create new decalogues." Within its original context, it has a meaning completely different from that which is implied by those who use it to argue that Christians are exempt from and beyond the ten commandments. The argument in Luther actually runs like this:

> We will make new decalogues...and these decalogues are clearer than the decalogue of Moses.... For when the gentiles in the very rottenness of their nature still could speak of God and were a law to themselves, Romans 2, how much more can Paul or a perfect Christian full of the Spirit design a decalogue and judge everything in the best way.... However, as for the time being we are unequal in the spirit, and the flesh is hostile to the spirit, it is necessary, also because of the sectarians, to stick to the certain commandments and writings of the apostles so that the Church may not be torn into pieces. For we are not all apostles who by the certain providence of God have been sent to us as infallible teachers. Therefore not they, but we may go astray and fall in the faith (Luther, in the disputation *On Faith*, Nov. 11, 1535).

The Spirit and Scripture are consonant because both are the Word of the same God. It is in the field defined by the decalogue—and nowhere else—that God will continue to instruct, prohibit and command. Because the ten commandments are the appointed place for the dialogue and communication of God and man, they remain valid for all of us.

I conclude with a quotation from a famous sermon of Martin Luther's on Matthew 22:36-46:

> Therefore learn, who can learn, and learn well, so that we may know, first the ten commandments, what we owe to God. For if we do not know this, then we know nothing and will not inquire about Christ in the least...the Law...must show me what my loss and disease are, or I will never ask for the physician and his help (Sermon on the 18th Sunday after Trinity, from his *Church Postil*).

Law and gospel must go together.

Secularism and Theology

Klaus Bockmuehl

Vol. XIX, No. 2 (June 1983):6-14

L et me begin with a statement about the relevance and rank of the topic, "Secularism and Theology." In my opinion the questions concerning the relationship between theology and secularism are about the most fundamental and decisive issues of our age. At stake, basically, is the question of the world's final authority. We are in the midst of an historic struggle for world dominion: will it be man's rule or God's rule, human autonomy or the Kingdom of God? It is my conviction that this basic alternative underlies most of the major and minor conflicts of the day: they can all be reduced to that deeper level. We are therefore also dealing with a perspective which has far-reaching practical consequences: if we understand the figures, designs and options of this *elemental* encounter, we will also be able to discern the positions and motivations in most contemporary issues of debate. In short, we are dealing with an aspect of the Christian world- view, and, in the last analysis, with the underlying problem of human existence.

To lead us into the discussion of this topic, we will first try to identify the concepts of "secularization" and "secularism" on two levels, on the levels of terminology and the historical movements themselves; then second, describe how theology has, so far, reacted to those movements; and finally, set out the nature and task of theology and the way in which it ought to assess, and deal with, secularism.

I. "Secularization" and "Secularism"

1. The Terminology.

The root term of the terminology in question, of "secular,"

"secularism," "secularization," is the Latin word *saeculum*. It can mean "century" as well as "world." In the Middle Ages it took the place of the Greek New Testament words *aion* and *kosmos*. These terms, *aion* and *kosmos*, can each be used with very different meanings. Coupled with the respective epithet, *aion* can stand for "this age" and for "the age to come," the one assessed negatively, the other positively. Again, *kosmos* can have two meanings: it can describe the world as God's good creation, and it can be used to describe the corrupted world that is doomed to destruction through man's fall into sin (John 8:23 and 3:16).

Saeculum seems to hold the same two connotations in the language of the Middle Ages. The positive meaning of *saeculum* can be found, for example, in the writings of St. Bernard, in a sentence like: "All boons that we have in this world (*saeculum*) we have by the grace of God," and the negative as in: "The total conversion of our hearts to God means total estrangement from the world (*saeculum*) and from ourselves" (*Sancti Bernardi Abbatis Clarae-Vallensis Opera Omnia*, ed. J. Mabillon, vol. 2, pars 2, Paris, 4th. ed. 1839, col. 1628A and 1605C). (*Saeculum* is here synonymous with *mundus*, another Latin phrase for "world," which again can be used either positively or negatively.)

To lead us one step further, it is important to observe that in the Middle Ages the term *saeculum* was predominantly used with an additional twist, namely to connote the antithesis to the monastic life. Monks and nuns stood in contrast to the *saeculares*, the people living in the world. The term describing the monastic existence is *religio*: not every believer is "religious," but monks and nuns are *religiosi*, the religious ones. The monk is one "who has been taken from the *saeculum* and planted into *religio*" (St. Bernard, col. 1617B).

From this it follows that the very first usage of the composite term "secularization" means the return of the monk from the monastery to secular, i.e., civil life. When he leaves the order, he is being secularized. Originally, then, the phrase "secularization" had a very specialized and distinct usage: it is a technical term, denoting an individual change of status as a topic of ecclesiastical jurisdiction.

However, since the Middle Ages we witness a dramatic broadening of the sense of the term "secularization." In 1646, at the deliberations for the peace treaty of Münster, which ended the Thirty Years' War in central Europe, the French delegate used the term "secularization" for the first time, in order to describe the forced seizure of church properties by secular political authorities (*"Sakulisation,"* an article by Art S. Reicke in *Religion in Geschichte und Gegenwart*, 3rd. ed., vol. 5, Tübingen, J.C.B. Mohr, 1961, col. 1280).

The next step was the "secularization" of all remaining ecclesiastical territories in central Europe in 1803 (actually the last major legislation of the then dissolved Holy Roman Empire). By this spoil Napoleon meant to compensate the German princes for those territories west of the Rhine that he had annexed himself (Reicke, col. 1284).

Since then the usage of the term "secularization" has shed all its former specifications and limitations. Today, in the twentieth century, we characterize as "secularization" any process by which not just the monastery, and not merely the organized church, but any religious influence as such, is replaced by strictly "secular," i.e., non-religious, considerations. Secularization nowadays is no longer a matter of material possessions, but of mental outlook, of the whole of human attitudes and activities. Since the nineteenth century, we have experienced the secularization of areas like education, social welfare and health care; moreover, the elimination of inherited Sunday legislation, as well as the secularization of institutionalized human behaviour as in weddings and funerals. Basically today we are faced with the secularization of the whole world of human thought, science and culture. A secular life is a life lived without relation to any religious point of reference, not just to church or organized religion.

The term "secularism" goes yet beyond secularization in that it relates to it as intention relates to act, program to event, theory to praxis. "Secularism" is to be understood as the program for overall secularization. "Secularism" establishes "the secular" as the highest norm and purpose of action, just as "socialism" pursues the social existence or the association of people by way of the "socialization" of all items, properties and activities that do not yet correspond to that postulate. Secularism, respectively, is the program and philosophy of a thoroughly secular, i.e., worldly, non-religious lifestyle.

It is of minor relevance at this point, that there existed in Britain in the nineteenth century a movement of free-thinkers who were the first to call themselves "secularists," agitating against Christianity, and for atheism, a movement initiated by George Holyoake (1817-1906). Today, secularism is no longer the brand name of some organizationally identifiable movement. It is, rather, an "ideology," i.e., an all-comprising, all-permeating, world-view, ethos and attitude. It is the antithesis to religion.

2. The Program and Some of its Phenomena.

It is at this point that we should move from exploration of

nomenclature to actual listing of the phenomena of the thing itself: the agenda of secularism as a worldview.

In one way, secularism is the positive equivalent to the negative concept of atheism or agnosticism, positively emphasizing this-worldliness and human autonomy. God here is not merely the rejected, but the forgotten factor. Let me list a number of characteristic phenomena of this intellectual and practical stance.

a) Regarding *nature*, secularism proclaims different theories of the genesis of the universe that exclude the idea of Creation and a Creator, e.g., the theory of the spatial and temporal infinity of the universe, the theory that the world has no beginning. Secularists today try to combine this somehow with the "Big Bang" theory in an attempt to keep the assumption of a Maker redundant. The response by Laplace, the astronomer, to Napoleon's question of the place of God in his worldview—"Sir, I have no need for that hypothesis"—neatly summarizes this attitude. Moreover, secularists have always decidedly held to Darwin's theory of evolution, or at least to their particular interpretation of it (since it is well known that Darwin himself thought evolution to be compatible with the belief in God as the Creator).

b) Another phenomenon of secularism seems to be that philosophy of *history*, so prominent today, which characteristically insists on the causality and the analogousness of all historical events. It thus declares history a closed entity with no possibilities of divine interference, be it in the form of miracles or of the Incarnation. In the words of Ludwig Feuerbach, the famed critic of religion: "There can be no messiah on principle." Moreover, in the secularist view of history, Christian eschatology is replaced by the idea of the immanent progress of humanity (one of the more obvious forms of secularization of Christian theology).

c) A third group of phenomena of secularism, or items on the agenda, concerns *ethics and the law.* Two hundred and fifty years ago Hugo Grotius insisted that the whole system of law must be developed strictly on the idea of a "natural law," understood as a law that was embedded in nature and could be picked up from there, obliging humanity *etsi Deus non daretur,* even if God didn't exist. Grotius, of course, positively presupposed the existence of God, but then argued that it made no difference practically. One result of the secularist dismissal of God as the guarantor of moral and legal norms is relativism in values, a general characteristic of secularism, and this furnishes relativism's further development towards anarchism, i.e., the rejection of all legal and political structure.

d) Another amazing phenomenon of secularism is in the vital

field of *economic doctrine*: the emergence of Adam Smith's philosophy of free trade capitalism. Replacing the ancient biblical concept of stewardship (i.e., the responsibility of the economic agent before God) with responsibility of that agent towards himself, he must make sure to most rationally serve his own self-interest, because only then would the economy, a balanced system of so many individual self-interests, work properly and to the profit of all.

It almost goes without saying that Marxism, as the antithesis to capitalism in the sphere of economics, nevertheless shares in capitalism's presupposition of secularism and human autonomy. It even sharpens the same to the utmost radicality, because it adds to its system of thought a programmatic, militant critique of religion, or rather, it begins with that critique. Capitalism did not do that. Marxism is consistently secular; capitalism is not.

The common denominator of all these phenomena of secularism is the attempt to reconstruct the world and human existence under that presupposition which Grotius had only employed as hypothetical: the assumption that God does not exist, that his reality and his commandments can and should be neglected, that man is fully autonomous and therefore must and can determine his ways himself, both in theory and practice. Secularism, then, is the apotheosis of man, setting man in the highest place, making man the measure of all things.

II. Theological Attitudes towards Secularization and Secularism

In this field, the phenomena seem to permit a classification into at least three basic groups of attitudes:

1. a movement of silent accommodation to the rule of secularism, and acquiescence in the ensuing removal of God from reality,

2. a daring attempt to openly acclaim the process of secularization and claim it as a genuine heritage of Christianity itself (re-interpretation),

3. the professed overall acceptance of secularity as the methodological presupposition also for doing theology, and the different stages of transition, toward factual or professed atheism. Let us look at these in turn.

1. A silent accommodation to the cultural ascendancy of secularism accepted as inevitable can be seen in the theological withdrawal from the reality of this world, or the evacuation of the contested territory, which makes God more and more unreal in terms of space and time. This abandonment of the world by theology has mainly taken place in two forms, a) as internalization of

God, and b) as transcendentalization of God.

Exemplary of the first process is the theological method of Friedrich Schleiermacher. Teaching during the first decades of the nineteenth century, Schleiermacher became the pioneer of all modern liberal theology in that he established the much-copied *model of doing theology under the presuppositions of the Enlightenment.* Revelation here is no longer seen in terms of God's action in nature and history; it is an existential event that takes place in the consciousness and emotions of the individual believer. The whole of theology is thereby developed from religious experience, without any reference to objective reality. It is subjectivity. The areas of nature and history are thus left free for the claim of the upcoming sciences, which argue "as if God did not exist."

The most prominent twentieth-century representative of this method of doing theology under the quiet acceptance of the domination of secularity, is Rudolf Bultmann. Bultmann confessedly abides by the rules that were set down by a secular philosophy of history, i.e., the causality and the analogousness of all historical events, which render closed the universe of history. The works of God must therefore be seen as strictly a matter of human self-understanding with no claim to space, time, and palpable reality. Memorable are those lines with which he wound up the debate of his proposal for the demythologization of the New Testament in 1952, when he expressly described faith as acknowledging the worldliness of the world or the secularity of the secular. Arguing from an assumed axiom of the essential invisibility of God, Bultmann wrote, "The framework of nature and history is profane, and it is only in the light of the word of proclamation that nature and history become, for the believer, the...field of the divine activity. It is faith which makes the world profane and restores to it its proper autonomy as the field of man's labours" (*Kerygma and Myth: A Theological Debate*, ed. H.W. Bartsch, New York: Harper Torchbooks, 1961, p.211). Secularization was the necessary corollary or the demythologization theory, or rather, the other way round: demythologization was the necessary consequence of Bultmann's acceptance of the dominance of secularism.

"Faith restores to the world its proper autonomy." Bultmann here echoes to the very word the precedent set down by Schleiermacher, who wrote, "Religion herewith yields all claims [on science and morality] and restores everything that it had been pressed to receive" (*On Religion: Speeches to its Cultured Despisers*, New York: Harper Torchbooks, 1958, p.35; this translation from the first German edition, ed. R. Otto, 6th. ed., Göttingen, p.49). Thus theology hands the world over to secularism and withdraws from the upcoming age of technology and world development. The opposite but complementary method of evacuating the world of time and space from the things of God on the grounds of the non-objectifiability of revelation was employed by the early Karl Barth of *Dialectical Theology* in 1922. He then, too, accepted the dictates of secular philosophy of history and so, in fact, surrendered this world's reality to secularist claims. Differently from Bultmann, the early Barth removed the contents of theology completely to the level of the transcendent, thus coming close to a position of Platonism. In those years, in the notorious second edition of his *Romans* of 1922, he ventured to proclaim: "No objectivity... There is no transcending of man and no entry of that kingdom into this world.... Ignorant, therefore, of God and of His kingdom, but familiar with the groaning of all creation, we lend our support to all honest, secular, scientific and historical research; but we dissociate ourselves from every semitheological interpretation of Nature and History" (*The Epistle to the Romans*, tr. E.C. Hoskyns, London: Oxford University Press [1933], 1976, p.318). This meant admitting that the world is empty of God. Secularism is right.

2. The second attitude taken by prominent Protestant theologians towards the ascendancy of secularism in our own time consists of declaring secularization to be the genuine product of Christianity or, so to speak, "christening" secularization.

The prototype of this argument had been developed by a colleague of Barth and Bultmann in their early days, Friedrich Gogarten. Gogarten seems to have proclaimed the "secularity of the secular" consistently all through his life. In the early twenties, it may have actually been Gogarten who inspired Barth to undertake that major revision of his book on Romans along the lines of the absolute transcendence of God (and the ensuing utter profanity of the world), that has been mentioned.

In 1933 and later, Gogarten consequently supported National Socialism ideologically by his insistence that the church had no right to interfere in matters of the state as an autonomous secular order. With this he gave a prominent example of that heretical interpretation, or rather, misinterpretation, of the Lutheran doctrine of the two kingdoms, i.e., of God's two-fold rule in salvation and creation, church and state.

After World War II Gogarten, by now Bultmann's weighty ally in the demythologization debate, addressed himself directly to the topics of secularization and secularism from those stated presuppositions. In his book, *Despair and Hope for Our Time* (trans. T.

Wieser, Philadelphia: Pilgrim Press, 1970), Gogarten establishes two basic theses about the secular. The first is the contention, already mentioned, that secularization is really the true daughter of the Christian faith. Gogarten tries to prove this from 1 Corinthians 10:23, where Paul says, "All things are permitted but not all things are helpful." To Gogarten, this signals that the world is given over to man to rationally decide what is good and what is not. It means the proclamation of the secularity of life in this world. Gogarten, claiming to be a modern day Lutheran, also pointed out eagerly that the worldliness of all our actions is required in order to safeguard the important Reformational doctrine of justification by faith without works: the works must be strictly secular and have no relation to the realm of salvation.

Secularization, then, was historically initiated by the Christian faith itself. However (and this is Gogarten's second thesis), once begun, secularization can also exist and continue without faith. The trouble is, in his view, that secularization can degenerate into secularism. Gogarten sharply distinguishes the two: secularism is a further stage of development when secularity (originally, as it were, the mere demise of the divine) is deified, enhanced, blown up into an ideology which encroaches on people. At this point, Gogarten believes, it is the task of the Christian to resist and to see to it that the horizons of thought remain wide open, that secularization remains secular and does not again take on religious overtones, developing into a religion of immanence.

In North America, Harvey Cox became the most spectacular pupil and partisan of Friedrich Gogarten and of the idea of "christening" secularization. His book, *The Secular City,* was also much celebrated in Europe. (Another very influential and, in its extreme conclusions, remarkable, product of this school of thought was the North American preparatory contribution to the Fourth Assembly of the World Council of Churches in Uppsala, Sweden, 1968, with the title, "The Church for Others.")

Cox, as is often the case with enthusiastic younger adherents of a given theological program, heralded Gogarten's basic thesis with a new and refreshing bluntness. Far from being something Christians should be against, secularization (which Cox defines as the process by which society and culture are delivered from religious tutelage and control) "represents an authentic consequence of Biblical faith." As Christians, rather than oppose it, we should see it as our task to nourish the secularization process, and to be on the lookout for movements which attempt to thwart and reverse the liberating irritant of secularization (*The Secular City: Secularization and*

Urbanization in Theological Perspective, London: SCM, 1965, p.l7f). It
is further characteristic of this advanced form of acclamation of
secularity that Cox should now see the primary danger not, as
Gogarten did, in secularization's possible deterioration into
secularism, but in the possibility that some Christians might not
embrace secularization willingly enough. With an unmistakable
note of threat in this direction, he says of the general relativization of
moral values (a characteristic element of secularization): "It
demands that all be drawn into the secularization process so that no
one clings to the dangerous precritical illusion that his values are
ultimate.... There is no reason that man must believe the ethical
standards he lives by came down from heaven inscribed on golden
tablets" (Cox, p.34f).

Cox also sports some kind of a biblical proof for his outlook.
Differently from Gogarten, he argues mainly from the Old
Testament. He thinks that the precedent of modern secularization
can be found, for one thing, in the book of Genesis and its accounts
of a "disenchanted nature," which is no longer full of deities and
numina, but is given to man for study and manipulation. Cox sees
those precedents further in the Book of Exodus, which he reads as
proclaiming the "desacralization of politics" because of what he sees
as a heralded revolt against a duly constituted monarch. Moreover,
the Sinai revelation is understood as the declared deconsecration of
values because of its prohibition of idolatry.

These interpretations of central topics of Old Testament theology
may not stand up to closer scrutiny even in terms of a secular
approach to the history of religion of Israel. Regardless, Cox rushes
on to the intended result: the Church must stop bewailing or
opposing secularization. It must get behind it.

3. In the immediately ensuing period, one witnessed a veritable
tidal wave of attempts to "get behind it," to be "with it," to "be a
truly secular" person—and on theological grounds (at least for the
time being). In 1964, in a sensational lecture, John A.T. Robinson, the
dashing Anglican bishop, posed the question, "Can a truly
contemporary person not be an atheist?" (who would not wish to be
"truly contemporary"?), and answered it with an exotic mix of no's
and yes's.

Dorothee Soelle, notably one of Gogarten's pupils, asserted the
possibility of a "Christian atheism," centering on a concept of Jesus
with God the Father removed. In North America, Paul van Buren
argued for the "secular meaning of the Gospel." With the quick and
impetuous manner of doing theology typical of those days, he
claimed that, as in all other idealistic philosophy, the term "God"

was meaningless to modern man; therefore one should no longer use it. Theological reviewers who did not wish to be left behind by the rapid development, praised Van Buren's book as "a fascinating attempt to be purely secular while remaining loyal to the gospel" (*A Layman's Guide to Protestant Theology,* by W. Hordern, rev. ed., New York: Macmillan, 1978, p.246f). Bishop Robinson's exertion of throwing out of the window anything in Christian life and doctrine that would seem to contradict secular culture remains one of the more bizarre spectacles of the whole movement.

This movement, at least its more picturesque promotions, may perhaps now be a part of the past. Some of the younger generation today have not even heard the names of those who managed to make the headlines with religious topics (even if logically for the last time), and whose success for a moment seemed to signal the death of Christianity, if not the "death of God." The names of these more sensational actors may soon be forgotten, but much of their preaching seems to have come to stay. It has hardened the general attitude of ignoring God, even within theology. There are many other phenomena of what Eric Mascall aptly called the "Secularization of Christianity" (see his book of this title, London: Darton, Longmans and Todd, 1965). Among them, a whole consistent liturgy of phrases and causes of secularized theology, is found in Cox's and Robinson's reduction of prayer to self-meditation, a rationalization of the widespread neglect of prayer altogether, a neglect that witnesses most to the power and influence of the secular lifestyle within Christendom. Another phenomenon is the reduction of the Double Commandment of love to its second part, love of neighbour. Again, a sign of the predominance of the secular mindset within theological ethics and social ethics is the matter-of-factness with which Christian spokesmen today set up ethical postulates without any reference to the necessity and possibility of a moral change in man, effected by God. The overall proof for the far- reaching sell-out of theology to the philosophy of secularism lies in the ubiquitous willingness of theologians to dabble with any given problem strictly within the confines of secular life, to leave out the basic question, the question of this generation's *rapport with God,* and to openly declare that "the God-question must be put on ice" until all the other pressing problems are solved. It is this attitude which shows that the unreserved acceptance of secularism has become the methodological presupposition for that type of theology: it is atheism in all but its name.

III. Theology and Secularism: A Necessary Confrontation

1. Identifying the adversary

Much could and must be said in criticism of these three main postures of accommodation of theology to secularism: the quiet withdrawal from reality, leaving it to be occupied by secularism, the coordination of secularization and Christianity, i.e., the bridge-building attempted by Gogarten, and the full identification with secularity on the part of his younger colleagues who actually cross the bridge.

At this moment, however, let us only point to one fallacy that undercuts the position of Gogarten, probably the most dangerous of the ones described: we have no way of dissociating secularism from secularization, regretting the one and welcoming the other. According to the rules of semantics, secularism and secularization relate to each other like theory and practice, intention and execution. There can, of course, be secularization without secularism, but human nature always tends to acquire a consciousness of, and an intentionality for, its actions—a tendency which none of us would wish to discourage. Today, in fact, we simply can no longer construe a situation of secularization without its program, secularism: it is always with us.

Moreover, we must make sure to understand the range of secularization: today we are no longer dealing with liberation from *ecclesiastical* tutelage, but as Harvey Cox was quite clear about, from any and all *religious* determination. In other words, in question is no longer merely the abolition of some hierocracy (or rule of the clergy), but of theocracy, or the Kingdom of God. Most important, however, is the fact that those theological advocates of secularization who point to the Old Testament, have not yet distinguished between a *monotheistic secularization* of a polytheistic environment, "disenchanting" nature in the Old Testament, and the present *atheistic secularization* of a monotheistic tradition, as pursued by contemporary secularism. This distinction is also a vital tool for the assessment of instances of secularization found today in many diverse situations all around the globe.

The same distinction is, of course, to be made with a view to the Protestant Reformation. In the eyes of the medieval theologian, the Reformation was a program of secularism: it advocated a secularization, the transferral of the "sacred" into the theatre of the profane. However, in this process the religious element, the relationship with God, remains intact and in power. The Reformation intended the *sanctification* of the "profane," the everyday life in the marketplace. It attempted a transferral, not a mutation of the sacred. Modern secularism aims at something quite different: it seeks the dissolution of the sacred in the profane, and its liquidation in the sense of its annihilation.

Martin Luther knew quite well that his adversaries called the Reformation a profanation of the sacred. Indeed, that it was, but in a different sense: it intended piety in the *profanum*, outside of the temple, *in* the world. Or even stronger, as in Calvin, it aimed at the permeation of the seeming profanity of life with the claims of God's Kingdom, instead of the inherited cultivation merely of a sacred precinct of religion, as in the concepts of the hermit and the monastery. The Reformation refuses to set the sacred apart; it moves into the profane world, declaring all of it sacred, because of its quality of being God's creation.

Today's ideologists depart from the world as creation into atheism, making the world the field of human autonomy. That is a new concept of secularism, a *second secularism*, as different from the first as human autonomy is from the hallowing of this world for God.

As it stands, secularism in the West means atheism and the apotheosis of man, or at least an attitude that denies God the honour of his kingship in creation. Theologians who accommodate to that position, who acquiesce in, or positively profess the autonomy of man, are therefore the twentieth century representatives not of the Reformational doctrine of the Two Kingdoms, but of its abolition.

However, more important than the exposure and critique of the fallacies of today's theological appeasement of secularism is the re-establishment of an adequate awareness of the true nature and task of Christian theology. From it all necessary insight into the right attitude of theology to secularism will follow.

2. The permanent task of theology

The paramount object of theology as a scholarly discipline is to gather and disseminate the knowledge of God. It is theology's constitutional task to create everywhere an awareness of the question of God, and to provide an answer to it. There should be no doubt about this; the very name of the enterprise states that theology is established to deal with God and things of God. Karl Barth, in order to dispel any confusion that might nevertheless have inexplicably arisen over this task, stated about dogmatics what must be taken to apply to theology as a whole:

> Dogmatics, in each and all divisions and subdivisions,...can first and last, as a whole and in part, say nothing else but that *God is*. According to the measure that it does this, it serves

the Church...and decides about its own scientific value or lack of value. In every train of thought, in every sentence which directly or indirectly serves the purpose of saying this, dogmatics does what it ought to do (*Church Dogmatics*, Vol.II/1, Edinburgh: T & T Clark, 1957, p.258).

It is, then, theology's permanent task to everywhere and at all times announce God to humanity, to each living generation. Any theory or practice, any discourse or silence that would not help to promote the revelation of God, any activity that resulted in concealing God and the things of God, would have to be judged as a failure, an evasion or a contradiction of the natural and stated task of theology.

The statement on the obligation of theology taken from Karl Barth's *Church Dogmatics* indicated that it is not sufficient for theology to proclaim the mere existence of God. Christian theology is duty-bound to render the whole of God's revelation given to man or, in the words of St. Paul, to "declare the whole counsel of God" (Acts 20:27). Theology cannot choose those things from the body of doctrine entrusted to it which it would seem to like best—in general, or at any given time—and hide those other things which it deems generally unpleasant, or unsuitable to the spirit of the times. Theology must make God known as the Creator, the Legislator, the Counsellor, the Saviour, and the Judge of humanity. In a word, it must make known God as the merciful king and Lord of the universe.

It is, then, the foremost responsibility of Christian theology to proclaim the Kingdom of God, just as this kingdom was central to Christ's own proclamation. Theology must go out, invite and warn humanity so to think, speak, and live that God's name be hallowed and his will done on earth as it is in heaven.

Moreover, theology must do this, as has been said, everywhere and at all times. Everywhere—theology must insist that God's claim to kingship over the world is a public claim, addressing the whole of society. God does not claim to be the Lord of the Church only. This is something which most Evangelicals still have to convince themselves of. They equate God's kingdom with church or chapel; they often are not even aware of the suppression of God's claim that takes place in the marketplace, at the hand of atheist secularism, and they spare themselves the pains that a partisan of God's kingdom must constantly feel in today's secular culture. Nevertheless, the task of theology is to represent God and the things of God publicly everywhere, to the ends of the earth.

Theology must also speak of God *at all times*, "in season and out of season." That can be a dramatic enterprise, as humanity, most of the time, is occupied with other seemingly more pressing problems. Karl Barth discovered this in 1933 when in a moment of revolution and national enthusiasm he nevertheless called for "Theological Existence Today." Barth warned of the danger that because of the forcefulness with which other claims are made, the intensity and exclusiveness of the claim of God's Word might no longer be understood. He concluded: "There are some things about which there is unanimity within the Church. One is, that there is no more urgent demand in the whole world than that which the Word of God makes, *viz.* that the Word be preached and heard" (*Theological Existence Today: A Plea for Theological Freedom,* tr. R. Birch Hoyle, London: Hodder, 1933, p.llf). That is theological existence; that is the true stance of Christian theology.

3. The attitude of theology towards secularism

If the above is a rough but correct sketch of the true nature and task of theology, then certain attitudes and activities of theology *vis-à-vis* secularism necessarily follow.

First, theology must identify contemporary secularism as that which it is: the attempt to ignore, evade, or rebel against the lordship of God. As distinguished from the theological friends of secular culture, secularists themselves are usually quite frank about this: they feel throughout that modern culture and its Christian past are mutually exclusive antipodes which must fight each other.

The Bible characterizes that struggle as part of the deeper opposition of mankind against God: "The kings of the earth set themselves, and the rulers take counsel together, against the Lord and his anointed saying, Let us burst their bonds asunder; let us cast their cords from us" (Psalm 2:3). It is this age-old disposition of man which Christ in his parables portrays as the attitude: "We do not want this man to reign over us" (Luke 19:14).

Second, a theology that is true to its task must also uncover the ever-recurring attempts made *within the church* to accommodate to the spirit of the times, to yield to, to legitimize, or even to celebrate secularism. Looking back to his experiences of the battle that the church had to wage during the time of the rule of National Socialism, Karl Barth described secularization as *the* great temptation and danger of the church, a temptation to heteronomy—to listen to alien voices; a temptation that, of course, comes with all the sweetness and plausibility that always goes with temptation. Secularization of the church takes place when the church lets itself be determined by what happens to be the most venerable or the newest or the strongest factor in its environment (ideological, political, economic) or by what its environment announces to be the most pressing or the most sacred aim or need at the moment. Secularization which then takes place can have the form either of withdrawal into some kind of theological or ecclesiastical fortress, *or* the form of bridge-building within Christianity and secular culture, a kind of baptizing of the non-Christian ideas, habits and enterprises, i.e., their Christian reinterpretation. We have seen that exactly this has taken place. And it is the task of all theology worth its salt to uncover and expose, and possibly to prevent the success of those accommodations, for, to conclude with Barth, "When the Church becomes secular, it is the greatest conceivable misfortune both for the Church and the world" (*Church Dogmatics*, p.667f).

IV. Conclusion: Affliction and Assurance

The theologian who takes these duties seriously might as well prepare himself for controversy and isolation. He probably will not be popular in his own time. He will, as Barth put it in the same context, "be a lonely bird on the roof." He will go through all the experiences and moods which the Psalter, especially Psalm 3-14, described of similar situations. He will feel the emotional drag of swimming against the stream when he is confronted with what "many say" (Psalm 3:2 and 4:6), with what almost everybody else seems to say. The success of secularism and its theological fellow travellers may be so overwhelming, the actual changes achieved in society may seem so definite, that this theologian finds himself on the brink of despair, speaking with the Psalmist, "The godless have destroyed the foundations; what can the righteous do?" (Psalm 11:3), or praying, "Help, Lord, for there is no longer any that is godly, for the faithful have vanished from among the sons of man" (Psalm 12:1).

The Psalmist, of course, knows that the rebellion of humans cannot make God's throne crumble: "The Lord is king for ever and ever .... Thou dost see, yea thou dost note trouble and vexation, that thou mayest take it into thy hands; the hapless commits himself to thee" (Psalm 10:16,14). Strikingly then, God turns round the minority existence of the true theologian into his becoming the salt of the earth and the light of the world. Correspondingly, it is a fascinating feature of the early Pietists in the seventeenth century (so unlike their present-day descendants) that they, in the midst of a seemingly dead church, a disoriented and ossified theology, and amidst all the hostility with which such a reform movement would be met, stuck to their conspicuous conviction of a *spes meliorum temporum,* the hope that God would yet give better times to the church.

What is the ground for such optimism? It may be based on the personal experience of regeneration that figured highly on the list of topics in Pietism. The ground for hope may lie in the respective conviction that "God who has resuscitated me to new life, can yet do the same for a whole church." It is the hope in a sequence that the Book of Psalms accentuates in another place: "I waited patiently for the Lord; he inclined to me and heard my cry. He drew me up from the desolate pit, out of the miry bog, and set my feet upon the rock, making my steps secure. He put a new song in my mouth, a song of praise to our God. Many will see and fear, and put their trust in the Lord" (Psalm 40:1-3).

The encounter with secularism is undecided, but it is not open-ended. We need to recover some of earlier Pietism's assurance that "Jesus is Victor!" The gospel is good news. For this reason, secularism, in its pursuit to liberate humanity from the gospel, can in the final analysis only become a *dysangelium,* bad news, and must be exposed as that.

We must surely distinguish between a dismissal of historically accrued ecclesiastical habits, which we may indeed need to be liberated from, and departure from the biblical Gospel—a distinction that was mostly missing in many of the proponents of the secularization of theology. Secularism, with its deliberate dismissal of God the Creator and Saviour will spell not liberation, but deprivation and destitution for humanity, a foolish course, however, which it is not our fate to follow.

Core Issues in Theological Debate

Linda Mercadante

Vol. XX, No. 4 (December 1984):7-11

All of us are engaged in one long, continuous theological debate. Whether you are always conscious of it or not, you are engaged in a process of theological reflection. Whenever you explain to your pastor that you don't agree women should be subservient to men, or find yourself arguing silently with sermons or books that stereotype you, or sadly justifying to family, yourself and friends why you can't attend that church anymore, you are at those times engaging in very serious theological work.

What I want to help you do is to pinpoint some of the core theological issues that keep popping up again and again as you try to explain, defend or convince that God indeed is a God of justice and mercy; a proclaimer of liberty to the captives, a God who loves women, as well as men, and wants us all to be free to serve God and to grow into the fullness of the divine image. If the Gospel is clear on this point, as we firmly believe it is, why, then, are we often so bogged down in theological arguments with other Christians? Why are there still many people who cannot accept this clear Gospel mandate?

I believe it is because certain core theological issues are behind many of these endless and often circular discussions in which we often find ourselves. Therefore, until we can recognize these issues for what they are and address them head on, we will never make the kind of progress we need to make in a world where wife-beating is often justified from Scripture, where nuclear weapons are called "a gift from God" and where blind prejudice is often defended as "following tradition."

The theological issues *are* important. In fact, they are crucial. For as long as people can justify oppression by pointing to religious arguments, we shame ourselves as Christians, hide the gospel under a bushel, and fail to give glory to God. But theological issues are important as more than just a way to hide sin. These issues are also important in themselves, for they are the underpinnings of our faith. As Christians, we need to seek both orthodoxy and orthopraxis: right thinking and right acting. And often the action can only come when the thinking has been resolved.

Haven't you met, on occasion, sincere people who honestly cannot understand Christian feminism? These people, while they may indeed be blinded by custom, sin or prejudice, are often just as significantly mired in theological dilemmas, whether they realize it or not, from which they cannot get out. And until they can see their way out, they are hesitant to accept anything you have to say about biblical feminism for fear of selling short the gospel.

And they are right in this: crucial issues are at stake in the debate over Christian feminism. Therefore, we need to have a firm grasp of them, so that in our own theological work we can operate with the sophistication, discernment, and wisdom necessary in order to give our work lasting value and contribute to the advance of Christian understanding and the proclamation of the gospel. Only as right thinking goes hand in hand with right action will we make any solid progress towards the goals we desire.

I want to focus on two of these core issues in the debate over Christian feminism, for I believe they will be most significant for you as you go about your own theological reflection. They are, *first*, the doctrine of God—in particular, feminine imagery for God—and *second*, the relationship between women's experience and theology.

The doctrine of God is obviously a key area of debate right now. We know that God is not somehow masculine rather than feminine, but that God as a spirit does not have gender as humans do. And we know that the exclusively masculine imagery for God used in our liturgies, our prayers and our theological language is not a complete representation of God's fullness.

There is a growing consensus on this point, and not just among feminists. But especially among feminist theologians there is an amazing consensus along the whole spectrum from evangelical to liberal, that we must increase our use of feminine imagery for God. The World Council of Churches inclusive language lectionary is one such attempt, and Virginia Mollenkott among others has done a good job of identifying in Scripture the hidden feminine imagery for God which has gone neglected for so long. And on the more radical end there are those women who urge a new religion of the Goddess, where *only* feminine imagery will be used.

So there is a consensus that we should increase our use of feminine imagery of God—but we still have a problem, and that is one of definition. What does "feminine imagery" for God really mean? Here is where the heart of the problem lies for those of us who want to make decisive changes in theology, in the church and in the culture. To put the matter simply, even if we take this imagery *solely* from Scripture, depending on *how* we use this feminine imagery for God, we will either help dispel the oppressive character of the gender stereotypes we have inherited, or we will reinforce these stereotypes and encourage, rather than discourage, their continuation.

So, what does feminine imagery for God look like? Is it restricted to nurturance, giving birth, comforting, feeling? Is feminine imagery to be used only when talking about these qualities of God, but not when describing God's righteousness, perfect knowledge, power, judgment of evil, and other characteristics traditionally thought of as masculine? Should we continue to use "Father" language here instead?

Think about this, for depending upon how we interpret and use feminine imagery for God, we may end up in a worse box than the one we are still trying to break out of now. Let's be careful *how* we incorporate feminine imagery for God into our worship, our prayers and our talk. For even if we manage to get feminine imagery for God into these areas, if we do it improperly we stand the danger of simply hardening the stereotypes.

Because even if we can admit that God somehow encompasses the ideal attributes of stereotypical maleness and femaleness, this, in itself, is a doubtful theological starting place. For if a man is only seen as best imaging God when he's being strong and a woman only when she's being comforting, have we really changed anything? No. In fact, we may have made our straitjacket even tighter: for the danger is that we will rank these attributes, even though they are all godly ones, making the "masculine" ones primary, and the "feminine" ones secondary.

In fact, such ranking is already being done. One evangelical scholar, Donald Bloesch, in his book *Is the Bible Sexist?* (1982, Crossway), admits freely that there is feminine imagery for God in the Bible. But he wants it known that "the biblical God is primarily Father and. . ." (p.121, n.38). So we must be cautious: not all feminine imagery for God is truly advantageous.

The core theological problem behind both the reaction *against* feminine imagery for God, and my warnings about a *lop-sided use* of this imagery is the issue of the transcendence and immanence of God. Is God primarily different from the world: transcendent over it and only acting into it through sheer grace and power? Or is God a part of the world, immanent in it, the ground of our energy and life forces? This is a perennial theological question and the answer to it is, of course, that God is both. God is other than the world, independent of it, but God has created the world and chosen to be in relationship with it and with us.

But the stress in certain dominant strains of Christianity has been on the transcendence of God, stressing God's independence, God's completeness without us, God's sheer strength, power and control. These attributes of God have been stereotypically linked with masculinity. And so males have had an investment both in keeping our focus on these aspects of God, and in imaging these aspects of God themselves.

Thus when someone deeply into this mindset hears you proposing feminine imagery of God, they have an immediate negative reaction even if they can't articulate exactly why. They think that you are denying God's independence, and otherness, the "infinite qualitative difference" between God and humanity. They think that you are offering them a weakling God, and a God who is passive, enmeshed in the life processes, but not in control of them.

But that is not the real problem. For what they fail to realize is that they have fallen into the trap of linking the attributes of God with human gender stereotypes. Why should a fatherly God seem more independent to them, while a motherly God seems more passive and ineffectual? The answer is clear: we associate independence with men and passiveness with women.

What can we do about this false notion? First, for your own theological health and for the health of your faith, you must realize the element of a very important truth in their spontaneous reaction. If they stress God's transcendence, you shouldn't get caught in the trap of even more loudly proclaiming God's immanence, even though divine immanence often *is* what they are forgetting. Remember that they have a point. If we give up on the otherness of God, we do end up with the idea of a relatively powerless and ineffectual God who cannot get extricated enough from the world to save it. But this balance has absolutely nothing to do with masculinity and femininty. That is the wrong connection.

Unfortunately, some feminist theologians have also operated out of this connection. And so in order to lean against both the over-emphasis upon God's transcendence, and its masculine associations, they have presented God, or the Goddess, as fully immanent in the world. And thus we look for God *only* in ourselves, in the world, in other people. This kind of God is *not* the biblical God, who is both actively present in the world, and yet also transcendent over it, lovingly guiding and leading the world according to the divine purposes.

What we must do, then, when faced with this problem (whether from ardent anti-feminists who oppose feminine imagery for God for the reasons I have named, or from ardent feminists who want to lean so hard against the lop-sided stress on transcendence) is to totally *break out of* this circular argument. God is both immanent *and* transcendent. The problem is not with God—the biblical presentation of God clearly has both sides of this issue in balance. The problem, rather, is with our association of transcendence with masculinity and immanence with femininity. The stereotypes are the problem. Once this false connection has been recognized for what it is, we can get on with the business of using feminine imagery for God.

But let your *feminine* imagery of God point to *both* the transcendent *and* the immanent characteristics of God, and let your masculine imagery of God to do the same. A motherly God is a strong shelter and a fighter for justice, just as a fatherly God is a comforter and nurturer, and *vice versa*.

The *second* issue which I find extremely crucial for our own theologizing is that of the relationship between women's experience and theology. Again there is on this subject a consensus along the whole spectrum of feminist theologians, from evangelical to liberal. They all say that the experience of women has been left out of traditional theology. Theologians and preachers have usually been male, and so when they have thought of sin and grace and other biblical concepts, they have thought of them in terms of their own life experiences. When male ministers talk, for example, about pride being the most deadly sin, they are talking about their *own* experience. Pride, in their experience, is the most serious problem.

But Valerie Saiving Goldstein has pointed out that pride is *not* women's chief problem—far from it. Instead, if we had to point to the chief failing or sin of women, it would more likely be overdependence—overdependence upon men, upon authority figures, upon society's opinion of us. And along with this overdependence comes a failure to trust our own judgment, to follow our own vision, and to trust in our own reception and perception of the Word of God. And so the majority of sermons you hear, and the theology which they reflect, do not include in them the religious experience of women.

The state of theology today is like a map which lists just those sights that men would likely visit. Of course some of these places would be very interesting to women, too. But the locations that would be visited primarily by women are not on this map. They have been left off. The map-maker considered them of minor importance, or perhaps didn't even take note of them at all.

Thus if you as a woman take a trip to this place, the map they have drawn is only partially useful to you. Much theology today reflects primarily the male experience with the biblical concepts of, say, sin, judgment and grace. Our experience of these things is not on the map yet. Therefore if we want to change the map of theology we must begin to speak about, write about, teach about, and counsel from our own attempts to hear the gospel message and our own experience in knowing God.

But back to the critics with whom you have to argue in order to accomplish these changes. As you may know, when you say to many a preacher or theologian that you want to theologize out of your own religious experience, you get a spontaneous and negative reaction. Why? Here the core question is this: What is to serve as the source and the norm of theology? Is it Scripture, or is it human experience? Again we are presented with a very difficult problem, and we seem forced to choose sides, just as we were tempted to choose in the transcendence/immanence issue. But again it is a false dichotomy.

Scripture has been, is and should always be the source and the norm of our theology and the pathway to faith in God. Scripture is the witness to the one supreme Word of God, who is Jesus Christ. Thus, while Scripture contains the revelation of God, and is the authoritive and unique witness to Jesus Christ, it is also a very human book, written by people who *experienced* the divine self-disclosure.

As we today read Scripture, it becomes alive for us as *we* experience the power of God through it, which is possible if we approach it with a "hermeneutic of consent." This does not diminish the authority and uniqueness of Scripture as the Word of God, nor its conceptual content, but it does point to the inevitable situation we are all in: The only way we receive, understand and interpret the Word of God—and thus theologize from it—is as humans, and out of humans' experience.

But if you propose that *women's* experience should begin to inform theology, you will likely be accused, directly or indirectly, of replacing the Word of God with experience as your source of theology. Is there a valid warning for us in this accusation? Yes. It is that the norm and source of our theology must never be solely human experience, whether male or female. God's self-revelation as witnessed authoritatively in Scripture is rightly the primary source of our theology. But as males read this book, they perceive it through the filter of their own experience—and inevitably their theology reflects that experience. Here again, we must point to the fact that all theology, all understanding of God comes, and can only come, through human understanding.

Is there a problem with the fact that, as far as we know, it was mostly males who wrote, compiled and edited this collection of writing recognized by the church as Scripture? Yes and no. Yes, in that the human authors were indeed products of their own age, and bound in their own cultures, which included a very patriarchal mindset. We cannot deny this, and it did colour their writings.

But we also know that the ultimate author of Scripture is God in that this is the *trustworthy* account of God's self-disclosure to humanity. So even if the human authors were not always aware of the deeper implications of what they were writing, we can count on the continuing presence of the Holy Spirit to interpret the ultimate message for us beyond any time-bound and human quality which inevitably will be there. As for our theologizing today, we must insist that the Word of God now be perceived through the lens of women's experience, as it has always been perceived through men's. As this is accomplished, we can be confident that the depth and richness of the gospel message will be better perceived.

This is a different approach from some of the more radical feminist theologies which have rejected Scripture as the source of theology because it is primarily written by males. They offer instead the experience of women as the primary norm and source. Some will grant that Scripture is authoritative in those places where it confirms women's experience, but where it does not, it cannot function as an authority for us. While they are correct at least in pointing out that some parts of Scripture are more important than others, we do not have to adopt their full position. It is possible to hold to Scripture as your authoritative source for theology, and still insist on the proper place of women's experience in that work of interpretation.

As with the first core issue we looked at earlier, what we need to do is to break through the false dichotomy that has been set up. We need to show that God's self-revelation is both trustworthily recorded in Scripture and also received through the means of human experience. As we perceive the Word of God through the lens of women's experience, new doors will open for us in our understanding of God.

I want to leave you with two things. First, a method: learn to break through these either/or situations. Don't get trapped in false dichotomies which make you a loser no matter which side you choose.

Second, I want to leave you with some homework. By all means begin to incorporate feminine imagery for God, starting from a biblical base, into your prayers, your talk and your worship of God, both publically and privately. But remember to avoid imposing the gender stereotypes once again. A motherly God is not simply barefoot and pregnant! And also, by all means, begin to incorporate your own experience into all your thinking and talking about God. What is sin *for you* as a woman? How have you experienced God's grace most profoundly?

But remember: You don't have to abandon Scripture as authoritative in order to do this. Learn to see it with new eyes, though; eyes that are truly your own and truly open to revealing the power of the Holy Spirit.

It is time for us to get down to the hard work of doing our own theology. We are *all* responsible for this work and it is an exciting and challenging opportunity for us. Let's get on with it.

This paper was first presented at the Evangelical Women's Caucus International Conference at Wellesley College, June 19-23, 1984.

The Means of Conversion

J.I. Packer

Vol. XXV, No. 4 (December 1989):14-22

My title steers me into choppy waters, for the question of the best means under God to induce personal conversion has been a debating-point among evangelicals for something like two centuries, and still is. It has in fact been part of a larger debate, not always clearly focused, about the set of ideological behaviour patterns that historians have labelled *revivalism*. Revivalism should not be equated with what was worked and prayed for, and actually experienced, in any one revival, nor with the hope of seeing revival again. Revivalism means, rather, a socio-cultural program shaped by a scheme of values that particular revival movements are held to have exemplified and validated. This program in various forms is still commended by some as canalizing the power of the Holy Spirit to quicken individuals and communities, but others criticize it as weakening the church, long-term, in at least four ways: by producing shallow, short-winded, poorly grounded Christians, with little concern about truth and little skill in its defence; by multiplying false conversions and unspiritual enthusiasms; by eroding churchly loyalty and the sense of churchly identity; and by idealizing a Christian ethos that for lack of intellectual formation remains naive, sentimental, and myopic. The debate, whether centred upon the phenomenon of revivalism as a whole or on particular priorities, procedures, and permutations within the larger reality, tends to be tense, for revivalism's defenders see themselves as God's faithful remnant, the spiritually alert people in the valley of dry bones, whereas revivalism's critics see themselves as fighting for rationality, sobriety, integrity, and maturity in discipleship, and for wisdom, order, and resilience in the institutional church, against wild men touting an emotional obscurantism.[1] I realise as I move into the territory of this debate that some listeners are likely to have personal involvements in it that are not identical with mine. I shall not feel free to pull any punches on that account, but I will try to express myself gently and keep my voice down.

Let me say at once where I anticipate disagreements. Shortly I shall decline to favour two revivalist developments that some advocate very strongly as means of inducing conversion. The first is the institutionalizing of the "crisis" conversion. This began with Charles Finney's "Anxious seat," or mourners' bench, a front pew which persons convicted by the preaching were asked to occupy for counsel and prayer; it grew into Dwight L. Moody's "enquiry room," and since has blossomed into the elaborate counselling network of today's crusade evangelism. At the heart of this procedure in all its forms lie two assumptions: first, that the counsellor's prime task is to try to clinch a commitment to Christ, striking while the iron is hot; second, that for concerned persons to identify themselves publicly by coming forward in response to an invitation helps them to be definite, whole-hearted, and permanent in their commitment. I am not happy about any of this, nor, on balance, do I think it gain that, as a result of a century and a half of it, everyone's knee-jerk reaction nowadays to the word "conversion" is to think of a sudden crisis of commitment such as is worked and prayed for at evangelistic meetings.

The second development is the insistence, characteristic of Pentecostal revivalism and its offshoots, that evangelism is not being biblically practised unless miraculous signs and wonders, chiefly healings, accompany the preaching of the word. Signs and wonders, it is argued, having convincing evidential force, whereas preaching without them lacks a degree of the credibility that it needs to have.[2] Here again I am unhappy, and shall in due course say why. But on neither issue can I expect that my caveats will convince everybody.

I make these introductory remarks not (I hope, and believe) out of egoism, but because I do not want anyone to be in doubt as to where I am coming from, or what is my angle of vision. My Christian life has been lived on the edge of revivalism, with one foot anchored in a revival-oriented, non-revivalist stream of Reformed thought, and no doubt some of the convictions that seem to me inescapably biblical will strike others as reflecting the limitations and blind spots of my heritage. However, like Popeye, I am what I am, and must speak what I think I see. You may not agree with me, but you will not, I trust, misunderstand what I say, or why I say it. It is the health of evangelism, the good of souls, and the glory of God, that I am ultimately seeking.

I plan to discuss three things: first, the nature of conversion, which I shall explore from a sociocultural and historical perspective with the Bible as umpire; second, the internal means of conversion, again with historial excursions; and, third, briefly, the external means of conversion, that is, the ways in which converting truth is communicated to the human mind and heart.

I. The Nature of Conversion

In the Bible, *conversion* (Greek *epistrophe*, Acts 15:3 only; verb, *epistrepho*, corresponding to the Hebrew *sub*) means "turn" or "return" to God. What one turns from is sin, i.e. self-deifying attitudes and self-serving conduct, which is lawlessness (*anomia*, 1 John 3:4); and that aspect of conversion is called *repenting* (Greek *metanoia*; verb, *metanoeo*, expressing the idea of change: change of mind, heart, and behaviour). That which one turns to is God promising mercy, God offering forgiveness, God in covenant, God in Christ; and that aspect of conversion is called faith (Greek *pistis*; verb, *pisteuo*, expressing the idea of trustful commitment and committed trust). *Epistrepho* and *metanoeo* are used both of initial turning to God and of subsequent returning after some lapse (Luke 22:32; Revelation 2:5; l6, etc.). Though the New Testament records several conversion experiences, some violent and dramatic (e.g. that of Paul, Acts 9:5 ff.; of Cornelius, Acts l0:44 ff., cf. 15:7 ff.; of the Philippian jailer, 16:29 ff.), no interest is shown in the psychology of conversion as such; Luke gives three accounts of the conversions of Paul and Cornelius (9:5 ff., 22:6 ff., 26:12 ff.; l0:44 ff., ll:15 ff., 15:7 ff.) because of the supreme significance of these events in early church history, not out of interest in the manifestations that accompanied them. The writers think of conversion dynamically, not as something one feels but as something one does, and they interpret it theologically, in terms of the gospel to which the convert assents and responds.

What has happened to the concept of conversion down the Christian centuries?

That turning to God means repenting of sin and believing the gospel, and that it is entry into a new supernatural life, was never forgotten, but possessing this blessing came at an early stage to be linked in Christian minds with the rite of baptism, in which sins were supposed actually to be remitted and the Holy Spirit actually conveyed. Then it came to be thought that post- baptismal sin was only remitted in the rite of penitential confession and priestly absolution, which by the middle ages in the West had lost its early character as public church discipline and become a private matter of periodically settling accounts with God and so maintaining one's personal standing in grace. In the static, non-evangelical Christendom of the five centuries before the Reformation, salvation was held to come through the life-giving ecclesiastical routines of infant baptism, penance, and extreme unction, mediating grace literally from the cradle to the grave, and the word *conversio* (which in itself can mean any kind of turning round) was applied to other things. Starting upon the purgative way, level one of mystical prayer, could be called conversion, and the transition to level two, the illuminative way, was sometimes called a second conversion. Sometimes becoming a "religious" (monk or nun) was called a second conversion, the first in this case being baptism. The story of Augustine's conversion from unbelief, as told in his *Confessions*, was not unknown, but the idea that it might model something for citizens of Christian countries seems never to have entered anyone's head.

Luther, the theological colossus of the early Reformation, gave the world the supreme demonstration of his theological and rhetorical power in *De Servo Arbitrio* (1525), where he expounds against Erasmus Augustine's idea of effectual prevenient grace changing the inmost nature of those whom God has predestined to life. The climax of his argument is a compelling *fortissimo* exegesis of New Testament passages showing that the fruit of this change is the self-despairing faith in Christ through which a guilty sinner is actually justified. Though Luther does not use the word conversion, the elements of the developed evangelical view are all there.[3]

Calvin, the great biblical systematizer, who once referred intriguingly to the "sudden conversion" (*subita conversio*) by which God "subdued and made teachable" his hard heart and gave him "some foretaste and knowledge of true piety,"[4] develops in the *Institutio* a concept of conversion as the practice of lifelong active repentance, the fruit of faith, spring from a renewed heart:

> The whole of conversion to God is understood under the term 'repentance'....The Hebrew word for 'repentance' is derived from conversion or return, the Greek word from change of mind and purpose: and the thing itself fits each derivation, for the essence of it is that departing from ourselves we turn to God, and putting off our former mind we put on a new one. So I think repentance may well be defined as a true conversion of our life to God, issuing from pure and heartfelt fear of him, and consisting in the

mortification of our flesh and old man and in the vivification of the Spirit.

When we call it 'a conversion of life to God,' we are requiring a transformation not only in outward works but in the soul itself, which can only bring forth fruits answerable to its renewal when it has put off its old nature *(vetustatem)*.

When God converts us to zeal for what is right, all that is of our own will is abolished, and what replaces it is all from God. I say that our will is abolished, but not as will, for in man's conversion what belongs to his original nature remains intact. I say that it (the will) is new-created, not so that it may thus begin to be a will, but so that it may thus be turned from a bad will into a good one.[5]

Using "conversion" as a descriptive rather than a technical, classificatory term, Calvin here projects with precision the thought of a radical affective and volitional change effected monergistically by sovereign grace—the pure Augustinian conception. Elsewhere he accounts for the sad phenomenon of "temporary faith" (*temporalis fides*) by explaining that those whose professed faith later fails were never regenerated with the incorruptible seed of life.[6] Calvin's interest is not in describing and dissecting personal spiritual experiences as such—he is too Christ-centred a thinker for that—but in making two points, as follows. First, the continual conversion (turning from sin and self to God and righteousness) in which the Christian's lifelong repentance consists is entirely God's work, inasmuch as it is the expression of a sinful heart that God has now made new and keeps new. Our "good works," to the extent that they are good, are thus God's gifts, not our achievements. Second, the active turning to himself that God works in Christians is the fruit of faith—a God-wrought disposition of assured and heartfelt trust in God as Father, in Christ as Mediator, and in God's promise of mercy as truth applying to oneself.[7] In substance these emphases correspond exactly to those of Luther controverting the idea of meritorious good works in *De Servo Arbitrio*.

The common evangelical view today is of conversion as a divinely triggered psychological event whereby a really and consciously lost sinner passes from death to life. This view, while contradicting nothing that Luther or Calvin taught, is more man-centred, experience-oriented, and evangelistically-angled, than the Reformers' teaching on repentance and faith ever was. This theologico-psychological perspective on conversion was developed within two parallel, interconnected seventeenth-century movements that sought the pastoral and devotional renewal of state churches: English Puritanism, exported in due course to America, and Pietism among Dutch Calvinists and German Lutherans. With small variations of emphasis (within as well as between their groups), they agreed on the following points:

(1) The event called conversion, regeneration, new birth (*Wiedergeburt* in German), and effectual calling[8] (in the seventeenth century these four terms were synonymous)[9], is a necessity for salvation, since the personal coming to faith to which they all refer is correlative to God's work of justifying us, of ingrafting us into Christ so as to share his death and risen life, of adopting us as children and heirs, and of sealing us as his own by the gift of the indwelling Holy Spirit. The quest for conversion is thus the most important issue of life.

(2) Self-conversion through one's own initiative, like self-justification through one's own works, is impossible, since fallen human beings are impotent and incompetent in relation to everything that would please God. "A natural man, being altogether averse from that [spiritual] good, and dead in sin, is not able, by his own strength, to convert himself, or prepare himself thereunto."[10] Conversion is in fact one aspect of new creation, in which the agent, as in the first creation, is and can be only God himself.

(3) Conversion involves the whole person. Faith starts in the mind as the reality of things already cognized as concepts comes to be felt. The things in question, in some shape or form, are the holiness and love of God; one's corruption, guilt, misery, and emptiness before God; and the personal approach of the Father and the Son with words of grace. Emotion may well be stirred (distress, shame, fear, joy), though the felt perception of spiritual realities is not an emotion as such, and unemotional conversions do in fact occur. Faith, beginning as cognitive *notitia* (knowledge), blossoms into volitional *assensus* (acquiescence) and hearty *fiducia* (trust), whence flows real repentance (actual turning from sin to follow Christ). Some conversion processes are sudden and others gradual, some are turbulent and others smooth, but the inner shape of them all is as stated.

(4) Conversion centres on Christ, and cannot occur where he has not been made known. It always brings some transition in consciousness from *angst* stirred by a sense of spiritual need to peace springing from a sense of God's acceptance through Christ. Its authentic fruit in subsequent life is not deadening complacency, but Christ-centred discipleship.

(5) Conversion requires preparation of heart in the form of a

radical humbling for sin (contrition). This is not because sorrow for sin has intrinsic spiritual value, or merits grace (though Puritan "preparationism" has often been misunderstood in these terms, and perhaps sometimes, in its less judicious exponents, so misunderstood itself). The reason why a "law-work" of contrition was demanded was rather this: that through it our corrupt love of anti-God independence, the love shown in unresponsiveness to God's word and misbehaviour in his world, withers, and desire for a new life of reconciliation to God and righteousness before men blossoms in its place. God, who is rational and made us rational, treats us as rational, and works conversion in us by a rational process that involves recognizing that our sin is repulsive as well as ruinous; begging Christ to save us from its power and presence as well as its guilt; and thanking him for freeing us from a sort of life that, quite apart from its woeful consequences, now seems to us intrinsically hateful. Hostility to one's pre-Christian ways is thus necessarily involved in entering upon peace with God, and this is what preparatory conviction of sin, misery, and need is all about.

(6) Spirit-given assurance, which is consciousness of one's faith, of one's salvation received by that faith, and of God's saving love towards one personally (see Romans 8!), comes with believing, sometimes vividly so from the start. Luther and Calvin spoke as if such assurance is of the essence of faith, and some of their followers preserved this emphasis, insisting that faith is not born till assurance is given. The Puritan consensus, however, was that "assurance doth not so belong to the essence of faith, but that a true believer may wait long, and conflict with many difficulties, before he be partaker of it: yet, being enabled by the Spirit to know the things which are freely given to him of God, he may, without extraordinary revelation, in the right use of ordinary means, attain thereunto."[11] All agreed, however, against Roman Catholics, that assurance is every convert's birthright, and that all who truly sought would truly find.

(7) The only proof of conversion is a life of convertedness (that is, continual turning from the calls of carnal self to God and his service). Persons loving, trusting, and following Jesus in this way are certainly converted, whether or not they know when it happened; persons not living thus have no right to be confident that they are converted, however strong the confidence that they actually cherish and proclaim.

(8) The false conversions (really, the non-conversions) of "temporary believers" are due to spiritual superficiality whereby people go through the motions of embracing Christ without fully seeing their need to seek and find the radical change of heart

described above. As Calvin had already phrased it, they "receive the gift of reconciliation...in a confused way and without sufficient discernment." [12] The best pastoral safeguard against this is depth and intensity of contrition, as described above.

(9) The church in idea is the company of the converted, and the conversion of those who attend should be the constant goal of the praying, preaching and counselling of the church's officers.

(10) The means of conversion is the revealed truth of the biblical gospel, received into mind and heart and responded to through the action of the Holy Spirit. Have the gospel sacraments any significance in this process? They well may; but when they do, their significance is not that they convey automatically to the non-resistant the grace of new life that they signify, as historic sacramentalism teaches; their significance is, rather, that they make visible, tangible, and thus certain, the promises of new life that faith must claim. As "visible words" (Augustine's phrase) they convey converting truth; they are sermons seen, reinforcing sermons heard. But the truth only converts through the agency of the Spirit working with and through it to renew the heart and call forth an acknowledgement of spiritual realities, a hatred of sin, a trust in Christ, and a love of God and godliness, of which we sinners were quite incapable before.

Such was the concept and theology of conversion among Puritans and Pietists in the seventeenth century and revival leaders both sides of the Atlantic, including the professed Arminian John Wesley, in the eighteenth century.[13] Common to them all was the Augustinian conviction that the turning from sin to God that God requires must be God's own gift, since full inward sincerity in turning is beyond fallen mankind's natural powers. Persons convicted of their present lostness should therefore be told of their need to look to God to renew their hearts, change their motivations, make their words sincere, and assure them of acceptance, as they seek to lay hold of Christ as their mediator and give themselves to him as their master. This was an integral element in the pastoral direction given to the unconverted by these evangelicals. It is an emphasis not found in later revivalist evangelism. I think we are the poorer for having lost it. To the extent that our preaching and counselling structures, especially in crusade evangelism, appear to assume that the volitional power of "decision" or "commitment" (which is how we indicate the first expression of faith and repentance) is at every sinner's command every moment, there is unreality, and unreality neither profits people nor glorifies God.

As a believer in the essential correctness of the view of conversion just set out, I am constantly troubled over this point. Today's crusade evangelism is an outgrowth of procedures developed by Charles G. Finney and Dwight L. Moody, neither of whom doubted that whole-hearted repentance was possible on the spot to anyone who had been sufficiently "broken down" (Finney's phrase) by the pressure or allure of the evangelist's persuasive speech. (You will recognize here a revival of the seventeenth century Arminian view that moral suasion is all the grace given or needed to induce conversion: a thesis that Augustinians, appealing to such passages as Romans 8:7-11, 9:14-24; Ephesians 2:1-10; John 6:43-45, would negate.) In line with this conviction, evangelists frequently orchestrate intense pressure-points at the close of each meeting of each crusade, seeking hereby to "draw in the net" and "reap the harvest." If, however, "decision" and "commitment" mean repentance and faith, and if faith and repentance can only occur as the convicting Spirit of God actually changes the inner man, in addition to convincing of need and assuring of God's love, and if the working of the Spirit is not ours to command, there is some unreality and some misdirection, as well as some manipulation, in making it appear as if coming forward for counselling, or responding with whatever other gesture is asked for, will eternally clinch, here and now, the issue of one's conversion. Even if it is said from the platform that this is not necessarily so, the procedure itself seems to tell a different story. I recognize that crusade evangelism may reach persons whom local church evangelism would not reach; nonetheless, local church evangelism, which, being continuous, does not need to institutionalize decision-this- moment in the intense, dragooning way I have described, is surely in itself a preferable thing. It is better to enforce the urgency of turning to God without projecting an erroneous view of man in the process.

II. The Internal Means of Conversion

Conversion itself is a process. It can be spoken of as a single act of turning in the same way that consuming several dishes and drinks can be spoken of as a single act of dining, and as we have seen, revivalism encourages us to think of a simple, all-embracing, momentary crisis as its standard form. But conversion, which was defined above as man's turning to God seen from man's standpoint, is better understood if viewed as a complex process that for adults ordinarily involves the following: thinking and re-thinking; doubting and overcoming doubts; soul-searching and self-admonition; struggle against feelings of guilt and shame; and concern as to what realistic following of Christ might mean. It may culminate in a personal crisis that will afterwards be remembered as "the hour I first believed." Sometimes, of course, it does so culminate, outside as well as within revivalist circles; think of Augustine hearing a child say "take and read," picking up a Bible and seeing Romans 13:13, and never being the same again. But sometimes it does not head up into a single conscious crisis, even for attenders at evangelistic crusades. God is Lord in conversion, as elsewhere, and experiences differ.

Some decisions that occur within the structural pattern of revivalist evangelism are preceded by very little of this kind of soul-travail, but then, as we also know, many of these decisions prove hollow, and if ten per cent of the professed converts in a crusade are still standing after a year we think we are doing well. It is surely healthier, at least among adults, when much thought and care about specific decisions go into the making of the umbrella-decision, as we may call it, whereby one comes to rely utterly on Jesus Christ for forgiveness, acceptance, and final salvation with God, and to enthrone him as Lord of the rest of one's days. (I dismiss here the strange idea, sometimes met in dispensational theology and child evangelism, that saving conversion means simply receiving Jesus as Saviour without regard for his Lordship. This view divides faith from repentance, and Christ's priesthood from his offices as teacher and king, and merits the comment: what God has joined, let not man put asunder. I move on.) Conversion, however simple in idea, is a complex process in life, just because we sinners are complex creatures, and our discussion of the means of conversion will be simplistic if this twofold complexity goes unrecognized.

Reformational theologians have always affirmed that the objective means of conversion is the gospel message, opened by the Spirit to the spiritual eyes that he opens as part of his renewal of our hearts. "Faith comes from hearing the message, and the message is heard through the word of Christ" (Romans 10:17). "He chose to give us birth through the word of truth" (James 1:18). "Believe in the Lord Jesus, and you will be saved" (Acts 16:31). The message is twofold: law and promise, law and love, law and grace. "Law" stands for declaring God's demands, our failure to meet them, God's threats, our need of a reconciled relationship with him, and our misery without it. "Promise, love, grace" stand for announcing Christ, the divine Saviour, crucified, risen, and reigning, living, forgiving, and befriending; for inviting sinners to come to him and through him to the Father; and for setting all that within the purpose of God who from eternity planned and promised the salvation that Christ now offers to us. Then the subjective means of conversion is the movement into evangelical faith and evangelical repentance that this message calls for, and that God through this message calls forth. By "movement into" I mean all that goes into the producing of the end-product: all that is involved in coming to believe against the pressures of unbelief, in centering upon invisible eternal realities despite the kaleidoscopic distractions of life's ongoing flow, and in struggling for self-denial against one's inbred instincts of self-assertion. This is our focus now.

Evangelical faith, we have seen, is knowledge, assent, and trust, with Christ and God's promise of grace through him as its object and one's personal destiny with God as its focus of concern. Evangelical repentance, we have seen, is turning from sin, now recognized as ruinous, to a new life of following Christ in righteousness, now embraced as the only way to go. How does a person come to faith and repentance? By coming to understand, believe, and perceive, the application to oneself of the gospel message. About this, several questions arise.

First: how much (or, how little) knowledge of gospel facts and truths does one need to come to a genuine conversion?

The answer has to be given in functional terms, thus: enough to make one certain, through the Spirit's convincing and convicting action, that one needs a new life that is right with God, and that the only way to have such a life is to trust oneself absolutely to the mercy and direction of Jesus Christ as living personal Saviour and Lord. In human relational contexts there is constantly more cognitive awareness than people can verbalize and more situational insight than was ever imparted by the utterances of others, so we need not wonder at instances of genuine faith and repentance resulting from amazingly little—we would have said, quite inadequate—formal instruction. (Some episodes in Jesus' ministry might seem to illustrate this: cf. Luke 5:18-25, 7:37-50, 8:43-48, 17:12-19, 18:35-43, 19:1-10.) Faithful preachers, teachers, and evangelists will conscientiously labour to instil full understanding of the whole gospel—creation, sin, God's holiness and love, incarnation and atonement, repentance and faith, new life in Christ with Christ and in the church with God's other children—and they will look to God to bless the truth that they teach, and not expect anyone to be converted without adequate knowledge. At the same time, however, they will be prepared to find that God has gone ahead of them, and has blessed very little formal knowledge to the production of real and virile faith in the Lord Jesus.

Second: is it possible to be specific about the preparation of heart that genuine conversion requires?

Once more, the only possible answer is the functional one: the preparation that is needed, along with belief that the gospel is true, is a sufficient falling out of love for sin and for one's life to date to produce gratitude to Jesus for opening the door to a new and godly way of living, and to make one want to follow him into it. This is not, however, endorsement of the doctrine (feared by many, though held by very few) that only one who has undergone a long period of heavy contrition is qualified to come to Christ, or will be received by him. The legalistic "preparationism" allegedly taught by Puritans and others who stressed the need for deep conviction of sin and laboured to induce it is in truth a figment of the critics' imagination. The position actually maintained by the Puritans and their admirers, past and present, is that only one who has come thoroughly to hate sin can turn whole-heartedly from sin to Christ. Contrition is necessitated not by the terms of the gospel, which calls us to Christ directly, but by the state of the fallen human heart. God uses the law to pave the way for the gospel by making us see not only our guilt but also the ugliness, nastiness, and repulsiveness of our previous ways, so that we cease to love them; and that sets us free to love Christ when he calls us to follow him into different ways.

The alternative is the false conversion modelled by the stony-ground hearers in Jesus' parable of the soils (Matthew 13:20f.). Under pressure one who received the word of pardon and peace with joy, and promised to follow Christ henceforth, finds the old way of Christlessness and sin more attractive than the new way of resisting sin out of loyalty to Christ and suffering in consequence (cf. Hebrews 12:3f.); so he goes back to it. That shows that such inner conviction and change as he experienced never went deep enough to make the life of sin intolerable for ever after, or to produce clear understanding that Christ will only save us from sin, never in sin. This has no bearing on the question whether a true believer can fall away; I speak here only of people who, though they profess faith without conscious insincerity, never in fact become true believers. The best we can do to avoid producing false conversions is to make much of the law, sin, and repentance in our communication, and not to press people for gestures of decision till we have done all we can to make sin hateful in their eyes, and have reason to judge that they have received this part of the message. But this deep conviction of sin, like the conviction that the gospel announces realities, and realities that impinge on my life, comes only from the Holy Spirit's application of the word we communicate.

Third: is it possible to be specific about steps for removing doubts and obstacles to belief?

Jesus' words, "If any man's will is to do [God's] will, he shall know whether the teaching is from God" (John 7:17), show that a reverent disposition and conscious openness to discover that Christianity is true is a means of moving from doubt to certainty. Willingness to be convinced will lead to the coming of actual conviction: not by auto-suggestion or wishful thinking, but by the work and witness of the sovereign Holy Spirit, both enabling one to see that unbelief is, after all, unreasonable and making one unable to doubt that the God and the Christ of the gospel, and one's own need of both, are inescapable realities.

Fourth: does confrontation with any sort of miraculous "signs and wonders" augment the convincing effect of gospel truth on the unconvinced?

Since Pentecostal Christians began to claim at the start of this century that all New Testament manifestations should in principle be constantly recurring in every age of Christian church life and mission, this question has been pressed in many forms, in the belief that the answer must certainly be "yes," and that Pentecostal Christians actually have many signs and wonders to show. About the latter claim I say nothing here, but my answer to the question itself is "not necessarily" for the following reasons. (1) It is always possible to doubt whether "wonders" are "signs" from God, or indeed works of God at all. (2) It is irrational to expect that persons not convinced by the Bible's narratives of miracles will be any more impressed by unusual occurrences under their own noses in connection with the ministry of the biblical gospel. (3) The essence of the Holy Spirit's convincing work with regard to gospel truth is to make one unable to doubt that the God and Christ of the gospel are realities confronting one here and now, and that one needs their mercy. Not even in Bible times did signs and wonders carry with them the guaranteed power of the Holy Spirit to bring this conviction in a way that the gospel word itself did not do. (4) The biblical case for expecting miraculous phenomena to accompany the gospel whenever and wherever it is ministered is not conclusive. The most that can be said is that, contrary to the opinion of some, God has not committed himself never to work miracles on earth again. It looks as if on occasion, in some pioneer missionary situations for instance, he has done so, and I do not suggest that no single one of the "signs and wonders" to which Western Christians of Pentecostal type would appeal is genuinely miraculous (however one glosses that word). But they are the exception, not the rule, when they occur; and the claim I am responding to is that they ought to be the ordinary attesting and convincing accompaniment of the gospel at all times.

In any case, the best evidence for augmenting the convincing power of gospel truth is the transformed lives of holy Christians—a much more telling demonstration of God's reality and resources than any physical wonder.

Fifth: how does the moment of regeneration relate to the subjective process of conversion?

The first thing to say here is that not all Christian teachers have admitted the concept of a "moment" of regeneration. For Calvin, regeneration was the whole process of our subjective renewal, from the first stirrings of faith to the completing of our sanctification. For the Puritans, regeneration was, as we saw, the whole process of conversion viewed as God's work. For most modern evangelicals, however, the "moment" of regeneration is the event signified by baptism, namely our implanting into Christ so that we become sharers in his death and risen life. Evangelicals who believe in the total spiritual inability of fallen man see conversion as necessarily presupposing regeneration; other evangelicals posit regeneration as immediately following the first genuine act of faith. Both viewpoints agree that its effect is to secure the sustained expression of Christ's risen life in and through us, and thus to supernaturalize our natural existence.

As a believer in total inability, I affirm a moment of regeneration and spiritual animation underlying the sinner's first true act of faith. But since the event occurs below the level of consciousness, in what Scripture calls the "heart," and since in any case the first exercise of real faith cannot usually be identified to the minute, this moment of animation is characteristically elusive, and speculation about it is profitless. Exegetically, my present view (I have oscillated!) is that the New Testament language of new birth, new begetting, and new creation points not to one vitalizing moment but to the whole conversion process, just as the Puritans thought. But a moment of quickening, causally linked with the exercise of authentic faith, has to be.

The infant regeneration about which the Fathers, mediaevals, Roman Catholics, Orthodox, sacramentalist Anglicans, Luther, Calvin, Wesley, Kuyper, and others have been so confident, namely a regeneration conferred or confirmed by baptism which lies latent for years, if not for ever, troubles me, I confess, precisely because of its lack of connection with conversion. There are biblical instances of infant and pre-natal piety (cf. Luke 1:15, 44), but in 1 John there is no spiritual regeneration that does not express itself in a changed life (2:29, 3:9, 4:7, 5:1,4). From this I infer that while no human is too young to be regenerated, the idea of a regenerated person not expressing the change at once is unbiblical; so no child should be presumed regenerate, even though born of Christian parents and baptized, till signs of active spiritual life appear.

III. The External Means of Conversion

Little remains to be said (which is as well, since this essay is now over length). The external means of conversion, as has already become clear, is the gospel message, the word of God, preached, taught, read, made visible in the sacraments, explained in books, and embodied in the life of the Christian community. Experiences of Christian worship and fellowship can mediate the reality of the things of which the message speaks, or rather they may become the occasion of the Spirit's action in creating awareness of this reality. Empathy with the hearers will help the preacher, teacher, or evangelist to get inside them with the message, applying it in a way that the Spirit will use to give knowledge of one's own need and of God's grace. Parents teaching their children gospel truths should seek a like empathy. Empathy in spiritual communication is a gift of God, and should be sought from him as such; it is essentially the ability to follow Paul in becoming all things to all men so that by all means we may save some (cf. 1 Corinthians 9:19-22). Fidelity to the revealed word, which keeps one under its authority, is the deepest secret of communicating it with authority, and authority of this kind is an abiding need in spreading the gospel.

Prayer, in which the church talks to God about people as earnestly as the evangelist talks to people about God, is also an external means of conversion, inasmuch as God's blessing is only ordinarily given where it has been sought. God the Holy Spirit is in the final analysis the evangelist who brings unbelievers to faith, and the means we use to this end will prove barren in our hands if we behave as if we thought that these means have converting power in themselves.

Conclusion

Throughout this paper my goal has been to appreciate, yet at the same time to transcend, the now largely international heritage of America's revivalism. Revivalism has always had its priorities right: it has gone all out for conversions and against specific social evils. But its pervasive anthropocentrism, its simplistic theology, hymnody, and spirituality, its streak of manipulative emotionalism, the personality cult that has entrapped many of its leaders, its developed style of worldly-wise, well-heeled pragmatism, its image of itself as leading the churches rather than supplementing and supporting them, and its unwillingness to be in any significant way accountable to them, are weaknesses that present longterm problems. Central to revivalism is its image of conversion, and how conversion is most effectively induced. My thesis is that if we substituted for this image the full-scale evangelical understanding of conversion that preceded revivalism we should not lose, but gain, theologically, evangelistically, pastorally, and in the quality of Christian humaneness, or humanism, that should always be blossoming in Christian corporate life and action. I write as for wise men; you judge what I say.

This paper was originally presented at a Consultation of the Lausanne Continuation Committee on World Evangelization which was held in Hong Kong in January, 1989.

Endnotes

1. George Whitefield, John Wesley, Archibald Alexander, Charles Finney, Arthur Wallis, and J. Edwin Orr, are among those who have in broad terms favoured revivalism out of concern for Christian spirituality; Charles Chauncy, George Lavington, Gabriel Hebert, and James Barr, are among those who in broad terms have opposed revivalism out of concern for Christian maturity; Jonathan Edwards, D. Martyn Lloyd-Jones, and Richard Lovelace are among those who have been cool towards revivalism out of concern for authentic revival.

2. See, for instance, John Wimber with Kevin Springer, *Power Evangelism: Signs and Wonders Today* (London: Hodder & Stoughton, 1985; San Francisco: Harper & Row, 1986).

3. See *Martin Luther on the Bondage of the Will* (i.e. *De Servo Arbitrio*), tr. J.I.Packer and O.R.Johnston (London: James Clarke, and Old Tappan: Revell, 1957), especially pp. 273 ff.

4. Calvin, Preface, *Commentary on the Psalms* (1557); cited and discussed by F. Wendel, *Calvin: the Origins and Development of his Religious Thought*, tr. Philip Mairet (London: Collins, 1963).

5. *Inst.* III. iii. 5 f., II. iii. 6.

6. *Ibid.* III. ii. 11.

7. "Firm and sure knowledge of God's good will towards us, based on the truth of the gracious promise in Christ and revealed to our minds and sealed on our hearts by the Holy Spirit" (*ibid.* III. ii.7).

8. Westminster Confession X dealing with conversion is titled "Of Effectual Calling." It starts thus: "All those whom God hath predestinated unto life, and those only, he is pleased, in his appointed and accepted time, effectually to call, by his Word and

Spirit, out of that state of sin and death, in which they are by nature
to grace and salvation, by Jesus Christ; enlightening their minds
spiritually and savingly to understand the things of God, taking
away their heart of stone, and giving unto them an heart of flesh;
renewing their wills, and by his almighty power, determining them
to that which is good, and effectually drawing them to Jesus Christ:
yet so, as they come most freely, being made willing by his grace"
(X.i).

9. Much modern Reformed theology presents regeneration in
terms of the biological or botanical analogy of implanting a living
seed, from which conversion grows. This highlights the monergism
of the work of internal grace, and is widely valued on that account.
It is mainly however a nineteenth century development. Most
Reformed theologians of the two previous centuries, and Lutheran
pietists and Wesley with them, treated conversion and regeneration
as correlative concepts, connoting the same process viewed from
different angles. Regeneration was God turning sinners to himself,
with all that that involved. "Turretin defines two kinds of
conversion: first, a 'habitual' or passive conversion, the production
of a disposition or habit of the soul, which, he remarks, might better
be called 'regeneration'; and secondly, an 'actual' or active
conversion, in which this implanted habit or disposition becomes
active in faith and repentance" (L. Berkhof, *Systematic Theology*
[Grand Rapids: Eerdmans, 1949], p.467. Turretin's *Institutio
Theologiae Elencticae* dates from 1688). KJV, wishing to project the
thought that man's conversion is God's work in him, mistranslated
epistrepho (active) by the passive "be converted" in Matthew 13:15;
Mark 4:12; Luke 22:32; Acts 3:19, 28:27.

10. Westminster Confession (1647), IX.iii.

11. *Ibid*, XVIII.iii.

12. *confuse nec satis distincte: Inst.* III.ii.11.

13. Warrant for this assertion will be found in many Puritan
writings, notably treatises by Richard Baxter (*A Treatise of Conversion;
Directions and Persuasions to a Sound Conversion; A Call to the
Unconverted*), William Whateley (*The New Birth*), Thomas Shepard
(*The Sound Believer, The Sincere Convert; The Parable of the Ten Virgins*),
John Owen (*Pneumatologia,* Book III); Philipp Jakob Spener (*Der
Hochwichtige Articul von der Wiedergeburt*); H. Heppe, *Reformed
Dogmatics* (London: Allen & Unwin, 1950), pp.520 ff., Timothy L.
Smith, *Whitefield and Wesley on the New Birth* (Grand Rapids:
Zondervan, 1986); etc.

Recovering Vocation Today

Klaus Bockmuehl

Vol. XXIV, No. 3 (September 1988):25—35

Introduction: The need for perspective and purpose

In recent years, we have witnessed a growing awareness of the human need for goals and perspective. One sees this in the trend towards goal-oriented management in business and industry, e.g., in the setting up of "quality circles" in industrial production which make room for individual initiative, and replace the traditional style of management by rule and duty. Recently, Peters and Waterman in their best-seller, *In Search of Excellence,* have built their remarkable theory of leadership and management around man's need for goals and meaning in life. They assert that to "formulate and define purpose" is essential to the role of the executive in his or her charge to secure commitment from people.[1] Those who study ideological developments in the Marxist world, encounter a similar movement, e.g., in the field of philosophy of education: Soviet theorists today propose education by goal, instead of by rule and command, on the presupposition that perspective engenders motivation.[2] We know that the organs and members of the human body are built to serve a purpose: they shrivel and atrophy if they are not employed in the higher tasks for which they were created. In some ways, this seems to be true also for the human individual as a whole. One can thus hardly over-emphasize the importance of the human need for goals and perspective.

Moreover, the importance of goals and perspective is not merely a category of the general nature of man; it is also a decisive factor in the formation of the Christian life. At this point we are not speaking of the universal hope of the Christian church (which also co-determines the life and walk of every Christian) but of the presence of goals that shape the life of the individual Christian. In one of his letters to Timothy, Paul touches upon this when he gives his young worker the testimony: "You have carefully followed my doctrine (*didaskalia*), manner of life (*agoge*), [and] purpose (*prothesis*)…" (2 Timothy 3:10). These three definitions identify the Christian: the believer is to be described not only by what one believes and teaches, or how one lives, but also by way of one's purpose (*prothesis*, literally: objective, proposition or intention).

However, an immediate qualification needs to be made: in its Christian usage, *prothesis* cannot be understood in the sense of a human project and program, i.e., of a self-styled plan and proposition. Rather, the proposition is God's. Therefore, to be precise, in the original, comprehensive meaning of the word "vocation," is the divine goal in life. Our purpose is set by our vocation.

Jesus said to his disciples, "My food is to do the will of him who sent me and to accomplish his work" (John 4:34). He saw himself as *a man with a mission*, in the literal sense of someone who has been sent. Jesus' goal in life, his perspective, had been set for him. They were a divine commission and assignment. This is exactly what we call "vocation" in the life of the Christian. Our "vocation" is derived from, and is the complement of, Christ's "mission."

It is therefore suggested that, for the Christian, "vocation" represents a far more comprehensive perspective of goal and vision, than the mere concept of "job" or profession. Admittedly, in the mind of the average secular person, the idea of vocation has a much narrower scope. Unfortunately, but for recognizable reasons, many Christians also have a concept of "vocation" that is equally limited. A good bit of removal of overgrowth and rubble is necessary in order for us to recapture and realize the range and breadth of the original biblical notion.

In probing the Christian concept of vocation, therefore, we will first look at Scripture and its concepts of vocation, then study the disintegration of the understanding of vocation that occurred in the history of the church, and conclude with some observations concerning the recovery of the original biblical synthesis of the concept of vocation today.

I. Three Aspects of a Biblical View of Vocation
A systematic outline of the concept of vocation as informed by the biblical material must deal with the concept of vocation on two levels: (1) a *general* level, regarding the whole of humanity, (2) a

special level, concerning all Christians, and within both of them, the particular vocation of the individual.

I. 1. Universal Vocation: The Cultural Mandate

The first and basic level concerns the creational vocation of man. This is a general vocation in the sense that it is addressed to all of humanity. Traditionally, this has been called the "cultural mandate" or the "culture commission," as found in Genesis 1: 27-28:

> God created man in his own image; in the image of God he created him. Male and female he created them; and God blessed them and said unto them: be fruitful and multiply and fill the earth, and subdue it and have dominion over the fish of the sea, over the birds of the air and over every living thing that moves upon the earth.

The cultural commission therefore consists of procreation, and stewardship over the earth and its creatures. Man is called by God to be his vicegerent in creation. This basic vocation again unfolds in different ways.

I. 1.1 General Specifications: The Divine Law and its Exposition

The creational "cultural mandate" is being specified in terms of ethics, i.e., in terms of how to act and implement the mandate in detail. Here, we will have to think first of that great Charter of Duties, the law divinely given in the form of the ten commandments. They are, as it were, the "Owner's Manual" for creation, giving the most general guidelines for humanity's life in it.

In addition to the actual text of the ten commandments, we must name their different expositions and interpretations, be it in the form of codes of legislation or of general ethical exhortation. Among them, with special relevance for the understanding of the cultural mandate, we encounter a vast body of moral orientation and instruction in the wisdom writings, partly in the canonical writings, partly in the so-called Apocrypha of the Old Testament. They are intended to guide the individual's walk in righteousness and are summed up in the commandment to love one's neighbour (Sirach 17:14). In them, one will find that in not a few instances, the wisdom of Israel comes close to the wisdom literature of the nations that surrounded it. This means that there exists a body of common knowledge of what is demanded to sustain God's creation, something which—although that is an ambiguous term—has been called "natural moral law."

I. 1.2. Individual Specification: the Civil Vocations

The wisdom writings, especially, give rise to a certain extent to that third level in the traditional disposition of man's "householding" or stewardship of creation, i.e., the individual's actual civil vocation. As individuals, all humans have vocations within the mandate to cultivate and sustain creation, such as the vocation of farmer, housewife, teacher, blacksmith, doctor, and all the other "civil vocations" that keep life together. So the Wisdom of Jesus Sirach (Ecclesiasticus) points every man to his particular task of husbandry which God has assigned to him (3:22ff.; 7:15), just as he has ordained a special role for all the forces of creation to work in unison (16:26ff.; 42:21ff.).

In sum, then, the cultural mandate means householding or stewardship in creation, husbandry in nature, and this is participation in God's own work of sustaining his world. A striking symbol and model of this basic creational vocation is Joseph in Egypt: Joseph the *Provider*, who says of himself that he has been called "to keep many alive" (Genesis 50:20). That is exactly man's task and calling in creation.

I. 2. Special Vocation: The Great Commission

In addition to the creational calling of man, we find Scripture speaking of the special vocation of the Christian. It is a special calling because it belongs to the church, to those who are disciples of Jesus, and not to humanity as such. It is thus a specifically Christian vocation, no longer a call on the level of creation, but on the level of salvation.

I. 2.1 General Specifications

Just as the creational calling of man is structured by the ten commandments and the ethics of wisdom, so the special calling of the Christian receives its instruction from the teachings of Jesus (e.g., the Sermon on the Mount), and the body of exhortations in the letters of the apostles. Looking at the specific content of the Christian vocation, according to the New Testament, one can speak of three different objects or goals of special vocation. The *first is that Christians are called to holiness.* The apostles Peter, Paul and John speak of this in their letters. Christians are called to belong to Jesus Christ and called to be saints. Vocation is indeed at the root of a Christian's commission and ministry and the basic Christian vocation is the vocation to holiness.

The *second calling of the Christian is the call to service* as the practical outworking of the commandment to love one's neighbour. This is best examplified in Jesus' parable of the Good Samaritan who ministers to a fellow human being in need. This Christian form of service sustains life. It re-employs the Christian in the original commission of preservation of life as man's creational calling, now understood not merely in the sense of prevention of harm, but in terms of measures of restoration and rehabilitation.

The *third*—and most clearly a call unique to the Christian—*is the vocation to witness.* This is spelled out, e.g., in 1 Peter 2:9, "You are a chosen race, a royal priesthood, a holy nation, God's own people...that you should declare the wonderful deeds of him who called you out of darkness into his marvellous light." Christians have been called from darkness to light, and been given the additional vocation of declaring God's great deeds. Theirs is a call towards a commission, towards an assignment. Christians are not simply called to be Christians, but called to exercise this task.

We have already sought to establish man's cooperation with God, and his participation in God's own work of sustaining of creation. To this we can now add that the Christian is called to cooperate with, and participate in Christ's own work and ministry of salvation. This happens by way of the Christian proclaiming with Christ "the acceptable year of the Lord" (Luke 4:19), the offer of God's fatherly goodness to a generation caught in revolt and confusion. Through witness, the Christian cooperates with Christ in his work of salvation and of discipling the nations.

In the New Testament, we find a number of pertinent formulae of this commission to witness as a special work for the Kingdom of God. In Philippians 1:7 and 12, the apostle Paul points out that his goal is "the defense," "the confirmation" and "the advance of the gospel." When we speak of the call to witness, we primarily think of the "Great Commission" in Matthew 28:18-20: "Go therefore and make disciples of all nations, baptizing them in the name of the Father, and of the Son, and of the Holy Spirit, and teaching them to observe all that I have commanded you; and behold I am with you always to the end of the age." Paul has a direct parallel to the "Great Commission" in Colossians 1:28-29 where he says, "Christ we proclaim, warning every man and teaching every man in all wisdom that we may present every man mature in Christ. For this I toil, striving with all the energy which he mightily inspires within me." This sentence resembles the Great Commission in that it four times over expresses the same universality that we find in Matthew 28: "Warning every man, and teaching every man, with all wisdom, to make every person mature in Christ." It indicates both the quantitative and the qualitative, the extensive and the intensive understanding of ministry: not only is "every man" to be reached, but he and she are also to become "mature in Christ."

What does it mean to be mature in Christ? One guideline for this attainment of maturity in Christ, the objective of all missions, is to be found in Christ's double commandment of love in Matthew 22:37-39, "To love the Lord your God with all your heart, with all your soul and with all your mind. That is the first and greatest commandment and the second is like it, love your neighbour as yourself." All the law and the prophets, says Jesus, depend upon and revolve around these two commandments. They are the pivotal point of Christianity, of its spirituality and of its dual ethic of worship of God and service to man. Therefore, the double commandment is a proper definition of maturity in Christ, and as such, the goal of holiness, service and missions. In other words, the content of Christian discipleship is to help people come to the point where they begin to love God with all their heart, and love their neighbour as themselves. This is the goal of the Great Commission, the Christian's special vocation to witness.

I. 2.2. Individual Specifications

Just as the creational "cultural mandate" is diversified into the many different civil vocations, so the distinct Christian commission in the realm of salvation is diversified by way of particular spiritual callings: there is, in addition to his or her general (creational) and the special (salvational) assignments, the *individual* vocation of a Christian to his or her own, separate, personal life work. It comes as a calling to some activity that not every human being and not every Christian believer is called to, but which is assigned to this particular person. One might be inclined to say that, if the cultural mandate came from the Creator, God the Father, and the Great Commission was the instruction of Christ Jesus, the Saviour, then the tutoring of the individual could be seen as the particular domain of the Holy Spirit.

I. 2.2.1 Through Individual Spiritual Tasks and Gifts

Again, this "very special," individual, particular vocation works in two ways. One way is through individual spiritual tasks and gifts. The New Testament clearly lays emphasis upon the individual appointment of the Christian's task. Jesus, in his parables about the disciples' deportment during his absence, characterizes himself as one who "gave...to each his work" (Mark 13:34). In a similar way, the apostle Paul describes himself as one who has planted, while Apollos watered, "as the Lord gave to each one" (1 Corinthians 3:5). Indeed, the "calling" of the Holy Spirit means to be "separated" for a particular work, as in the case of Paul and Barnabas (Acts 12:3).

The same can be expressed in terms of gifts of the Spirit, insofar as each gift represents a corresponding task. As the apostle Peter puts it: "As each one has received a gift, minister it to one another, as good stewards of the manifold grace of God" (1 Peter 4:10). St. Paul has a whole chapter (1 Corinthians 12) developing his thesis: "To each is given the manifestation of the Spirit for the common good" (1 Corinthians 12:7). Some Christians are thus gifted and commissioned to speak from inspiration, some to shepherd and teach, some for evangelism, some to help. There is a whole universe of different gifts which together make up a vibrant church. So it is first through the spiritual tasks and gifts, the *charismata*, that the Holy Spirit appoints and instructs the individual to a personal vocation.

I. 2.2.2 Through Actual Guidance

Second, the Holy Spirit also instructs in terms of actual individual guidance. The *charismata* seem to be given to individuals for a whole life-span but there is also the possibility of a specific calling and guidance for an individual in a given situation.

We find many instances of this described in the Bible. One example is Simeon in Jerusalem, the old man who came to the Temple to meet Jesus the Messiah, upon the prompting of the Holy Spirit, "because the Holy Spirit was on him" (Luke 2:25). In the book of Acts one can hardly open a single chapter where one would not find examples of these divine instructions and assignments, as they take place in the course of the propagation of the gospel.

It is highly relevant, therefore, to study those cases within their proper context: they occur within the overall Christian vocation to holiness, service and witness. These three horizons also form the framework for the guidance of the individual. Simeon was "righteous and devout" (Luke 2:25). His call came within the framework of God's greater work of engendering holiness. Similarly, in Acts, individual calls come in course of the pursuit of the Great Commission, as for Philip in Acts 8, Peter in Acts 10, or Paul in Acts 16. Thus, in order to find God's instructions one must begin to pray, "Lord, I need to be more conformed to Jesus, I need to become more holy. Where?" "Lord, I want to help to serve and to lift up people. Whom?" "Lord, you have called me to promote the Gospel and to strengthen the brethren. How?" This is the way in which Christians will have to pray for particular guidance within the framework of the divine commission already received.

In sum, then, Christian vocation is to exercise husbandry or householding, simultaneously in the fields of nature and grace, in humanity and in the church. The Christian vocation is to help both towards preservation and regeneration, to sustain and invigorate the physical and spiritual life of people. The Christian is called to be a "provider" in a physical and spiritual sense. And he or she will find direction added for personal conduct in both fields.

II. Breakdowns in the Understanding of Vocation

We have identified several biblical understandings of vocation and calling. Unfortunately, however, all of history seems to reveal a human incapacity for balance. Perhaps due to the habits and structures of our natural reasoning, we seem to be unable to understand a "both/and" position. We find it impossible to hold together both the "cultural mandate" and the Great Commission. In consequence, we constantly seem to be splitting up into groups which parade opposing half-truth positions: one group extolling the Great Commission, e.g. giving every last penny to the work of overseas missions but paying little attention to the concerns of ecology or the just ordering of social relations at home; the other doing just the opposite. Many movements in the history of the church conform to this apparent human incapacity for true biblical balance.

An exemplary disintegration of the biblical synthesis and an ensuing confrontation between divergent concepts of vocation can be found in medieval and Reformation times. Let us look first at the medieval concept of vocation.

II. 1. The Medieval Bias

In the Middle Ages, monasticism, the lifestyle of the monk and the nun, claimed to be the "real" Christianity. The monks reserved for themselves the term "the religious" which could easily be understood as saying that those outside monastic orders were not religious. When the orders emphasized the church they did not mean the local parish church; for them the church was the monastery. In their eyes, the monastery was the house of God and when they sang "let us go into the house of the Lord" (Psalm 122:1), they took it to mean entering the monastery. The monastic lifestyle as a type—not withstanding exceptions in certain areas (like the agricultural exploits of the Cistercians)—implies a strong ethos of withdrawal from society and culture, abandoning of the world, having nothing to do with humanity.

The monastic lifestyle is supposed to be a very exceptional Christian ethic. Monks are not interested in the creational duties that are valid for everybody. They strive for a peculiar holiness beyond the observation of the ten commandments, a holiness or "perfection" laid out in what they call the three evangelical counsels, i.e. the vows of poverty, chastity (by which they mean never to marry), and obedience to their superior. In terms of the double commandment of love (which humanity never finds easy to keep in balance), their emphasis would be on love for God, to the detriment of love of neighbour.

Monastic theology, however, did not speak about vocation. Vocation was not a term of any consequence to the monks. Rather, they spoke of electing this particular lifestyle—not being called to it but *electing* it themselves. The reason for this is that, by and large, their philosophy was bound up with the concept of merit before God. If one were called by God to a certain assignment, the whole idea of merit would be undercut because it was God's inspiration and God's call, not human volunteering. However, if it was human election, if one did not have to, but freely chose to do it because of love of God, then it could seem to be meritorious. So the monks "elected" what they called the "state of perfection" in which they lived a special life-style which was not commanded but which they offered as a sacrifice and gift to God—specifically, abstinence from marriage, poverty and obedience to a superior. This stance must be understood as the background of all of Reformational and Protestant ethics.

II. 2. The Reformational Reaction

II. 2.1 Against Monasticism

The Protestant Reformation attacked monasticism and turned its ethics upside down.

For one thing, the Reformers replace the "Evangelical Counsel" of monasticism with a new emphasis on the ten commandments. They condemn the monks' quest for extraordinary good works:

"Just think, is it not a devilish presumption on the part of those desperate saints to dare to find a higher and better way of life than the Ten Commandments teach? They pretend, as we have said, that this is a simple life for the ordinary man, whereas theirs is for the saints and the perfect. They fail to see, these miserable, blind people, that no man can achieve so much as to keep one of the Ten Commandments as it ought to be kept....Therefore all their boasting amounts to as much as if I boasted, 'Of course, I haven't a single groschen to pay, but I promise to pay ten gulden.' "[3]

The Reformers constantly remind the monks of the verses from Sirach 3:22ff.: "Search not for things beyond your ability, but the things that God has commanded you. For you have already been commanded more than you can manage."

Therefore, Reformational ethics develops as a comprehensive and elaborate exposition of the ten commandments. Both Luther and Calvin believed in what they called the "sufficiency," "plenitude," or "perfection of the law"; that is, that each and every issue that confronts us in life can be answered by an exposition of one of the commandments. Thus the whole of life is covered by the decalogue.

In addition to the ten commandments, one's civil vocation takes on paramount significance. "True Christianity" is now located in the life of the lay person in his or her everyday work. The real "saint" is now the "secular saint"—not the one who withdraws from society. From this follows that the primary emphasis tends to be no longer on the church but on the state, society, the family, which now becomes a primary location of God's church. One does not withdraw from the world anymore; rather, the Reformation returns the Christian into the world. This has to be understood literally: thousands of monks were encouraged to leave their monasteries and re-enter civil life.

Christian perfection is now to be found in the normal working day. To put it in Luther's classical and drastic phrase:

> "A godly maid-servant if she goes within her command and station and according to her duties sweeps the yard or carries the manure, or a man-servant who with the same mind goes and drives his cart, they move straight into heaven on the right road; whereas another one who runs into the monastery or goes to St. James [on a pilgrimage] or to church, and leaves his duties and his station and work on the side, goes straight into hell."[4]

So it is the "worldly Christian," the secular working person who is on the right road to heaven, who is the incorporation of true saintliness.

Sanctification takes place within one's civil vocation. The New Testament exhortation "to flee the world" is to be understood spiritually, not in the sense of becoming a hermit or running into a monastery, but it is to be realized within one's station in life. Luther the Reformer interprets Scripture consistently in this fashion: for him, the Beatitudes of the Sermon on the Mount as well as Jesus' image of the fruit of the good tree speak of a life of faithfulness in one's civil vocation and station in life.[5] He will say the same of the pericope about the weapons of the Christian's spiritual battle, Ephesians 6:10ff.[6] And when Paul, in Galatians 6:4, admonishes the church "Let each one test his own work...and not boast in his neighbour," he immediately takes this to mean the realm of civil vocation, and that "someone who is a magistrate, a householder, a servant, a teacher, a pupil, etc., should remain in his calling and do his duty there, properly and faithfully, without concerning himself about what lies outside his own vocation."[7] If everybody did what he must in his station, it would be the Kingdom of God in this world. In this vein, Luther even justifies Peter's resolve, "I am going fishing" (John 21:3) by pointing to the great number of fish he subsequently caught, and comes to the surprising conclusion that Jesus does not call the disciples away from fishing, and— generally—"lets politics and economy stand undisturbed."[8] Nor is the Reformer disquietened by the phenomenon of Anna, a prophetess, "who did not depart from the temple, but served God with fasting and prayers night and day" and thus might be seen as a prototype of the monastic life. No, says Luther, prayer and fasting is rightly the task of a widow. A housewife should never leave home and children and think of doing the same.[9] Moreover, one also gets the impression that Luther secularized the New Testament doctrine of the Spirit's gifts and tasks in the church (Romans 12:4; 1 Corinthians 12; 1 Peter 4:10) in applying it to the interplay of vocations in civil society which for him, of course, was identical with the church.[10]

This ideal of worldly holiness is summed up in the famous section on monastic vows in the *Augsburg Confession*: true perfection and the right service of God consists not in being a monk or "wearing a black or gray cowl" but in these four points: 1) fear of God; 2) trust in God's providence; 3) good works; and 4) commitment to one's civil vocation.[11]

It is immediately evident that in such a system, one's particular civil vocation—understood, as it is, less as one's trade or craft, than one's position in society, or "station in life"—was very often the station in life into which one was born; it was one's "birth station." The very fact, e.g., that one was born a woman already determined one's station in life: women were to become mothers. Thus for half of humanity—and more—the circumstances and duties of life and existence were already set down by birth. Centuries later this concept of station in life was still reflected in the verse: "The rich man in his castle, the poor man at his gate, God made them high and lowly and ordered their estate." It is all set down, and to leave one's vocation and hang on to alien works amounts to, as Martin Luther put it: "walking on one's ears, veiling one's feet, and putting shoes on one's head." It would turn everything upside down and destroy the fabric of society.[12]

Indeed, one's vocation is decided by the circumstances, "as it came to be without you," as Luther puts it.[13] God "calls" through the circumstances of one's milieu. Normally, one would relate the concept of "vocation" and "calling" to a voice that speaks. But in this instance God does not speak with a voice; we are faced with a mute concept of vocation, with the God of Providence. God speaks to the individual only indirectly, through circumstance. He will also speak through one's parents. If they make a decision about one's career then that is God's will because parents are the earthly representatives of God. If children are uncertain of what they have to do, they must go and ask their father, and the father will tell them, and what he tells them is to be taken as the will of God. The Reformational concept of vocation is therefore also strongly patriarchal. The combination of a parent's or superior's decision and general circumstances together act "as if" God had spoken to us directly.

This concept of vocation is not only the particular bent of Lutheranism; equally strong statements on the individual's vocation and station in life can be found in Calvin's writings. Calvin links up the whole set of duties of the individual to his particular vocation: "The Lord bids each one of us in all life's actions to look to his calling...[He] has appointed duties for every man in his particular way of life. And that no one may thoughtlessly transgress his limits, he has named these various kinds of living 'callings.' "[14] In fact, in the thought of Calvin, the Reformational doctrine of vocation is even strengthened by his powerful doctrine of predestination. It is by the Providence of God that each and every person has his or her particular station and vocation in life; and they have to stay in it because where they find themselves is exactly where they are meant to be. The *status quo* is God-ordained. Similar to Luther, Calvin rejects monasticism as not commanded in Scripture and incompatible with the Christian duty to work in a (civil) vocation.[15]

Thus the Reformational critique of the monastic lifestyle establishes the Protestant axiom that the decalogue and one's vocation together cover the whole of Christian ethics and strictly limit and define one's role and action in society.

II. 2.2 Against the Anabaptists

There is a second Reformational reaction that informs the Protestant concept of vocation. This is a reaction not against monasticism but against the Anabaptists: the early Swiss Brethren, the Mennonites, and various other Anabaptist groups.

The Reformers criticized what they saw as their withdrawal from society, separation from the church, and their huddling together in small groups of believers. Because of this withdrawal from the world the Reformers actually called the Anabaptists "the new monastics."

The Anabaptists indeed did not put much weight on civil vocation. Also, they did not stop and enlarge upon the ten commandments. They took their ethics primarily from the New

Testament, especially from the Sermon on the Mount with the emphasis on life in the fellowship of the brethren. In addition they were the ones who in the sixteenth century held the idea of individual guidance from the Holy Spirit. Both the Lutheran and Calvinist Reformation fought the Anabaptists on all three counts. There were certainly people in the Anabaptist movement who felt called by God to leave their civil vocation, wife, children and family behind and go out to the mission field to proclaim the word of God. In Luther's and Calvin's view that was *not* something that befitted the believer.

Because of this, Calvin in particular was positively hostile to the Anabaptists. Testimony to this can be found in his *Institutes* and in a separate book which he wrote entitled *Against the Anabaptists*. He had encountered groups which seemed to combine the concept of the idea of individual spiritual guidance with an attitude of rejection of the commandments, and went on to condemn the whole Anabaptist movement because of them.

These "fanatics," he said, "invent secret revelations of the Spirit for themselves" and despise the external ministry of the Word.[16] For Calvin, divine guidance today could only come through the exposition of Scripture.

In sum, the genesis and peculiar nature of Protestant ethics, especially its concept of vocation, is very much determined by the Reformers' struggle with monasticism and, secondarily, Anabaptism. The consequence of the Reformational rejection of these movements for the Protestant concept of vocation is that it reduces the much broader biblical concept of vocation to civil vocation, and it seriously restricts the second, specifically Christian vocation. Also, it eliminates the third level of vocation in terms of the individual believer's calling through a spiritual gift and commission as well as through actual guidance in a challenging situation. The disintegration of the biblical synthesis in the concept of vocation can be paralleled in a separation of the two constituents of Christ's double commandment of love: monasticism wants to be seen as pursuant of the love of God—to the exclusion of love of neighbour (as their Protestant adversaries put it)—whereas the Reformation emphasizes love of neighbour, to the detriment of the notion of love of God. Finally, the breakdown of the biblical synthesis regarding vocation may well be responsible for that striking impairment of vision concerning cross-cultural missions which is characteristic of the first two hundred years of the history of Protestantism.

III. Recovering "Vocation" Today

III. 1. The Present-Day Situation
We have been looking into history with the intention of trying to understand the present. What then is the present day situation? Where do we stand? The surprising answer is that we find ourselves very much in the same situation where the Reformational undertaking left us. The disintegration of the biblical synthesis of the concept of vocation is, unfortunately, still very much in force within the Protestant churches, in the sense that the so-called mainline churches continue the Reformational emphasis on civil vocation whereas many of the so-called "believers' churches" have adopted the Anabaptist position. This division also more or less explains the differences that are found between the situation in Europe and in North America.

III. 1.1. In Europe
Europe has inherited the "Magisterial Reformation" of Martin Luther and John Calvin; therefore, the situation in the European church and the mainline denominations generally, reflects their ethic of the decalogue plus civil vocation. Decisions are supposed to be made by expounding the ten commandments and applying them to the situation by means of human reason. In addition, a powerful movement in nineteenth century Protestant theology recovered and extolled the concept of civil vocation. There is, of course, less reference nowadays to the duties that spring from one's station in society. Nevertheless, the concept of a God who calls one to one's station and vocation in life—the silent God of Providence—is still very much in evidence. Therefore, much more than in North America, one may find a fairly impersonal relationship with God on the part of the believer in the European churches. Many mainline Protestant theologians actually teach that it is the church that has a relationship with God, not the individual Christian. Consequently these churches often suffer from a lack of spirituality, i.e. of instruction for the individual believer's conversation with God, as part of Christian ethics.

Moreover and, as we have seen, understandably so, these churches show comparatively little activity in the direction of foreign missions. If it is true—as their traditional teaching goes— that you do well to stick to your trade and stay where you are, who would dare to go into other countries and into cross-cultural missions? To be sure, Pietism in the early eighteenth century, going back to Scripture itself, rediscovered and cultivated missions in the Protestant camp. However, on the level of the church in general, uncertainty as to the place of missions has continued to the present day. Therefore, it hardly comes as a surprise that a country like Germany has the lowest percentage of missionaries of any Western nation.

Divine guidance, too, is an alien concept in this milieu. The *charismata*, the individual spiritual gifts, are under suspicion. The result of this is that there is much less lay participation in the work of the churches in Europe. The local church often is a one-man show, run by the pastor (not seldom over-worked), whereas the laity has long been accustomed to playing the role of the audience. This is very much the rule, although there are (which almost goes without saying) laudable exceptions.

III. 1.2. In North America

North America is different from Europe, for several cultural reasons. Compared with its counterpart in Europe, North American society is much more mobile. Many people actually came from Europe to North America in order to "better their situation." So they have a living consciousness of an "exodus" at least in the sociological sense, i.e. leaving behind a more stratified and stationary society. So right from the start we are faced with an altogether different background and perception of social life.

In addition, in North America traditions different from the dominant Lutheranism and Calvinism of Europe form the general Christian mindset, i.e. through the preponderance of the "Believers' Church" and the Evangelical and Anabaptist movements. Hence, the Sermon on the Mount will be stressed, but the ten commandments are sometimes an unknown entity. In contrast to Europe, individual divine guidance is a familiar theme in North America. However, together with it one also finds much subjectivity, individual arbitrariness and caprice. Indeed, one can find some of the very phenomena of lawlessness which Calvin criticized, e.g., the claim to be guided by God even if the road leads into a (divinely ordained?) transgression of God's commandments. Among Evangelicals one can also encounter a low concept of civil vocation: all attention is here focused on the Kingdom of God, so there is little energy left for the concerns of one's civil vocation and of society. Similarly, Christians representing this stance also seem to have little awareness of the need for the tasks of stewardship in creation.[17]

So the "cultural mandate" is something which especially needs reconsideration in North America and among North American evangelicals. They would also be wise to go back and memorize the ten commandments again. The enormous ease with which North American Christians take to divorce today, seems to be evidence that they don't build their house on the solid ground of these God-given laws.

III. 2. The need for balance and structure in understanding the Christian vocations

In a quest, then, for recovery of the biblical synthesis in the concept of vocation, we first need to rehearse again the creational commission, or the "cultural mandate" given to humanity by its Creator. It is the commission to work as householders and stewards in God's Creation. This includes the commandment of love of neighbour as well as responsible dealings with animals and inanimate nature, all of which are entrusted to our care.

Next, what we must recover at the specifically Christian level of vocation and ethics is the Great Commission—the commandment of missions. We need to undertake a theological critique of the Reformational reduction of vocation to its civil and creational understanding. A theological critique of the Protestant concept of vocation is much more important than the usual sociological critique. Many people today say, "we can't hold to the traditional understanding of vocation and station of life, because we have become a mobile society. That particular ethic doesn't help us anymore." That is the sociological argument. The real problem with the Protestant concept of vocation is not the throttling of *social* mobility but its throttling of *spiritual* mobility. It brings about a loss of spiritual mobility: the loss, generally, of Christian commitment in the laity, and a loss, specifically, of geographic mobility in terms of people willing to go into cross-cultural missions.

In Protestantism, we also need to recover the biblical concept of individual Christian calling as happened to Barnabas and Paul (Acts 13:2). We, all of us, generally and individually, need to have our ears open and our vision re-opened to the possibility of a personal vocation to full-time Christian ministry. This includes a renewed understanding of spiritual gifts and calling. We even need to recover the possibility, e.g., of someone living a single life for the sake of the Kingdom (Matthew 19). Voluntary celibacy and poverty for the sake of the Kingdom must again be a possibility amongst us—as callings, not for merit's, but for ministry's sake. We must also reconsider individual Christian calling in the sense of actual personal guidance. There must be room in the Christian life for actions like the anointing of Jesus with the precious ointment by the woman in Bethany (Mark 14:3ff.). Such actions of love, instilled by the Holy Spirit, go beyond the call of duty and commandment.

There is indeed more to the Christian life than civil vocation. Karl

Barth, among other useful innovations in *Dogmatics and Ethics*, re-designed the traditional presentation of the Doctrine of Salvation, insisting that it contained not only the theme of Vocation, and spoke of the believer's vocation to witness. He later spoke about this vocation in two different places of his *Church Dogmatics*: (1) in the framework of the Ethics of Creation; and (2) in the context of the doctrine of salvation.[18] In connection with a critique of the Reformational apotheosis of civil vocation Barth, moreover, left no doubt about the preponderance of the Christian vocation to witness.[19]

This needs to be said, because according to the New Testament one's civil vocation can even become a hindrance to the call to the Kingdom: in Jesus' parable of the invitation to the great banquet (Matthew 22:5; Luke 14:18ff.) one sees how civil vocation, i.e. occupation, matrimony and economic concerns, can become obstacles preventing someone from entering the Kingdom.

Finally, how should we structure and *coordinate* the three vocations of the Christian? We have discussed 1) the creational level—that is our vocation in sustaining life and Creation, and the social life in which we all have a part. This is our cultural mandate from God the Creator. 2) On the second level we have dealt with the special call to Christians, the call to holiness, the call to service (as in Christ's parable of the "Good Samaritan") and the call to witness. 3) Finally, within the special Christian call comes the spiritual calling of the individual. We may perhaps envision these three in the image of a pyramid, or a wedding cake, where the basic layer represents creational vocation, followed by the higher level of Christian vocation and the particular individual calling on top. This image helps to point out that the individual guidance of the Holy Spirit will always fall within the larger framework first of the special Christian calling to holiness, service and witness, and, secondly of the ten commandments. The Holy Spirit never leads one outside of the teaching of Jesus, and Jesus does not guide us outside of the perameters of the decalogue.

Christian Ethics is made up of both *law and spirit*, basic commandments and actual individual guidance. We should never be one-sided for the sake either of safety, or of liberty. We must have both. Clearly, divine guidance in the sense of an actual vocation needs to be safeguarded. Subjectivism, arbitrariness and personal whim will be avoided as soon as we apply the three biblical measuring rods: one, God's commandments; two, the principle of community, i.e., checking and sharing with our brothers and sisters and seeking their counsel and judgment; and three, the horizon of the Kingdom. Thus, as we search for the instruction of the Holy Spirit, it cannot be for the sake of sensational experiences or personal fulfillment but must be for the defense and advance of the Gospel, and the furthering of love of God and love of neighbour. The Holy Spirit is the giver of love and the leader of Christian missions, and it is to this end that he gives his guidance, and not for the pursuit of personal goals in life.

For the rest, if God does not call us to a particular task at a particular time, we must fall back on the creational and salvational tasks that we have already been given: to sustain and to further physical and spiritual life in the family and in the community, in the neighbourhood and in the nation.

Today, we find ourselves in a highly mobile society. In addition to that, we are in a volatile ideological situation globally in that many of the guard-rails and guidelines that Scripture and the Reformation put in place have been lost. Ours is a situation where we, more than at any other time, need to develop a consciousness of where we are and where we are meant to go.

This brings us back to the absolute necessity of purpose and perspective in the Christian's life. That is especially true today where the world horizon has been opened to us through the media as never before. Therefore we must learn to take responsibility to serve and to support the defense and advance of faith and love everywhere. "Think globally, but act locally!" We can begin to do so through our prayers of intercession. On that basis we will also be ready for God to show us the areas of our particular commitment and of our individual vocation.

Endnotes

1. T. Peters and R. Waterman Jr., *In Search of Excellence: Lessons from America's Best-run Companies.* New York: Harper & Row, 1982, p.97, also cf. pp. 83ff.

2. Cf. my "Marxism and Education: A Survey Report," In J. Vander Stelt (ed.), *The Challenge of Marxist and Neo-Marxist Ideologies for Christian Scholarship.* Sioux Center, IA: Dordt College, 1982, pp. 210-244.

3. Luther's Large Catechism, in *The Book of Concord: The Confessions of the Evangelical Lutheran Church,* T. G. Tappert (Trans. and ed.). Philadelphia: Fortress, 1959, p.408 (315).

4. *Luther's Works,* Weimar edition (WA), Vol. 10, I, 1, p.431 (not in the Am. Ed.). Also cf. Large Catechism, l.c., p.381 (120).

5. Cf. eg., *Luther's Works,* Am. Ed., Vol. 21, St. Louis: Concordia, 1956, pp. 20; 37f.; 256ff.

6. WA, Vol. 32, p.152 (sermon preached in 1530).

7. *Luther's Works*, Am. Ed., Vol. 27, p.119.

8. WA, Vol. 32, p.66f (sermon preached in 1530), cf. p.153.

9. Am. Ed. Vol. 52, p.123f.

10. WA, Vol. 10, I, 1, p.152.

11. *The Augsburg Confession*, art. 27, 49ff., in *The Book of Concord*, l.c., p.78ff.

12. Am. Ed. Vol. 52, p.124.

13. WA, Vol. 10, I, 1, p.435 (not in the Am. Ed.).

14. J. Calvin, *Institutes*, III, 10, 6.

15. *Institutes*, IV, 13, 2f.

16. *Comm. Ephesians* 4, 12.

17. Cf. F. Schaeffer's critique in *Pollution and the Death of Man—The Christian View of Ecology*, Wheaton, IL: Tyndale, 1970, ch.3.

18. Karl Barth, *Church Dogmatics*, Vol. III, 4, sect. 56.2 and Vol. IV, 3, sect. 81.

19. *Church Dogmatics*, Vol. III, 4, p.522f.

The Serenity of Christ

James M. Houston

Vol. XV, No. 1 (March 1979):3-6

The Christian life can be described in many ways, for it is all embracing and so richly faceted. But in the wealth of its attributes, we sometimes have to distinguish between a key trait which is the source of many other features, and a lesser trait, which is only part of a more masterful theme. For example, we talk about being "sincere" Christians and we also describe Christians as "serene." Which is the more masterful of these words, sincerity or serenity? Perhaps we are tempted to believe sincerity is the greater virtue, as Lionel Trilling has traced in literature, in his book *Sincerity and Authenticity.* Perhaps we remember the paternal advice of Polonius in *Hamlet* as he speeds Laertes on his way:

> This above all: to thine own self be true
> And it doth follow, as the night the day,
> Thou canst not then be false to any man.

For a moment Polonius has been persuaded of his own self-transcendence, and thus believes sincerity is the essential condition of virtue. How that promise seems to ring in our ears! A concord is proposed—a marriage of my own self-image and me—were ever two things better suited? Me as I think I am, and me as I really am.

But is such concord possible if I spend my life repressing or rejecting those unlovely traits of my life and temperament, so that I cannot really see how ugly is my face? Instead, I plaster it with cosmetics. Therefore, our self-concealment makes it impossible to be true to ourselves because we do not even know who we are. Matthew Arnold realized how hard it is to discern our own selves when he wrote:

> Below the surface-stream, shallow and
> light
> Of what we *say* we feel—below the
> stream
> As light, of what we *think* we feel—there
> flows
> With noiseless current strong, obscure and
> deep,
> The central stream of what we are
> indeed.

Since he wrote, modern psychoanalytic theory has further
demonstrated this difficulty. Perhaps we shall have to wait until we
enter into God's presence to "know even as we are known."

The poet Yeats, himself a great role player and lover of *personae,*
discovered the futility of sincerity.

> Those masterful images because complete
> Grew in pure mind, but out of what began?
> A mound of refuse or the sweepings of a
> street,
> Old kettles, old bottles, and a broken can,
> Old iron, old bones, old rags, that raving
> slut
> Who keeps the till. Now that my ladder's
> gone,
> I must lie down where all the ladders start
> In the foul rag-and-bone shop of the heart.

If, as Paul saw it, "in me, that is in my flesh, dwelleth no good
thing," then sincerity as a Christian virtue really does not take us
very far. Instead, I would opt for serenity as a far richer and more
profound quality of life to describe Christ's presence in our lives.

Serenity is not a word often circulated today. To describe
someone as serene is strange to youth's ears. Why? Because words
are driven out of currency by our own self-conscious avoidance of
them. For example, many words used to describe the body today
would have deeply embarrassed our Victorian great-grandparents.
Perhaps now, instead, we have grown embarrassed to use terms of
the soul. Serenity certainly does not describe our age, for to quote
Yeats again:

Things fall apart, the centre cannot hold;
Mere anarchy is loosed upon the world.
The blood-dimmed tide is loosed, and
everywhere
The Ceremony of innocence is drowned.

Likewise, the crying out of our own anxieties prevents personal
security. And yet, would we not wish it to be said of us: "So- and-so
is such a beautiful, serene person." And so we pray in that lovely
hymn,

O grant unto our souls:
Light that groweth not pale with day's
decrease.
Love that never can fade 'til life shall
cease.

Joy no trial can mar,
Hope that shineth afar,
Faith serene as a star,
And Christ's own peace.

Yes, I would opt every time for serenity as one of the most
meaningful experiences and descriptions of the Christian life. A
serene star shines calmly and clearly in the night sky. The essence of
such a description is that serenity is both light- admitting and
calm-diffusing. From a source not its own, serenity glows clearly.
Great works of art have this quality of serenity, and the true artist has
the ability to change the opaque into the serene—which glows with
light. Serenity transforms a wall into a window, so making the
whole of life penetrable by light.

A second quality of serenity is its appropriateness. It has an
imperishable quality of timelessness that belongs to the realm of
harmony, order, structure and rhythm—all those things that are
comprehended in the idea of form. Somehow serenity casts a spell
over us, creating expectations that are always and continually
fulfilled. Giovanni Bellini has a masterpiece entitled "The Agony in
the Garden." In this picture of Gethsemane, it is appropriate that
lesser men are painted with halos for they have little else to
distinguish them in the sleep of the night. But Jesus seems to have
the whole sky as his halo, and it is as if he lightens up the whole night
with his presence.

Finally, serenity has a celestial quality, as if earthly life is suffused with heavenly light. And because of this it has an invincible power that no earthly circumstance can take away. For serenity is not a temperamental trait, not the luck of the genes, not some personal idiosyncracy contributed by family background. To see the serene countenance of a vitally alive Christian is like viewing life from a window where an angel has appeared. Indeed it is far more, for it is the beholding of "the beauty of the Lord." It is the realization that the most wonderful reality in the whole world and in all of life is the beauty of God himself. When Malcolm Muggeridge first became a Christian, he began to identify those who are "beautiful for God." He called them "the light people"; "the children of the light," as John the apostle describes them.

What then is the secret and the source of Christian serenity, of Christ's own serenity? We see how Jesus was serenity incarnate. Asleep in the boat while his creation rages, the serene Christ calms his disciples' fears. Serene on the mountain, he teaches his disciples the illuminating realities of the Beatitudes. And because he is the Beatitudes incarnate, we find him later transfigured before them. The full glory of what they had heard on the mountain is metamorphosed before their eyes. Later still on yet another mountain, he is caught up into glory as they witness his ascension. How marvellous it all is. And yet, serenity is not stoicism. Where there are mountains there are always valleys. So the serene Christ does not only carry the light of the heavens to the mountain tops, but also takes it into the gloom of the valleys. Moreover, he carries the needs and interests of the valleys up to the mountains in his prayers and teaching. After the Sermon on the Mount, we read in Matthew 8:1- 2, "And when he was come down from the mountain, great multitudes followed him. And behold there came to him a leper." Again after the Mount of Transfiguration, "as they were coming down...there came to him a man kneeling to him saying, Lord have mercy upon my son...for he is epileptic, and suffered grievously" (Matthew 17:9, 14-15). That is to say, the light that glows over the mountains provides serenity also in the valleys with their disease and afflictions.

The eight Beatitudes are the true principles of Christian serenity, revealing a penetration of God-given light into our souls that is timeless, imperishable, ordered, appropriate and invincible. This is the true meaning of the term "happy" or "blessed," not the superficial happiness that depends upon circumstances, such as too much alcohol, or too little sorrow, or a too-superficial life. It is serenity that provides confidence, peace, contentment, and joy deep in the heart, soul-satisfying. It is not synthetic like many features of conventional Christian appearances. It is real, personal, and authentic. Moreover, the biblical use of the term "blessed" indicates it is what God does, how he has acted or will act on behalf of man. The glow, the source of light, that we associate with serenity is his and his alone. No one reading the Beatitudes can help being struck, moreover, that the eight traits outlined describe Jesus himself. He is the Beatitudes. So if we are to find the true source of serenity, we must find it in Jesus Christ and the traits that characterize him.

Blessed are the Poor in Spirit

According to Jesus, happiness and serenity are associated with some kind of poverty. But it is poverty in the inward man, not in outward circumstances. Nor is it being poor in spirit, as in someone demoralized with an inferiority complex. Rather it is a recognition of one's inadequacy before God. It means one must look to God for everything. It means therefore that it is "not by works of righteousness that we have done, but by his mercy he saved us." No one, however mature and radiant a personality, who lives independently of God and therefore unrepentant as a sinner before God, can actualize the Beatitudes. God in his grace alone can make all these traits possible. The glow of the truly serene is the manifestation of God's spirit.

To be poor in spirit must imply, therefore, being empty vessels that God can fill. And until we are empty we cannot be filled by God. Too often when we are threatened by inadequacy, we set up defences around our personalities, so that we live in a make- believe world of our goodness, our righteousness, our usefulness. C.S. Lewis once wrote in *Mere Christianity*, "Whenever we find that our religious life is making us feel that we are good—above all, that we are better than someone else—I think we may be sure that we are being acted on, not by God but by the devil. The real test of being in the presence of God is that either you forget about yourself altogether, or you see yourself as a small, dirty object" (pp. 96,97). Like Isaiah, the poor in spirit cry out, "Woe is me! For I am undone, because I am a man of unclean lips, and I dwell among a people of unclean lips, for mine eyes have seen the King, the Lord of Hosts" (Isaiah 6:5). But it is by this sense of inadequacy before God that they can live in the Kingdom of God, where Christ rules as king. Note that the verb "to rule" is in the present tense: God rules now. And so this first Beatitude has always been the key-note of the Christian life, the foundation of all else. Thus we sing:

But tho' I cannot sing, or tell, or know
The fullness of Thy love while here below,
My empty vessel I may freely bring:
O Thou who art of love the living spring, my
vessel fill.

I am an empty vessel—not one thought
Or look of love, I ever to Thee brought;
Yet I may come, and come again to Thee
With this, the empty sinner's only plea—
Thou lovest me.

Blessed are They that Mourn

Heaven, I believe, will be filled with praise, for earth is full of groans, and celestial joy is the redemption of earthly sorrow. Here again is the spiritual principle that serenity actually comes through sorrow, pain and distress, and not just in spite of them. William Barclay has quoted the Arab proverb in this context that says "all sunshine makes a desert." People who have had things all their own way, with little suffering in their lives, are really very poor in character. As 2 Corinthians 7:10 indicates, "the pain that is borne of God has an effect too salutary ever to regret." It enriches life with so much that is creative and meaningful. All the blows that hit our personalities can be the very means of God to give us serenity, a true blessedness of spirit.

To mourn is to be aware of other people, of their difficulties and problems. We can apply this to social conscience, to philanthropy, and to a general concern for the feelings of others. But we can only have this when we are serenely blessed in our poverty of spirit. The self-defensive are too busy "looking after number one" to take a thought for the feelings and suffering of others. They do not see the world of other people, how they feel and react. Self-inadequacy that is unconfessed leads to self-centred blindness. So it is a step forward in life to learn the ability to mourn for others.

But the most profound mourning is that done over the presence of sin in the world. Twice Jesus wept over sin: once for the unbelief of those who watched at Lazarus' tomb, and again for the stubborn hardness of heart of the inhabitants of Jerusalem. Nevertheless, Jesus promises that God's comfort is given to those who thus mourn: "Weep not," says the elder to John, "for the Lion of the tribe of Judah has prevailed to open the book" concerning the destinies of sinful man.

"Fear not," says the angel to the shepherds, "for behold I bring you good tidings of great joy, which shall be to all people. For unto you is born this day in the city of David a Saviour, who is Christ the Lord" (Luke 2:10-11). Yes, it is the comfort of God, given to those who mourn over sin in our lives, over sin in the world, that is the secret of the Christian's serenity.

Blessed are the Meek

Meekness is not a natural gift; it is supernatural. It is expressive of God's gentle folk. But meekness is not weakness. It refers to a disciplined and balanced virtue and indicates both self-conquest and profound reliance upon the grace and will of God in all things. It reflects on the imagery in the apocalypse, where it is a lamb that rules from the throne of God in the efficacy of its death. As such, it is a reversal of human values and human conceptions of power. We assume that it is the elbow-pushers and the go-getters who have power. But this is because we only have a horizontal perspective on the sources of power. The meek are those aware that the vertical God-ward relationship, rather than the man-ward one, is the profound source of all power and authority.

Such meekness is humanly impossible, but it is Jesus who makes it possible. "Come unto me all ye that labour and are heavy laden, and I will give you rest. Take my yoke upon you, for I am meek and lowly in heart, and ye shall find rest unto your souls" (Matthew 11:28-29). It is from such a source that Paul, owning little, could speak of "possessing all things" (2 Corinthians 6:10). Indeed he says, "All things are yours; whether Paul, or Apollos, or Cephas, or the world, or life, or death, or things present, or things to come; all are yours; and ye are Christ's; and Christ is God's" (1 Corinthians 3:21-23). Thus it is true that those who have the serenity of such meekness inherit the earth.

Blessed are They who Hunger and Thirst after Righteousness

The first three Beatitudes point to man's need and show the essential approach. Bankrupt before God, sorrowing for sin and meek before his will we express what the Old Testament describes as "the fear of the Lord." It is the essence of godliness. This in turn leads to a more profound longing, to hunger and thirst after righteousness. The grammar in the Greek suggests the desire for a perfect righteousness, not merely a hungering to be more righteous, but to have it absolutely. It is indeed the desire to hunger and thirst as Christ himself hungers and thirsts, not an impartial desire but a perfect desire for God. As an intense desire, desiring a perfect satisfaction, it is focussed upon Christ who claims: "I am the bread of life; he that cometh to me shall never hunger, and he that believeth on me shall never thirst" (John 6:35). Therefore we should rejoice in our restiveness, emptiness, and longing to be filled more and more by the reality of God in Christ. For these things that, at one level, might make us discontented and miserable, at a deeper level are a great joyous gift; in needing God we find God.

Too often we are content to merely seek techniques whereby we may pray more effectively or counsel more wisely or speak more eloquently. But in this Beatitude we are reminded how much more powerful is simply our absolute need of God, of his presence in our loneliness, of his riches in our poverty, of his power in our weakness. So we are literally blessed when we express the feelings of emptiness, for only thereby are we drawn to God. It is again a complete reversal of the value-system of the world around us. Through our tears and brokenheartedness we are truly blessed, for how else would we need God and desire that absolute righteousness, the corrective to our whole awareness and behaviour in life. These traits of the godly life are inward, expressing profoundly our personal, private relationship with God. But it is out of them that flow extrinsic connections, so that we are enabled to have serene relationships with other people too.

The External Traits of the Christian Life

The four remaining Beatitudes describe our relationships to other people and spring from the inward relationships we have towards God in Christ. We now find described that vivid greenness of a desert oasis, manifest in its fruitfulness because it draws upon deep hidden wells. It is like the righteous man of Psalm 1, planted by rivers of water and expressing this in the way he relates to others.

First, serene is the person who is merciful and through him grace in action is expressed to the world around. The merciful are those who have obtained mercy, just as the Lord's prayer reminds us that we forgive others as we ourselves are forgiven. To exercise mercy is therefore to explore the ways of the Redeemer. There are even many Christians who do not understand the nature of mercy. Pragmatically they assume that people's characters are so fixed that all they can do is judge them, avoid them and live independently of them as if they are already cast away by God's own judgment. At one level this attitude can be very effective and such people can be most efficient and economic in their personal relationships. But ultimately it is implacable and totally inconsistent with the redeeming grace of God. For "God who is rich in mercy, for his great love wherewith he loved us...has made us alive together with Christ." The serenity of the Christian must therefore spill out with the same spontaneous graciousness and love which Christ has had for us. There are no laws of determinism in his mercy for such love does not keep accounts and therefore is not concerned about settling its scores.

Another serene quality of the Christian is purity of heart. In the ministry and character of Jesus we see no shadow of the self- life. In its flawless perfection he expresses only one relationship to his Father, one source of joy in doing his Father's will, for he finds that his identity is also in his Father. Indeed, even his love was that of his Father. It is impossible to write a biography of Jesus, for there was no self- life to write about. "He that hath seen me hath seen the Father also." Serenity has this quality of translucence and can be likened to a beautiful alabaster vase, taken from a dingy oriental bazaar out in the sunshine, thus revealing its true, flawless quality, its translucence showing its perfection. So too is the Christian given the privilege of being wholly committed to Christ, not bound to him by ties of legalism, nor by the practice of asceticism, nor by any other self-endeavour. We rest in the joy of knowing we are "in Christ," the source of our identity and therefore all we need. To such is given the privilege of seeing God. Too often, perhaps, we confuse our tactics with the only one, proper strategy for the Christian: to love God, to glory and honour him. All else are but tactics, however important our role-playing may appear to us. Only as lovers of God can we enjoy this purity of heart.

A third expression that radiates the serenity of Christ is that of peacemaker. We are so because Christ is our peace, "having made peace by the blood of his cross." By the efficacy of his work and his gracious life in us, he enables us to be peacemakers. How frequently we make his cross of no effect by our own anxious bickering and bad tempers. Again we have forgotten that the self-life with its vested interest can only be a source of friction and ultimately of self-destruction, "for he that loveth his life shall lose it," and in our self- defensiveness we are totally incapable of being ministers of his peace. The glorious word *shalom,* used so frequently in Scripture for the ultimate blessing of the believer, expresses wholeness, health and a total experience of well-being. The serene person in Christ radiates this health which heals all the wounds of divided mankind, including the differences of culture, colour and status. But it is indicative of the state of our hearts that if we do not have peace within we cannot radiate this peace without.

Finally, our Lord expresses to us the blessedness and serenity of those who are persecuted for righteousness' sake. Too frequently we are persecuted, but it is because of our own nasty temperaments and hasty reactions towards others. When persecuted for the right reasons, however, there is given that inner support which is expressed in its outward confidence. Such was the serenity of Jesus when he was reviled and yet did not return rebuke. A conqueror's calm dignity is expressed so eloquently in his silence during the trial, mockery and flogging to which the soldiery subjected him. It is the serenity of one who cries from the cross "Father forgive them for they know not what they do." This serenity gives him the royal title of true "Son of Man," as he subsequently inspired his first witness in martyrdom, Stephen, to see him as the Son of Man standing at the right hand of God. For in spite of all external pressures seeming to contradict the Christian's source of serenity, there is an ultimate awareness that the victory is God's and justice is his sceptre. We are therefore exhorted to rejoice in this serenity (Matthew 5:12) realizing that, for the Christian, blessedness and serenity are one source of inward provisions for outward relationships.

The Prayer-Life of
C.S. Lewis

James M. Houston

Vol. XXIV, No. 1 (March 1988):2-10

Prayer, perhaps more than anything else, is a true test of a Christian's devotion and intimacy with God. Its presence in a Christian's life says it all. Its absence is the evidence of a merely theoretical framework of faith. So to try to enter into the understanding of Lewis' prayer-life is an attempt to penetrate his very mind and spirit in the most intimate way. Can we do so without presumption? Is it speculative to try to do so? I knew Lewis personally, enough to have a clear impression of his personal faith in the years between 1946 and 1953, when we met in a group discussion that was held in the home that I shared with Nicholas Zernov, during those years. Zernov was then leader of the Society of St. Albans and St. Sergius. It was through him that I got to know Lewis.

While he was a witty raconteur and provocative debater, Lewis was essentially shy about his inner life, so it would be an impossible task to describe his prayer-life unless he had written significantly about prayer. But he made a substantial contribution to the theology of prayer. His last work, published posthumously, *Letters to Malcolm,* he completed in April 1963, just seven months before his death. It deals frankly with issues that he faced privately in prayer. His *Reflections on the Psalms,* published two years earlier, deal with his personal difficulties in reading the Psalms, and also his appreciation of the Christian liturgy of the Psalter. But Lewis was never enthusiastic about his own church life, which in the setting of college chapel was atypical of parish life. So his own focus upon prayer was more personal than corporate. Several of his essays, notably "Work and Prayer" and "The Efficacy of Prayer," challenge us with specific issues of personal prayer. His autobiography, *Surprised by Joy,* and

The Screwtape Letters also contain personal comments on prayer.

In my own encounters with Lewis, he never spoke about prayer. I did communicate once with him directly about the daily prayer meetings of the Oxford Inter-Collegiate Christian Union where much prayer had been made for the conversion of Sheldon Vanauken, whose wife was active in our prayer-group. Indeed, I told Lewis of Sheldon's conversion the day after it happened. But Lewis was never forthcoming about his own prayer life. A shy man, he was all the more sensitive to the Oxford atmosphere then prevailing, that you no more discussed religion too intimately than you talked about your kidneys. So he simply responded positively to Vanauken's news as a confidant who expected it anyway.

Lewis suffered enough from the cynical reactions of some of his colleagues when his first religious books were published. For he, an English don, should not be dabbling in theology, much less getting cheap publicity in this way. To trespass into another academic discipline was questionable to say the least. So Lewis was very careful to introduce his own theological views modestly, though he did have the support of his friend Austin Farrar and other theologians, when he did so. In his *Reflections on the Psalms* he begins, ''I write as one amateur to another, talking about difficulties that I have met, or lights I have gained, reading the Psalms, with the hope this might at any rate interest and sometimes even help, other inexpert readers. I am 'comparing notes,' not presuming to instruct.''[1] It is only now that some of us have wakened up to the fact that if all of life is carved up among the professions, so that there is likewise no room left for being dilettantes or amateurs in the arts or culture generally, then we shall all be cheated of humanness itself. Lewis got away with it in his day, for when he was questioned about his preaching as a layman at R.A.F. stations during the Battle of Britain, he could genuinely reply he was just doing his warwork, like any other old don who did his duties as an air-raid warden, certainly not very trained but doing his best in an emergency. In such a crisis there is no need for any further apology than what he writes in the preface to his published B.B.C. talks given during the war, when he first came to public attention:

> There is no mystery about my position. I am a very ordinary layman, of the Church of England, not especially 'high' nor especially 'low,' nor especially anything else.[2]

When I first met him in the 1940s he looked like Mr. Badger from *The Wind in the Willows*[3]: stout, in an old rumpled brown tweed jacket, brown shoes, pipe in mouth, looking like an Oxford farmer. However, once he began to speak, I realized that few people I had ever met, other than perhaps his friend Dyson, could articulate so well, so humorously, and exactly to the point.

In this paper, I want to describe six traits that I think characterize the personal prayer-life of Lewis, and then to look at three aspects of his own theological reflections on prayer.

1. The Earthy Realism of His Prayer-Life

Lewis was no mystic. He admits this several times in his letters. Others might climb daringly in the mountains of mysticism, but he simply slogged around in the foothills. Rather then, his spirituality is earthy, full of realism, for he was dead scared of sentimentalism. It was expressive of a no-nonsense kind of faith. The first poem of his collection edited after his death, spells out his similar poetic credo:

I am so coarse, the things the poets see
Are obstinately invisible to me.
For twenty years I've stared my level best
To see if evening—any evening—would
    suggest
A patient etherized upon a table;
In vain. I simply wasn't able.
To me each evening looked far more
Like the departure from a silent, yet
    crowded shore
Of a ship whose freight with everything,
    leaving behind
Gracefully, finally without farewells,
    marooned mankind—
I'm like that odd man Wordsworth knew,
    to whom
A primrose was a yellow primrose, one
    whose doom
Keeps him for ever in the list of dunces,
Compelled to live on stock responses,
Making the poor best that I can
Of dull things...[4]

Lewis is admitting to us all that his spirituality, like his poetry, is prosaic, ordinary, about the world around him. This down-to-earthness about him, is perhaps the greatest impression he left upon me. Neo-platonism was anathema to Lewis. So instead of saying "we must be spiritually regenerated," he confesses, "we're like eggs at present. And you can't go on indefinitely being just an ordinary, decent egg. We must be hatched or go bad."[5] Thus his style is vivid, concrete, practical, empty of "gas," full of solid stuff. So too his faith is all for "sound doctrine," not the woolly-mindedness of contemporaries he debated with, who wanted "religion without dogma." Growing up as a child in a "low" church milieu, he felt later that it did tend to be too cosily living at ease in Zion,[6] not the tough, realistic faith and prayer-life Lewis was to develop later.

2. The Practical Realism of His Prayer-Life

Prayer is not something simply to talk about. It is not even something we "do," for Lewis. "Saying one's prayers" was for Lewis only a small part of his experience of prayer. "For many years after my conversion," he admits, "I never used any ready-made forms except the Lord's Prayer. In fact I tried to pray without words at all—not to verbalize the mental acts. Even in praying for others I believe I tended to avoid their names and substituted mental images of them. I still think that the prayer without words is the best—if one can really achieve it."[7] But we have to remember that our exercise of prayer is only effective as we take ourselves as we really are, and not idealize how we would like to be, and thus try and exercise an unrealistic form of expressing prayer. So Lewis had to learn himself, that "to pray successfully without words one needs to be at 'the top of one's form.' "[8] Thinking that we can do always, what we can do on occasion, is an error that makes our prayers also unrealistic, and this Lewis had to discover, as we all must.

The practical rhythm of Lewis was simple enough each day. He would rise at about 7 a.m., take a walk, attend matins at 8 a.m. in college chapel, breakfast, and start tutorials at 9 a.m. Late in the afternoon he would make time for prayerful thought and contemplation, as he walked around the college grounds. Never would he recommend saying one's prayers last thing at night. "No one in his senses if he has any power of ordering his own day, would reserve his chief prayers for bed-time—obviously the worst possible hour for any action which needs concentration. My own plan when hard pressed, is to seize any time, and place, however unsuitable, in preference to the last waking moment. On a day of travelling...I'd rather pray sitting in a crowded train than put it off till midnight when one reaches a hotel bedroom with aching back and dry throat, and one's mind partly in a stupor and partly in a whirl."[9] In a letter to a friend in 1955, that is to say shortly after he had taken up his professorship at Cambridge, when he used to return home to Oxford at weekends, he said:

Oddly enough, the week-end journeys (to and from

Cambridge) are no trouble at all. I find myself perfectly content in a slow train that crawls through green fields stopping at every station. Just because the service is so slow and therefore in most people's eyes *bad*, these trains are almost empty—I get through a lot of reading and sometimes say my prayers. A solitary train journey I find quite excellent for this purpose.[10]

All this is consistent with Lewis' earlier observations, that much of prayer is really a disposition of heart that is in tune with God's presence in one's life, so that the more our hearts are in tune with and obedient toward God, the less fuss do we need to make about how vocal and articulate we are in "saying our prayers"; provided, of course, that we do not succumb to merely having "warm feelings" or vaguely imaginative thoughts we mistake for real communion with God. This will always demand the most rigorous attentiveness and serious intent to be called real prayer.

3. His Natural, Simple, Unstructured Attitude to Prayer

As we have noted, Lewis was a private person, concealing his soul in the midst of convivial friendships. He remarked on one occasion that friends are not like lovers who look at each other, but in what they hold in common. So friendships were outward looking, not introspective for him. Several times he observes the importance of "looking at," rather than looking "through" things. So he would never have analyzed his prayer-life as we are attempting to do. He would bury us in a loud guffaw of the absurdity of such action.

While still agnostic, in October 1929, Lewis read the *Diary of an Old Soul* by George MacDonald. "He seems to know everything," Lewis confided to Greeves, "and I find my own experience in it constantly."

My surgent thought shoots lark-like up to Thee,
Thou like the heaven art all about the lark.
Whatever I surmise or know in me,
Idea, or symbol on the dark,
Is living, working, thought-creating power
In Thee, the timeless Father of the hour.
I am Thy book, Thy song—Thy child
would be.[11]

By the following summer term he had also perused *The Practice of the Presence of God*, by Brother Lawrence, and *Centuries of Meditation* by Thomas Traherne. By the following term he was attending 8 a.m. chapel regularly. But on Christmas Eve, 1930, he writes his friend Greeves, "I think the trouble with me is *lack of faith*. I have no *rational* ground for going back on the arguments that convinced me of God's existence; but the irrational deadweight of my old sceptical habits, and the spirit of the age, and the cares of the day, steal away all my lively feelings of the truth; and often when I pray, I wonder if I am not posting letters to a non-existent address."[12] The reason for the remoteness of Lewis' faith at that time was he was still a deist rather than a Christian. So after a long talk one night with Tolkien and Dyson in July 1931, Lewis wrote Greeves further: "I have just passed on from believing in God to definitely believing in Christ—in Christianity—my long talk with Dyson and Tolkien had a great deal to do with it."[13] Later that year he also read William Law's *Serious Call to a Devout and Holy Life.* Lewis was now finding it meaningful to pray for his brother Warren in Shanghai. So he wrote to him at the end of 1931:

> When you ask me to pray for you—I don't know if you are serious, but the answer is yes, I do. It may not do you any good, but it does me a lot, for I cannot ask for any change to be made in you without finding that the very same needs to be made in me; which pulls me up also by putting us all in the same boat, checks any tendency to priggishness.[14]

All this may seem to be biography about prayer rather than theology. But to Lewis the one was impossible without the other. To look at prayer in detachment from its exercise was inconceivable. And since most of one's existence is usually pretty dull and routine stuff, one's prayers are not exceptional either. Indeed, the more honest we become with ourselves, the more "normal" our prayer life will be. As Lewis said early on in his B.B.C. talks on Christian morality, at first Christianty seems to be all about rules and regulations, guilt and virtue, only to find its members are really living in another country. "Every one is filled full with what we would call goodness as a mirror is filled with light. But they don't call it goodness. They don't call it anything. They are not thinking of it. They are too busy looking at the source from which it comes."[15] So too, in prayer, Lewis sees that it should become so natural to the believer, that we do not make any fuss about it, but simply do it because that is the nature of the Christian life. Speaking about the struggles we may have in prayer, the distractions and dryness in our lives, he comments: "The disquieting thing is not simply that we skimp and begrudge the duty of prayer. The really disquieting thing is that it should have to be numbered among duties at all. For we believe that we were created to glorify God and enjoy Him forever. And if the few, the very few, minutes we now spend on intercourse with God are a burden to us rather than a delight, what then?...if we were perfected, prayer would not be a duty, it would be a delight."[16] Clearly our sins handicap us from the openness that prayer requires, while the unreality of the unseen realm of prayer only shows how distant we may be from God and his ways. Like friendship with a dear friend, however, prayer is never forced nor irksome. It grows as the relationship grows too.

4. Supplicatory Prayers for Others

Praying for his brother was perhaps the first step that Lewis made in supplication for many other people throughout the rest of his life. In the correspondence to an "American Lady," begun in October 1950, we read Lewis promising again and again, "I will have you in my prayers," "of course we'll help each other in our prayers," "let us continue to pray for each other," "of course I have been praying for you daily, as always, but latterly have found myself doing so with much more concern." On this last occasion, he narrates an event that was of special circumstance. He had felt one night with strong feeling how good it would be to hear from her with good news. "Then, as if by magic (indeed it is the whitest magic in the world) the letter comes today. Not (lest I should indulge in folly) that your relief had not occurred before my prayer, but as if, in tenderness for my puny faith, God moved me to pray with special earnestness just before He was going to give me the thing. How true that prayers are His prayers really: He speaks to Himself through us."[17]

Lewis was not prepared merely to hold that while petitionary prayer is expressing personal need before God, supplication is praying on behalf of others. Early he had seen that to supplicate for others to be changed by prayer, implied the pray-er was also willing to see changes in his life as he prayed for others. But petition and supplication are also part of a greater, more mysterious reality of divine soliloquy, since God intends to be not merely "all" as pantheism declares, but "all in all." If the Holy Spirit is the one who prompts us and gives us the gift of prayer itself, are we not in our supplications and petitions actually entering into divine soliloquy, to celebrate the sovereign good that God has intended for all his creatures? So Lewis quotes a poem he found in an old notebook, author unknown, to illustrate this.

They tell me, Lord, that when I seem
To be in speech with you,
Since but one voice is heard, it's all a dream,
One talker aping two.

Sometimes it is, yet not as they
Conceive it. Rather, I
Seek in myself the things I hoped to say
But lo!, my springs are dry.

Then, seeing me empty, you forsake
The listener's role and through
My dumb lips breathe and into utterance wake
The thoughts I never knew.

And thus you neither need reply
Nor can; thus, while we seem
Two talkers, thou art One forever, and I
No dreamer, but thy dream[18]

"Dream" does suggest pantheism, so Lewis adds, perhaps it is more accurate to call it rather "soliloquy." In fact, Lewis sent Bede Griffiths this poem in 1938, to describe the growing convictions of what prayer meant in his life.[19] For this reason, he worked over this poem several times.[20]

5. Prayer as Friendship with God

Perhaps many of us find that the growth of prayer is also associated with the cultivation of friendships. It is as if the relational quality of life that is nurtured and cultivated in personal friendships on the horizontal level of companionship, assists us also to deepen friendship with God in prayer on the vertical level. This then, is another trait of Lewis. He grew in prayer as he grew into friendships. Sometimes they were boon companionships, at other times they sprung from correspondence with strangers who became real friends, like "the American Lady." Perhaps too, as Lewis leaned on confidants in his distresses, so he should reach out to others in their needs too. "Forgiveness," he once said, "is another name for being forgiven." This reciprocity explains perhaps the largesse he gave to others in his enormous correspondence, indicative of what he felt he received from his trust in God.

So at the outbreak of the war in 1939, he wrote to his old pupil and friend Bede Griffiths, "I was terrified to find how fearful I was by the crisis. Pray for me for courage."[21] Again he writes to him in 1954, "I had prayed hard for a couple of nights before that my faith might be strengthened. The response was immediate, and your book gave the finishing touch" (that is, *The Golden String*, Griffith's autobiography).[22] Again, on December 20, 1961, Lewis wrote Griffiths after his wife's death: "I prayed when I buried my wife, my whole sexual nature should be buried with her, and it seems it has happened. Thus one recurrent trial has vanished from my life—an enormous liberty. Of course, this may be old age...."[23]

Another special friend was Sister Penelope Lawson. His first letter to her he wrote in 1939, saying: "Though I'm forty years old, I'm only about twelve as a Christian....So it would be a maternal act if you found time sometimes to mention me in your prayers."[24] Then on October 24, 1940 he told her: "I'm going to make my first confession next week, which will seem an odd experience. The *decision* to do so was one of the hardest I have ever made; but now that I am committed (by dint of posting the letter before I had time to change my mind) I began to be afraid of the opposite extreme—afraid that I was merely indulging in an orgy of egoism."[25] A month later, he wrote again to say, "well—we have come through the wall of fire, and find ourselves (somewhat to our surprise) still alive and even well. The story about an orgy of egoism turns out, like all the Enemy propaganda, to have just a grain of truth in it, but I have no doubt that the proper method of dealing with that is to continue the practice as I intend to do. For after all, everything—even virtue, even prayer—has its dangers and if one heeds the grain of truth in the Enemy propaganda, one can never do anything at all."[26]

A particular thorn in the flesh for Lewis was Mrs. Moore who was the mother of a friend killed in the First World War, and with whom Lewis had had an unfortunate romance that turned sour. She continued to live with Lewis and his brother for many years, and her last years in the household got progressively worse. During one particular crisis over her, Lewis wrote to Sister Penelope, "It was a bad time, but I almost venture to say I felt Christ in the house as I have never done before." Signing himself "Brother Ass," he added contritely, "but alas such a house for Him to visit!" Years before his brother had wistfully compared their own troubled household with that of the Dysons, where life seemed one long series of delightful picnics! So again Lewis wrote to Sister Penelope on January 3, 1945: "Pray for me, I am suffering incessant temptations to uncharitable thoughts at present; one of those black moods in which nearly all one's friends seem to be selfish or even false. And how terrible that there should be even a kind of *pleasure* in thinking evil."[27] As Mrs. Moore sunk into senility and kept the household in constant discord, he wrote, "I have been feeling that very much lately: that *cheerful insecurity* is what our Lord asks of us."[28] Again, on June 5, 1951, Lewis wrote her "I especially need your prayers because I am (like

the pilgrim in Bunyan) travelling across a plain called Ease!
Everything without, and many things within, are marvelously well
at present."[29] It was at this time that he began to think of writing a
book on prayer.

Perhaps it began to dawn upon him that he could not do this
without more experience of its reality in his own life, for on February
15, 1954, Lewis wrote again to Sister Penelope, "I have had to
abandon the book on prayer, it was clearly not for me."[30] He kept
this postponement for the next nine years of his life, indeed to the
year he died. But while he was writing it, his wife Joy Davidman
commented how excited she was about his project, as perhaps one
of the most important things Lewis would ever do.

6. Prayer-Life is Matured by Suffering

Perhaps in the meantime, Lewis began to think of what was
involved symbolically in the change of locale from Magdalen
College, Oxford, to Magdalene College, Cambridge. "My address
will be Magdalene, so I remain under the same patroness," he wrote
to Sister Penelope on July 30, 1954. "This is nice because it saves
'admin.' readjustments in Heaven." At the end of the year, he wrote
to his friend Veta Gebbert, "I think I shall like Magdalene better than
Magdalen." "It is a tiny college (a perfect cameo architecturally) and
they're so old-fashioned, pious, and gentle and
conservative—unlike this leftist, atheist, cynical, hard- boiled, huge
Magdalen" that had caused Lewis so much hurt.[31] In a letter to Bede
Griffiths on November 1st, he asked: "Has any theologian (perhaps
dozens) allegorized St. Mary Magdalene's act in the following way,
which came to me like a flash of lightning the other day!...The
precious alabaster box which we have to *break* over the holy feet is her
heart. It seems so obvious, once one has thought of it."[32]

So Lewis had come to see that prayer grows in the breaking of the
human heart before God. His perhaps was broken since Oxford
never recognised his worth to offer him a university professorship,
and later still, it was broken again by the far more poignant grief of
losing his wife in bereavement. Like all of us do, Lewis continued to
struggle with God when,

> By now I should be entering on the
> supreme stage
> Of the whole walk, reserved for the
> late afternoon.
> The heat was over now; the anxious
> mountains,
> The airless valleys and the sun-baked

rocks, behind me....[33]

Yet in June 18, 1962, he writes: "the plumbing often goes wrong....I need to be near a life-line." [34] Worse was to come.

After the loss of his wife, he asks the raw and naked question: Where is God? This is one of the most disquieting symptoms. When you are happy, so happy that you have no sense of needing Him, so happy that you are tempted to feel His claims upon you as an interruption, if you remember yourself and turn to Him with gratitude and praise, you will be—or so it feels—welcomed with open arms. But go to Him when your need is desperate, when all other help is in vain, and what do you find? A door slammed in your face, and the sound of bolting and double bolting on the inside. After that silence. You may as well turn away. The longer you wait, the more emphatic the silence will become. There are no lights in the windows. It might be an empty house. Was it even inhabited? It seemed so once. And that seeming was as strong as this. What can this mean? Why is He so present a commander in our time of prosperity and so very absent a help in time of trouble?[35]

In times of such bitter sorrow, Lewis admitted that "I am not in much danger of ceasing to believe in God. The real danger is of coming to believe such dreadful things about Him."[36]

> Of this we're certain; no one who dared knock
> At heaven's door for earthly comfort found
> Even a door—only smooth, endless rock,
> And save the echo of his voice no sound.
> It's dangerous to listen; you'll begin
> To fancy that those echoes (hope can play
> Pitiful tricks) are answers from within;
> Far better to turn, grimly sane away.
>
> Heaven cannot thus, Earth cannot ever, give
> The thing we want. We ask what isn't there
> And by our asking water and make live
> That very part of love which must despair,
> And die, and go down cold into the earth,
> Before there's talk of springtide and re-birth.[37]

Yes, this is perhaps one of the deepest experiences of prayer, to be able to say to our Heavenly Father, "Lord, not my will but thine be done."

Lewis' Theology of Prayer

If Lewis' personal experience of prayer has these six traits—an earthy realism, a practical import, a natural and simple attitude, a strong supplicatory concern for others, warm and honest expressions of friendships, and matured by suffering—how do these characteristics shape his theology of prayer? Perhaps two features he stressed most in his writings were: the problem of causality in prayer, and the nature of petitionary prayer. But like other human beings he had first to overcome morbid experiences of childhood before he could enter into a more truthful realism about the nature and exercise of prayer, so this we must consider as a necessary prelude.

A child tends to relate to God, as he relates with his parents. This correlation, unless corrected and healed, may persist, unconsciously so, throughout life. "My real life—or what memory reports as my real life—was increasingly one of solitude," Lewis reports. He had bad dreams, "like a window opening on what was hardly less than Hell."[38] As a child of seven, he admits "solitude was nearly always at my command, somewhere in the garden, or somewhere in the house....What drove me to write was the extreme manual clumsiness from which I suffered," so that he hated sports. His early years he described as "living almost entirely in my imagination," or at least "the imagination of those years now seems to me more important than anything else."[39] Then at the age of ten his mother died. He remembered what he had been taught, that prayer offered in faith would be answered. Then when she died he shifted his ground to believe he now needed to believe in a miracle, seeing God merely as a Magician. It left him with theological confusion about God for years to come. All happiness left him, and like the solid continent of Atlantis that disappeared under the waves, "all that was tranquil and reliable, disappeared from my life...it was all sea and islands now."[40]

At boarding school later, Lewis says he began "seriously to pray and read my Bible and to attempt to obey my conscience."[41] But his slight alienation from his distanced father increased, and there was emotionally no solid ground for the child. Sometimes he would awake at night afraid that his only brother had slipped off with his father to America, and left him behind. His prayers became sheer acts of despair. Having said them at night, his conscience would whisper he had not said them properly enough, so he would try and try again until he fell asleep in frustration and lack of abiding assurance. A deepening pessimism eventually led him at university to decide he was an atheist, which for many has been the cold comfort of forgetting God in a conversion of relief. Perhaps the dread of frustrated prayers at night-time never fully left him, and the issues of a reasoning faith about prayer were coloured perhaps as much from his early alienation as from his heightened intellectual search for the appropriate enquiry that would serve the logic of the mind, more than the rest of the heart. Perhaps Lewis' cure was to rest in the presence of God, rather than be always enquiring about its appropriateness.

1. Lewis' Emphasis upon "Festoonings in prayer"

The bad situations of imagination and conscience that Lewis had placed himself in, as a child, explain perhaps the emphasis he placed later in life upon the importance of placing one's self in what he called "prayerful situations," or "festoonings." Perhaps he learnt this from his own failures as a child to ever pray "properly" at all. Francis de Sales might also have helped him when he advises that in meditation, "place yourself in the presence of God." In honest humility, Lewis also learnt to see that at prayer one is in a more "real" situation than ever one could be in the "real world." Prayer is the struggle to come to grips with "rock-bottom realities." Prayer, then is the struggle for the "real I" to meet with the reality of God. Prayer then is saying, "may it be the real I who speaks. May it be the real Thou that I speak to." This is the prayer that precedes all prayers. Then as the great Iconoclast, God in his mercy may shatter all our false ideas and conceptions of him, that so hinder our real prayer in life.

Another area where "festoonings" of prayer are needed is in the realm of causality. Several times in his writings, Lewis recites the *Pensées* of Pascal: "God instituted prayer in order to lend his creatures the dignity of causality." Lewis' comment is that God perhaps "invented both prayer and physical action for that purpose."[42] For God has granted us the dignity of both work and prayer together. So a proper attitude to both is to pray as we work responsibly with the gifts that God has given to us, as well as to go on praying when we can work no more. Indeed, prayer is a stronger force than causality, not a weaker form. For if it "works" at all, it does so unlimited by space and time. Prayer then, is not a direct action over nature, it is action in co-operation with God, so we are most in harmony with God's provident action when we are in prayer before him. Perhaps the post-Einsteinian worldview ahead of us, still little appreciated in Lewis' day, now frees us from being so "hung up" with causality, as some his contemporaries were, but neither is God. Our relationship with God in faith that pleases him, is therefore still the vital prayerful situation for all praying.

2. Lewis and Petitionary Prayer

Wisely then, Lewis argues that it is a wrong kind of question to ask, "does prayer work?" It misleads us about the true nature of prayer. The quiet composure of heart before God rests in a relationship that is deeper, far deeper than words can ever express. This is where Lewis so clearly rested, and explains why so little need be said really about prayer. It is to be experienced rather than superficially talked about. At the same time Lewis honestly had difficulty with the apparently inconsistent character of petitions he noted in the gospels. For he observed two different types of prayer which appear inconsistent with each other.[43] Type A is the prayer taught by our Lord: "Thy will be done." In the light of the great submission of his passion, nothing can be asked for conditionally, only submissively so. It is asked in the Garden of Gethsemane, with any reservation whatever: "nevertheless, not my will but Thine be done." Type B is the petition in faith, able to "move mountains," to heal people, to remove blindness, and do much else. The apostle seems to advocate it when he urges us to "ask in faith, nothing doubting" (James 1:6-8).

Lewis asked many wise people about this apparent inconsistency and received no clear answer or solution. Hesitantly, Lewis suggested himself that until God has given us the faith to move mountains, it is perhaps to leave them alone, for he created them, and that is his business. Instead, it is advisable to concentrate more attention on Type A prayers, that indicate the surrender of self-will and self-love is more important than getting our own way, for we can easily mis-interpret our perception of things in foolish, wilful ways. Perhaps what Jesus actually did when he prayed submissively as he did on the night of his betrayal, was actually to identify himself with our weakness, so that even the certitude of the Father's will was withdrawn from him, so that in his extreme humiliation, Jesus prayed as we tend to pray in our weakness. Our struggles may be, says Lewis, to even believe that God is a Listener, not just that he is an Enabler.

Thus Lewis remained modest, extremely so, about his prayer life. Perhaps nothing keeps us humbler than a healthy realism about the inadequacy of our personal relationship with God. Lewis knew times of dryness in his prayer life, what the medieval monks used to call *accidie*. He warns us wisely against viewing our prayer life in relation to our emotions. "Whenever they are attending to the Enemy Himself," wrote Screwtape to his assistant Wormwood, "we are defeated." The Devil's advice to his evil apprentice is to distract their attention from God himself, to their feelings about God. "So when they ask for charity, let them also be deflected by having charitable feelings. When they pray for courage, let them feel brave. When they seek forgiveness, divert them with feelings about forgiveness. Teach them to eliminate the value of each prayer by the success in producing the desired feeling."[44] At all costs avoid the real nakedness of the soul before God in prayer. It is that, argued Screwtape, that is so deadly, of being in the living Presence of God himself.

These then, are some of the things Lewis teaches us by his life and honest reflections. They are home-spun, for the truth is always simple, if it is lived rather than being mere theory. As the primary language of the soul, prayer is like saying the alphabet. It may not appear very profound to describe, yet it is essential, the basis of all communication with God, that leads us forward into mysteries yet unknown and still to be experienced. In the mercy of God, he takes our childhood wounds and memories, to show us how deeply we need to ask, "Lord, teach us to pray." Then in the lessons he gives us through the lives of others, as well as our own, he unfolds the most wonderful journey for the soul we could ever conceive. Little did Lewis realize as a child where that journey would take him. Nor can we. But prayer remains its pulse-beat. We give the last word to Lewis about his own experiences of prayer. "Prayer," he says, "in the sense of asking for things, is a small part of it; confession and penitence are its threshold, adoration its sanctuary, the presence and vision and enjoyment of God its bread and wine. In it God shows Himself to us. That he answers prayer is a corollary—not necessarily the most important one—from the revelation. What He does is learned from what He is."[45]

Endnotes
1. C.S. Lewis, *Reflections on the Psalms* (London: Collins, Fount Paperbacks, 1984), p.9.
2. C.S. Lewis, *B.B.C. Talks* (London: Geoffrey Bles, 1941).
3. Kenneth Grahame, *The Wind in the Willows* (New York: Charles Scribner's Sons, 1908).
4. C.S. Lewis, *Poems,* edited by Walter Hooper (New York: Harcourt, Brace, Jovanovich, 1964), p.l.
5. C.S. Lewis, *Mere Christianity* (London: Geoffrey Bles, 1952), p. 155.
6. C.S. Lewis, *Letters to Malcolm: Chiefly on Prayer,* edited by Walter Hooper (New York: Harcourt, Brace, Jovanovich, 1964), p.13.

7. *Op. cit.*, p.11.

8. *Ibid.*

9. *Op. cit.*, p. 28.

10. C.S. Lewis, *Letters,* edited by W.H. Lewis, (New York: Harvest Books, 1966), p.265.

11. George MacDonald, *Diary of an Old Soul* (Minneapolis, Minn.: Augsburg Publishing House, 1975), p.111.

12. William Griffin, *Clive Staples Lewis, a Dramatic Life* (San Francisco: Harper & Row, 1986), p.76.

13. *Op. cit.*, p.79.

14. *Op. cit.*, p.84.

15. C.S. Lewis, *Christian Behaviour* (London: Geoffrey Bles, 1943) p.64.

16. C.S. Lewis, *Letters to Malcolm,* p.114.

17. C.S. Lewis, *Letters to an American Lady,* edited by Clyde Kilby (London: Hodder and Stoughton, 1967) p.21.

18. William Griffin, *Clive Staples Lewis,* pp. 149-150.

19. C.S. Lewis, *Letters to Malcolm,* pp.67-68.

20. C.S. Lewis, *Poems,* pp.122-123.

21. William Griffin, *Clive Staples Lewis,* pp.162

22. *Ibid.*, p.357.

23. *Ibid.*, p.428.

24. *Ibid.*, p.162.

25. *Ibid.*, p.181.

26. *Ibid.*, pp.181-182.

27. *Ibid.*, p.241.

28. *Ibid.*, p.316

29. *Ibid.*, p.324.

30. *Ibid.*, p.349.

31. *Ibid.*, p.356.

32. *Ibid.*

33. C.S. Lewis, *Poems,* pp.118.

34. William Griffin, *Clive Staples Lewis,* pp.429.

35. C.S. Lewis, *A Grief Observed* (London: Faber & Faber, 1964), pp.9-10.

36. *Ibid.*

37. C.S. Lewis, *Poems,* pp.126.

38. C.S. Lewis, *Surprised by Joy* (New York: Harcourt, Brace, Jovanovich, 1955), p.11.

39. *Ibid.*, pp.15-18.

40. *Ibid.*, p.21.

41. *Ibid.*, p.34.

42. C.S. Lewis, *God in the Dock,* edited by Walter Hooper (Grand Rapids: Eerdmans, 1970), pp.104-107.

43. See the essay "Petitionary Prayer: A Problem Without an Answer", in C.S. Lewis, *Christian Reflections,* edited by Walter Hooper (London: Geoffrey Bles, 1967), pp.142-151.

44. C.S. Lewis, *Screwtape Letters* (London: Geoffrey Bles, 1967), p.28.

45. C.S. Lewis, *The World's Last Night and Other Essays: The Efficacy of Prayer* (New York: Harcourt, Brace, Jovanovich, 1949), p.8.

Godliness in Ephesians

J.I. Packer

Vol. XXV, No. 1 (March 1989):8-16

I

This article is a Bible study—but, quite specifically, it is a theologian's Bible study, carried out with a theologian's special concerns in mind. And I had better be explicit about what these are, for many Christian people do not know. They see theologians as interested in making simple things difficult and complex, and in exploring questions that have nothing to do with life. But, putting it in homely imagery, theologians are in fact the church's water engineers, plumbers, and sewage specialists, whose job it is to ensure that pure truth, fully fit to drink, is constantly supplied, and that nothing which threatens spiritual health gets absorbed unwittingly. Intellectual garbage keeps fouling the springs of the church's life, and no one who swallows its poison is likely to stay healthy. So the church needs theologians to detect and dispose of all such unedifying matter.

Theologians are the church's nutritionists, too. "Sanctify them by the truth," was Jesus' prayer. Some people talk as if knowledge of God's truth, and soundness in faith, do not bear on the life of godliness, but Jesus' words teach the opposite: without divine truth, the life of true consecration cannot be. Health requires a health-giving diet, and the theologian's positive role is to see that such a diet is provided. That is why he sometimes ventures to ride herd on teaching that does not constitute a balanced menu, or that allows poisonous fungi to get into the food in the guise of edible mushrooms (once more, please accept the homely imagery). Such action on his part may not advance his popularity, but it may help to preserve the church, and that is what chiefly matters.

II

Our theme is *godliness*. Is that a word you often use? Probably not. Does it sound to you faded and old-fashioned? I fear that to many of us it does, and that the reason why we rarely use it is that we rarely think about the reality that it signifies. But that is not as it should be. What, after all, is godliness? It is a life, a life-style (as we say these days), a lifestyle compounded of personal practices with which the Ephesian letter is deeply and directly concerned: holiness, righteousness,· and love; purity, praise, and prayer. Do other biblical books expound godliness? Yes, one way or another, they all do. Is there any pressing need to study Bible teaching on godliness? Yes, there is, for mistakes about it abound: three especially, with which I must try to deal before we go any further.

First: some think that godliness is really *unimportant*. I was once asked to write a journal article on the question: "Is personal holiness passé?"—that is, outdated, trivial, and no longer mattering? Did I do well to be shocked, and to burn up the paper with my answer? I thought so then, and I think so now; for, however modern Christians view the matter, Ephesians shows it to be one of God's chief concerns that believers be godly. The Father chose us in Christ before time began "to be holy and blameless in his sight" (Ephesians 1:4). Christ "loved the church and gave himself up for her to make her holy...and to present her to himself as a radiant church...holy and blameless" (5:25-27). The sanctifying Holy Spirit is "grieved" (4:30) when Christians retain sinful habits. Thus Father, Son, and Holy Spirit are at one in purposing that we saved sinners become godly. But if our godliness is important to God, it cannot be unimportant for us.

Second: some think that godliness is *self-generated*, as if we could manufacture it simply by going through the motions of spiritual disciplines and routines (prayer, meditation, worship, fellowship) as one goes through the Royal Canadian Air Force exercises for total physical fitness (eleven minutes daily for a woman, twelve for a man). But this is not so. Though there is no godliness without the disciplines, it is not the disciplines in themselves that make us godly. Godliness is God's own gift and work; it is from the Three-in-One, and specifically from the Holy Spirit, the third divine Person, that the power effecting growth in grace, and so in godliness, derives. This is part of the point of the present imperative—passive, not active—in Ephesians 5:18: "Be [continually] filled with the Spirit." Paul means: be open to all the Spirit's work, be totally taken up with the Spirit's concerns, let him have his way with your lives, let him make you into a singing, rejoicing, praising, ministering Christian, by a supernatural transformation of you that goes beyond anything you could have produced in yourself. When Paul speaks of Christians being "filled to the measure of all the fullness of God" (3:19), and of Christ as being the source of the spiritual growth of his "body," the church (4:16), he is making the same point: godliness is a quality of life that God works into us, not one that we work up in ourselves. We cannot rise to Christlikeness by tugging at our own bootstraps; we shall only be changed this way as divine power changes us.

Third: some think that godliness is irrelevant to *usefulness*, as if spiritual gifts do not need to be backed by solid Christian character for fully effective service. That was evidently the view of the Corinthians; not, however, of Paul! It is striking to see how in Ephesians 4, in spelling out his plea for a worthy walk, Paul calls for the moral qualities of humility, gentleness, patience, forbearance, and love (vv. 1-2) before saying a word about ministry and growth (vv. 11-16). The necessity of godliness for fruitfulness is also brought out by Jesus' words in Matthew 5:16: "Let your light shine before men, that they may see your good deeds and praise your Father in heaven." Jesus is declaring that his servants, having already spoken of their Father in heaven (otherwise, how would "men" know whom to praise?), must now give credibility to their good words by good works. The good works show that the speakers know what they are talking about, having themselves been transformed in the manner specified. We have all known situations that prompted the cynical comment, "your life shouts so loud that I can't hear a word you say"—but Jesus has in view the opposite: namely, situations in which the quality of the speakers' lives opens the hearts of skeptics to receive truth that they would otherwise have shrugged off as fantasy. There is no credibility in a bald man peddling hair restorer, but if the salesman, once certifiably bald, now has a fine head of hair, the case is altered. From this we see why gifts must be grounded in godliness if they are to be fully fruitful, and why good ministry is made barren by a bad or worldly life. Godliness is in fact supremely relevant to usefulness.

III

Our theme is godliness *in Ephesians,* and it will help us forward if we now spend a moment reminding ourselves of Paul's strategy in this letter.

Paul wants his readers to know God's grace in order that they may grow in it. Accordingly, he devotes chapters 1-3 to celebrating the greatness and glory of the saving mercy that has created the new society to which they belong (that is, the church, the Father's family and temple, the body, bride, and building of Christ the Son); after which he spends chapters 4-6 begging them to behave in a way that is worthy of their calling, maintaining unity, ministry, and charity within their diversity, doing good, fighting evil, and honouring Christ no less in the family than in the church. The dictum that for Paul—doctrine is grace and ethics is gratitude—is verified by almost every verse.

What Paul is doing pastorally in all this is following out his philosophy of *raising steam.* In former days on the railways trains of over a thousand tons were moved at high speed by the expansive power of steam. Such trains could not be moved by passengers pushing, but when the fire in the firebox of the locomotive had raised steam in the boiler and that steam was piped into the cylinders, movement began at once. By dwelling upon grace in a way that calls forth gratitude, Paul is lighting the fire that raises moral and spiritual steam for spontaneous, whole-hearted godliness as his readers' response to divine love. The four propositions that I shall now present constitute a demonstration of how he does this, and an analysis of what he sees to be involved.

IV

(1) Godliness according to Ephesians starts with *acknowledging God's grace and power in Christ*: which is an activity of the mind, reasoning, and thereby grasping truth.

"Grace" is in effect a technical term. In secular Greek it signified simply elegance of various kinds, but Paul regularly uses the word to mean divine love shown to the unlovely in the form of mercy that defies demerit by bestowing eternal salvation on them when otherwise they were eternally and deservedly lost (see 1:6f., 2:4-8 with 1-3). Then, by extension, Paul uses it also for the God-given privilege and capacity of furthering God's saving work in others by one's own grateful service (see 3:2, 7f., 4:7). Both Paul's greeting and his farewell take the form of prayer for grace for his readers (1:2, 6:24); no doubt he is expressing the comprehensive desire that they may both receive fulness of salvation and render fulness of service continually. Grace is Paul's focal theme throughout chapters 1-3, for he knows that it is precisely from an understanding of grace that authentic godliness grows.

"Power" is also for Paul a technical term. Secular Greek, like modern English, would use the word for any show of strength of any sort, but Paul uses it with regular reference to God's redemptive energy in renewing and re-creating that which physical, moral, or spiritual death has for the moment ruined. This divine power, first displayed in the resurrection and exaltation of Jesus, is now imparted by the Holy Spirit in and through ministry of the gospel to bring new life in Christ to persons spiritually dead, morally disordered, and personally, as we nowadays say, destroyed (see 1:19-23, 3:7, 16-20, 6:10-13; cf. 2:4-10, 4:17-24, 6:14-20). God's life-giving, life-changing, life-preserving power, the power that gives vigour for "good works" that displace habits of sin, valour for witness to a hostile world, and victory against evil in all its many forms, is highlighted throughout Ephesians, for Paul knows that authentic godliness presupposes a proper appreciation of it.

"In Christ" is yet a third Pauline technical term, pointing first to the centrality of the incarnate Lord in God's plans to restore his ruined world (1:9f., 3:10f.) and then to the multidimensional solidarity with Christ that is given us by grace and is, first to last, the source and means of our salvation. It is a union that was predetermined before creation (1:4-6) and will last for ever (2:7, 3:21). It is representative, with Christ acting on our behalf as our mediator, our substitutionary sin-bearer whose death reconciled us to God and our avenue of present access to the Father (2:13-18), and it is also real, with Christ as our indwelling source of change, growth, and joy through the Spirit (3:17, 4:12-16 with 2:21f., 5:18-20). It is vital (a life-union) as well as covenantal (a federal union), for it introduces us to living communion with Christ as he exercises his headship over us and imparts to us his life-flow within his body, as well as involving us in the Father's acceptance that is now his and in the sure hope of sharing his glory eventually. It is worth illustrating what wealth of divine giving is covered by the phrase "in Christ" by following it through the first half of the letter.

We who now have faith (1:1) may know that we were chosen from eternity *in Christ* for final glory, says Paul (1:4,11). *In Christ* we now have our redemption through his blood, that is, we have been sealed as God's through the gift to us of the promised Holy Spirit upon our believing (1:13), that is, the Spirit fulfilling in us his distinctive new covenant ministry of making us perceive the glory of Christ and his salvation (cf. 1:17-21) and drawing us into fellowship with the Father through the Son (1:17, 2:18, 3:12). (*Sealed* gives the picture of a purchaser, say of a stack of lumber, using his signet ring to put his seal on a wax tablet that would then be affixed to the woodpile, doing duty as a "Sold" notice, until the purchaser sent his cart to collect what he had bought. The Holy Spirit within us is God's seal upon us till he comes to take us home to himself: see 4:30.)

But this is not all; indeed, it is hardly half. Paul goes on to tell us that *in Christ* we have been raised from spiritual death, in fellowship with Christ who was himself raised from physical death, and *in Christ* we have been enthroned with Christ (that is what "sit" means) in the realm of eternal spiritual reality, the order of things that abides unchanged when this world passes away (2:6). (The pictures here are, first, of ourselves as lifeless corpses now animated for conscious responses to God that were impossible to us before and, second, of ourselves as consciously living "on top" of all that happens, appreciating that it is all for our benefit and so is "ours" [cf. 1 Corinthians 3:21ff.] because we are linked to the Lord of love, who is "on top" of everything in the sense of actually controlling and shaping it so as to bless us through it [cf. Romans 8:28f.].) And God has thus enthroned us with Christ, Paul continues, so that "in the coming ages he might show the incomparable riches of his grace, expressed in his kindness to us *in Christ Jesus*" (2:7). Being in Christ, therefore, guarantees us an eternity of ecstatic enrichment. Meantime, as of now, we know ourselves to be new creatures in Christ, programmed for godliness ("good works") (2:10), new creatures who have been brought permanently near to God (brought, that is, into his abiding favour and fellowship) *in Christ* through the cross (2:13, cf. 14-18, 3:12).

To see all this is to begin to realize something of the breadth and depth of meaning contained in the great initial statement that chapters 1-3 seek to open up to us—"God...has blessed us in the heavenly realms with every spiritual blessing *in Christ*" (1:3)—and to appreciate why he feels obligated to call the riches of Christ *"unsearchable"* (3:8). But Paul has no doubt that authentic godliness requires some awareness of what believers are and have in Christ.

All Paul's letters are pastoral communications, calculated to have a certain effect on their readers, and Ephesians is no exception. As we have already noted, Paul wants the readers of this letter to *know* God's grace (see 1:9, 17-19, 3:2-11, 17-19) in order that they may grow in it, both individually and as a fellowship, or series of fellowships (see 2:21f., 3:19, 4:12-16). Paul's rhapsodic celebration of grace through chapters 1-3 is meant to help readers "grasp how wide and long and high and deep is the love of Christ, and to know this love that passes knowledge" (3:18f.), and from this appreciate how blessed they are, as objects of such love. Their *election* is a fact; they were chosen in Christ from eternity (1:4f.); that means that they are eternally secure in him, and need not fear anything, human or Satanic, that rises to obstruct their path as their Lord leads them on to holiness and home

(1:4f., 2:6f., 19-22, 3:20, 6:10- 13). Their *redemption* is a fact; they were reconciled to God at the cost of Christ's cross (2:16); that means that they are forever forgiven, accepted, and sharers in the *shalom* of God (1:7, 2:14-18), and need not be anxious anymore as to where they stand with their Maker. Their *renewal* is a fact; their acts of repentance have been matched by God's work of regeneration (4:20-24), and now they know themselves as new creatures (2:10, 4:24), indwelt by the Holy Spirit (1:13f., 4:30), and called to work out what God has wrought in them by living a new life (4:17-5:17). Their *incorporation into Christ* is a fact; they are now units (limbs, organs, moving parts) in his body (4:15f., 25), with a lifelong ministry of caring and sharing to fulfill. Realize who and what you are through God's almighty grace! says Paul. Godliness starts here.

Paul's concern that his readers should grasp the *greatness* of God's grace and power comes out clearly. He speaks of the *riches* (wealth) of divine grace (1:7, 2:7) and of divine glory (3:16)—meaning by glory, God's display in action of his saving love and power; and he exults in the God-given privilege of preaching "the unsearchable riches of Christ" (3:8), and so becoming the human means of God's transformation of lives. He deploys the stark image of spiritual *deadness,* in sin (2:1,4), a corpse-condition of total non-response to the stimulation of the gospel, followed by the equally startling idea of God's quickening touch as *co-resurrection with Jesus* (2:5f.), to enforce the same realization, that the grace of God is a great, wonderful, and altogether supernatural thing. He speaks of *election* and *predestination* to holiness and heaven (1:4f.), not to start arguments or stir anxieties (Paul would, I think, be mystified at the bellicosity of some, and the worries and embarrassments of others, in our day about predestination); he does it, rather, to call forth in his readers the great joy of knowing that the great change that God has wrought in them is the outworking of a great plan to save them, a plan which was formed before the world was and will be sovereignly carried on until they arrive safely home, to the praise of the divine grace and glory that has brought them there (1:6, 12, 14). All these themes are presented to believers as belonging to the good news about God's great grace: from knowing which, as Paul sees the matter, true godliness springs, on the principle that the greater the gratitude, the more robust the response. As it has been put:

> I will not work my soul to save,
> For that my Lord has done;
> But I will work like any slave
> For love of God's dear Son.

That leads us to our next propositions.

V

(2) Godliness according to Ephesians grows by adoring God's grace and power in Christ: which is an activity of the heart, responding, and thereby practising worship.

The fact we must notice now is that though the content of chapters 1-3 is doctrinal instruction about God's plan and work, their form is praise, punctuated by prayer. Paul has chosen to make the whole section doxological and devotional in tone. Why? Because he sees thanksgiving for grace already given, coupled with desire for more, whether on one's own behalf or on behalf of others, as the proper mind-set—soul-set, if you prefer—for all saints. He does not write out his materials this way at random; he knows what he is doing; he is modelling godliness, of which praise and prayer are the basic modes of expression. Talking, doing, helping, leading, fighting do not add up to godliness if they are not rooted in praise and prayer. And praise, as we shall now see, has priority.

Doxology is the note struck by Paul's very first word after his greeting. "Blessed be the God...who has blessed us with every spiritual blessing..." (1:3). The New International Version renders "Praise be to...God," thus underscoring the fact that this is worship at the price of obscuring Paul's deliberate juxtaposition of the two blessings, for which he uses two Greek words from the same family (*eulogetos, eulogesas*): surely the New International Version is here losing more than it gains. Paul wants us to see the two blessings as connected, the second called forth by the first. His thought is that as God blessed us by the decision and acts of power that result in our salvation, so we should now bless God by declaring his goodness in this and voicing our gratitude for it. Because he blesses us by showing us his glory in our redemption. He shows himself praiseworthy, and our mouths are to show forth his praise. Grateful adoration of God, from the heart (cf. 5:19f.) is the branch on which all the additional fruits that go to make up godliness have to grow. What grows on a different branch should be given a different name: it is not true godliness, whatever else it is.

Doxology rounds off the letter's celebration of grace, just as doxology began it. 1:3 was Paul's invitation to join with him in worship; 3:20f. is Paul's own concluding word of worship. "Now to him who is able to do immeasurably more than all we ask or imagine, according to his power that is at work within us, to him be glory in the church and in Christ Jesus [the two phrases are a hendiadys: in the church, that is, in Christ Jesus, is what Paul means] throughout all generations, for ever and ever. Amen." Paul ends as he began,

practising and modelling praise; for he knows that if godliness is a
house, gratitude expressed in adoration and praise is its ground
floor.

I will not ask you whether you pray—I am sure you do—but I will
unapologetically press the question, do you praise? How large a
place does adoring, heartfelt praise take in our personal lives and the
lives of our churches? If the place of praise in our lives is in fact small,
that argues, not only that we have not as much godliness as perhaps
we thought, but, more basically, that we have no adequate idea of
how to honour God in our approaches to him. Let Dr. Martyn
Lloyd-Jones, commenting on Ephesians 1:3, speak to this.

> Because of our wretched subjectivity our tendency always is
> to concentrate at once on the blessings; we always want
> something for ourselves. The Apostle insists, however, that
> we start with God, and with worship. We are not to rush
> into the presence of God in prayer or in any other respect;
> we must always start by realizing who God is. What would
> be thought of a person who tried to rush into Buckingham
> Palace to see the Queen of England and refused to consider
> matters of etiquette? Such an approach would be regarded
> as insulting, and yet we all tend to act in that manner in
> respect to Almighty God on account of our great concern to
> obtain a blessing. But the Apostle insists upon the right and
> appropriate order; and we must only consider the nature of
> the blessings after we have worshipped God and praised His
> Name....Indeed it is only as we adopt this Apostolic order
> that we shall really begin to enjoy the blessings. I can
> certainly testify after many years of pastoral experience that
> the people who give me the impression of being most
> miserable are those who are always thinking of themselves
> and their blessings, their moods and states and conditions.
> The way to be blessed is to look to God; and the more we
> worship Him the more we shall enjoy His blessings. This is
> most practical. The practical man is not one who runs after
> the blessings, but the man who considers the Source of the
> blessings and is in touch with that Source.[1]

Dr. Lloyd-Jones is right; God-centred adoration must come first,
and be the ground-base, so to speak, shaping all our dealings with
God on every occasion. Paul, who as we have seen models this in
chapters 1-3, clinches the point in 5:18-21, where after saying "be filled
with the Spirit" (that is, live a life in which what most concerns the

Spirit most concerns you too) he adds four descriptive clauses to show what this will mean. It is unfortunate that no English version since the American Standard Version, apart from the New King James Version, lets us see this; they all detach at least one of the clauses, sometimes more than one, from the command to the Spirit-filled, and thus conceal more or less of the truth that all there to show us what the Spirit-filled person is like. The are there to show us what the Spirit-filled person is like. The fourth clause specifies humble submissiveness in Christian relationships (21); the first three items are hymn- and psalm singing, a song to Christ in one's heart, and habitual thanksgiving (19f.). Such is the godly person's basic temper.

The word to us, then, is: catch the spirit of praise! Ground your devotion in doxology! Let adoration become an ever bigger element in your spiritual life! This is the route that authentic godliness always travels. The characteristic pentecostal and charismatic insistence, based on the King James Version of Psalm 22:3, that God inhabits the praises of his people in the sense that they find him near as they adore him, is profoundly true, however much the translation of that verse may need amending. Genuinely godly souls know this truth, and stay on the path of praise.

VI

(3) Godliness according to Ephesians demands *alteration of behaviour through God's grace and power in Christ*: which is an activity of the will, resolving, and thereby obeying the gospel.

The gospel calls on sinners to change their ways. That is what it means to *repent*, and there is no real salvation and no real godliness save as we learn repentance (see 5:5f.). Our faith is no more genuine than is our repentance; indeed, repentance and faith are two sides of the same coin, for turning to God in Christ means turning from sin. And, as the first of Luther's 95 Theses declared, repentance is meant to be lifelong. Our ongoing life of faith must also be a life of ongoing repentance—that is, of grief over our various follies and resolute change for the better.

The task of breaking bad habits and forming good ones is never over, and woe betide the Christian who at any point thinks it is. To be sure, most of us have conservative instincts, and the prospect of change rarely pleases, and the older we get in years the less attractive we find it, so that the chilling words of W.H. Auden, "We would rather be ruined than changed," tend to apply to us increasingly, in all sorts of ways. But it is a terrible thing when a Christian says, on a question of obeying God, "I'm too old to change." That is nothing less than defiant impenitence—something that itself needs to be repented of.

Paul's awareness of the necessity for ongoing moral change, and also of the frightening ease with which Christians whose first zeal has cooled slip back into the ways of the world around them, leads him into a theologically-based exhortation to Christian living in chapters 4-6 that is quite as weighty as (and slightly longer than) his celebration of God's saving grace in chapters 1-3. The hinge statement linking the two halves of the letter is in 4:1: Christians must walk worthy of their calling. "Walk" is a regular Bible picture of living, and Paul uses the word repeatedly (2:10, 4:1,17, 5:2,8,15), though neither the Revised Standard Version nor the New International Version allow the reader to see this. His six admonitions (walk in good works...worthy of your calling...not as the Gentiles do...in love...as children of light...in wisdom) make clear the direction of the changes called for; and of the new behaviour-pattern as a whole, from inception to maturest fulfilment, he has these four basic things to say.

First, this changed life is a matter of being *different*. In 4:17-24 Paul teaches the principle of a clean break with pagan ways (which is, of course, what repentance—a word not used in Ephesians— actually amounts to). You have been taught, he says, in terms of "the truth that is in Jesus," "to put off your old self, which is being corrupted by its deceitful desires, to be made new in the attitude of your minds, and to put on the new self, created to be like God in true righteousness and holiness" (4:21-24). By resolution from your side, and by regeneration from God's, you are now different from what you were and what pagans around you still are. So identify with your new identity in Christ, and live out that difference! Don't deceive others, but tell the truth (25); don't bear grudges, but make up quarrels (26 f.); don't steal, but do some honest work (28); don't talk disgustingly or maliciously, but helpfully (29, 5:3f.). Godliness means being thus different.

Second, this changed life is a matter of being *Christlike* and *Godlike*. Paul invokes Jesus' example of costly love for us (5:2), and goes on to apply it to the way in which a husband must love his wife (5:25-33); he also invokes God the Father's example of freely forgiving us, and tells us to be kind, compassionate, and forgiving to others in the same way (4:32-5:1). These divine models for our behaviour must always be kept in view: we fall short of godliness if we ignore them.

Third, this changed life is a matter of being *Spirit-filled*. Paul has already introduced us to the indwelling Holy Spirit as God's seal upon us, assuring us that we are his (1:13); as a foretaste ("earnest," meaning first instalment, down payment, deposit, pledge) of our coming inheritance (1:14); as the "giving gift," to use Thomas Smail's phrase, of heart-insight into gospel truth (1:17-20; "spirit" in 1:17 is the Holy Spirit, as in the New International Version); as the source of experiential access in peace to the Father (2:18), and experiential knowledge of Christ's love (3:16-19); and as the Sanctifier, to whom our sins bring sorrow and distress (4:30). It is with this Spirit, servant of these purposes and executor of these ministries, that Paul now charges us to be "filled." (If we render "filled" as "taken over, drawn forward, led on, absorbed, preoccupied, and satisfied," we shall not be far wrong.) Godliness requires this too.

As we said earlier, being Spirit-filled means living a life in which the things that most concern the Spirit—the glory of Christ, and the sanctity of saints—are the things that most concern us also; and the marks of being Spirit-filled, according to Paul, are, first, praise and thanksgiving to God out of inward joy (5:19f.), and, second, mutual submission within the fellowship "out of reverence for Christ" (5:21). The meaning of "submit" here seems to have nothing to do with chains of command within non-reversible, hierarchical authority patterns such as we meet in the armed forces (how could submission ever be *mutual* in that kind of one-way street?); it has to do, rather, with neighbour-love, which puts itself at another's service in order to do that person good. Love has been well defined as activity planned to help, please, and exalt the loved one, and mutual submission means practising love by living in terms of the old tagphrase, "at your service." The "reverence for Christ" that Paul specifies as the reason for this submission crystallizes in the thought that as Christ has loved us, and does love us, according to this formula, so we must imitate him in loving others according to the same formula. That is godliness in action.

Godliness, like charity, begins at home, so we should not be surprised at Paul's move from 5:21 straight into *Haustafeln*, prescriptive analysis of domestic relations between married couples (5:22-33), children and parents (6:1-4), slaves and masters (6:5-9). (The present-day relevance of this last section will appear if one adapts it to employees and employers.) Home life in the ancient world was often a brutal business, in which wives, children, and slaves suffered much, but in Christian homes, says Paul, loving care and respect on both sides within the given shape of these asymmetrical relationships must prevail throughout. So husbands must love their wives as Christ loved the church, and wives must respond to their husbands as the church responds to Christ. Children must not defy their parents, and parents must not exasperate their children. Slaves must see service rendered to their owners as part of their service of Christ, and masters must be considerate to their slave, knowing themselves accountable, not indeed to the slaves themselves, but to God, who is Owner and Judge of master and slave alike. It is a negation of godliness, a grief to the Holy Spirit, and a demonstration that one is far from being Spirit-filled, when one mistreats one's family and employees.

Fourth, and last, this changed life is a matter of being *natural*. By that I mean not that godliness ever comes easily (it does not; Satan sees to that), but that, since new creation in Christ means that the behavioural instincts and desires of Jesus' perfect humanity have become our own deepest instincts and desires also (that is one side of what union with Christ involves), we now find fulfilment, just as Jesus did in doing God's holy will, and at the deepest level we experience only frustrated unfulfilment if we flout that will. As obeying God was unnatural to us in our fallenness, so unnatural that we could not do it at all while we lived under the power of sin (cf. Romans 6:17-22), so now disobeying God, though all too possible when carelessness prevails and conscience sleeps, has become equally unnatural. When, however, we follow the promptings of what we call our new nature, and Paul calls "the new man which was created according to God, in true righteousness and holiness" (4:24, New King James Version), we are doing what has become natural to us, as the resulting inner contentment clearly shows. Naturalness in Christ means being uninhibited about acting on the urgings of our renewed personal being; such naturalness always marks the Spirit-filled life, and is an integral element in true godliness. So I say: Christian, understand yourself, and be natural!

VII

(4) Godliness according to Ephesians requires *aggression against evil through God's grace and power in Christ*: which is an activity of the person, crusading, and thereby becoming a light in the world.

Godliness is not a passive, but an active disposition, and godly persons attack evil as well as being attacked by it. The passage on spiritual warfare in 6:10-18, which teaches us how to fight back when Satan puts us under mental and emotional pressure, whether by direct or (as most often) indirect means, is familiar ground, and justly so. Clearly, Paul wrote it out of his own struggle with the feelings of uncertainty, tending to depression and despair, that must have swept over him again and again as he languished on in prison; clearly, the temper of analytical adoration, passionate calm, ecstatic exaltation, and triumphant tranquility, which so distinguishes Ephesians among Paul's letters, is the fruit of his own successful use of the armour of God in battling with these feelings; and clearly, he wants us to see that godliness calls for similar resistance whenever Satan deploys his deceitful cunning in attempts to ruin us by commandeering our thought-life. But from the standpoint of our present interest the more arresting passage on opposing evil is 5:3-14, where the key thought is: "having nothing to do with the fruitless deeds of darkness, but rather expose them" (11). Realize that you are light that must shine, says Paul (8f.); it is the testimony of your life, your words and actions together, that must encompass the exposure. This, too, is godliness in action.

Though the paragraph is slightly elliptical, the flow of thought seems clear. Do not talk about the world's immoralities as if you can approve or tolerate them, says Paul (3f., 12), and certainly never fall back into such ways yourselves (5-7,11). Find and follow the will of the Lord Jesus, and live as those who, having once been personal black holes of moral darkness, have become through new creation light in him. Practise goodness, righteousness and truth, expressing in action what you now are in essence, and you will inevitably expose the world's evil ways, just be being there and being purposely and purposefully different. The effect will be of light shining into a dark corner, revealing everything in its true colours and in the process showing up all the dirt (cf. 13): an action which, though Paul does not mention this, may well be resented deeply by those whose murky ways are exposed. But the happier result may be that persons who were spiritually asleep wake up, see their need and lostness, and are drawn to Christ, recognizing that their past immorality has been ugly and destructive and leaving it behind (14). Thus we should hope and pray that our witness, weak and faltering as it often is, will be used to the conversion of others and with that a raising of moral standards around us. Both of these are goals that true godliness actively seeks.

Do we accept this? Do we live this way? How often, and how seriously, do we go on the offensive against evil in our local, civic, or national community? Paul would, I think, tell us that Christians today are much too timid and low-key when faced with scandalous corruptions; much too ready, he would say, to tolerate the intolerable. He would remind us that sometimes speaking out is the right thing to do, and that sometimes testimony that is not forceful will not seem credible either. Our own present idea of godliness may

be altogether too narrow, in-turned, and acquiescent: who knows?
We had better look, and see.

VIII

It should by now be clear that godliness according to Ephesians,
the godliness that starts with a growing appreciation of God's grace
that blossoms continually into pure worship, good works, and hard
warfare, is actually the high road to human wholeness. Those who
practise Pauline godliness are being led on towards the maturity of
the "perfect (full-grown) man" who is "the measure of the stature of
the fullness of Christ" (4:13, New King James Version, cf. 1:21). This
"perfect man" is a corporate figure; he is the "one new man" that
Christ created in himself through the incarnation and reconciled to
God through the cross (2:15); he is the church, the building, body,
and bride of Christ, but the church viewed from a particular angle,
namely as the fullness of the humanity of all who compose it. Paul's
thought in 4:13 seems to be that it will take all the grace and power
that Christ has shown in every single Christian to display his
fullness. In other words, the combined testimony and experience of
all the millions of believers that have ever been is needed to make
known to the admiring angels, who are the spectators of God's work
in the church (see 3:10), the full resources of divine saving wisdom.
If you have ever been in a gathering where a series of people have
testified to God's grace and power and wisdom in their lives, you
could by extrapolation form some idea of at least one of the activities
that will make new Jerusalem into a city of unending joy. In the
togetherness of all God's perfected saints the fullness of Christ—his
entire resources of wisdom, love, and power—will be open to view,
open to exploration and adoration perpetually. It is thus that glory
(praise) will come to be given to God "in the church and in Christ
Jesus throughout all generations, for ever and ever" (3:20); and it is
as one tiny element contributing to this great goal that our godliness,
such as it is, finds its ultimate significance. So Paul indicates in this
marvellous letter to the Ephesians, of which so far we have but
scratched the surface. But there are limits to what one can do in a
single article, and I must stop.

Endnote
1. D.M. Lloyd-Jones, *God's Ultimate Purpose* (Ephesians 1:1-23),
Edinburgh: Banner of Truth, 1978, pp.57 ff.

Confessions of a Failed Archaeologist

Carl E. Armerding

Vol. XXV, No. 1 (March 1989):5-7

In 1968 I went to Palestine, fresh with a Ph.D. in ancient Near Eastern languages and history, a love for everything Semitic, a zest for life, and a year to devote to a post-doctoral fellowship in Biblical Archaeology. During that year I listened to lectures by G. Ernest Wright, tramped the deserts of the Sinai with Nelson Glueck, and explored Negev ruins with Yohanan Aharoni and William Dever. There were some great moments: the camaraderie, the excitement of finding another "floor level" (we never discovered earthshaking things like the Dead Sea Scrolls; such serendipities were reserved for Bedouin tribesmen), and the sheer delight of returning to Jerusalem or Beer Sheba for a cool shower and a night's sleep in a good hotel.

And I learned much of the archaeologist's craft. My teachers were enthusiastic about the subject, there was a sense of relevance as we uncovered ancient civilizations, and the work, although hot and dirty, carried its own rewards. In a very real sense, the little band of diggers, from all nations and religious backgrounds (or lack of same), was a remarkable fraternity. Oh yes, they could, and did, frequently dispute one another's conclusions. They had their share of professional jealousies, and like chaplains in the Navy, they flocked in groups of like-minded colleagues. But, in the final analysis, archaeologists are not unlike other professionals, including ministers in a pluralistic environment. They are bound together by a common loyalty to the profession, and they are proud of what they have, corporately, achieved.

Why, then, did I turn out so badly in the eyes of my fellow archaeologists, or aspiring archaeologists? With all my training, with the ability to sight a straight baulk, discover a floor-level where others had failed, and a penchant for reading any kind of ancient script available, why have I resisted the lure of the tell for almost twenty years?

Of course, the answers to these questions are never simple. Some of my colleagues would readily divide diggers into categories of the weak and the strong, the courageous and the timid, those with conviction about their discipline and those who are readily drawn aside to lesser pursuits. Among my acquaintances are even some who attribute my failure to an inability to withstand the rigours of desert life (they have never seen me charging around Twenty Nine Palms in Marine cammies!). But, in fact, I had my reasons, and they related less to personal preferences for the cool summers of the Pacific Northwest over the heat of the Sinai than to the question of what archaeology can and cannot do. Let me try, in the remainder of this article, to elaborate on that statement, and in the process tell why I prefer the sanctuary of the Old Testament scholar's library to the working life of a Palestinian tell.

Archaeology: The scorecard

1. Archaeology provides the artifacts of historical research, but can often miss the ideas. In Palestine we dug up unlimited supplies of the most mundane household utensils, but frequently had no idea, from this base, what made people tick. What were they thinking when they cooked their meals on rude ovens, or smashed those broken potsherds into the floor under their feet? What caused the migrations of whole peoples as a city was abandoned? Was it enemies, a dried up water supply, a search for Lebensraum, or a scrap between brothers? Near Hebron we discovered a magnificent set of tombs, from roughly the time of Abraham, but we had little way of knowing just what made nomadic people return year after year to deposit the bones of their deceased neatly in small, circular cells in the soft limestone.

Even the archaeologists who probe the relatively more grandiose civilizations of Egypt, Mesopotamia and Hatti-land (the Hittites) frequently struggle to know what ideas were bound up in the hearts of those remains they must disturb. When we possess texts or monumental inscriptions (the Nile valley and the Tigris-Euphrates have produced their share of both), our information is usually limited to the political and military history of those who made the inscriptions. Even that is suspect; today we would readily label much of it (dis)information.

But did the march of armies across the fertile crescent really determine history? Was the destruction of a defenseless Canaanite city important to subsequent generations in the ongoing struggle of humankind to develop their potential? For myself, I would far rather know the simple thoughts of a shepherd meditating on the meaning of life as he "considered the heavens" than examine the boastful statements left us by a few kings sufficiently powerful and ruthless to produce monuments in stone and effusive claims in clay.

2. Archaeology not only can overlook the important ideas of civilization, it also finds the people themselves elusive. Archaeology can discover Diogenes' tub, but miss Diogenes. It can uncover Abraham's bedstead but have no clue as to Abraham. But people are far more interesting than artifacts. True, we can know much about the people from the artifacts they have discarded, but can we know them in themselves? Were they melancholy or lighthearted, courageous or timid, loving or quarrelsome? What did they think of the gods (or God)? Did they live in constant fear of the unknown, or were their beliefs able to generate confidence about the future?

It is the people who love, laugh, cry, create, procreate, migrate, plant and harvest, hunt and fish, discipline and direct offspring, build altars and offer sacrifices, raise up laments and thanksgivings and in a thousand other ways work out the destiny of the race. I must confess, I found too little in the artifacts to satisfy my longing to know the vanished inhabitants of the deserted cities.

3. Archaeology cannot make moral judgments about the history it uncovers. Again, archaeology provides much material for a disciplined and accurate judgment, but archaeology has no philosophy of history. As such, it has no determining cosmology, no guiding light on human behaviour, no ability to commend the destroyers of one tell while reproving those who burned the city next door. It is even jokingly admitted that archaeologists love nothing better than a record of utter and complete destruction in a tell. A six-inch burn level makes a far superior distinction between generations than do the remains of a peaceful village where for years fathers taught their sons to plant and reap, grandmothers passed on the lore and traditions of a civilization, and old men sat by the fire repeating and creating the epics of their race. But the archaeologist, as such, has no way of making that judgment. The stones reveal little that separates good from evil, better from best. Such judgments, and surely they are the important ones, come more from the accumulated wisdom of the civilization, found frequently in its ancient traditions, than from the monuments built by the mighty, or the destruction wreaked by the tyrant.

4. On the positive side, the developing science of archaeology has produced a context for our study of the traditions of the ancient world. In addition to the fact that many of our most ancient records were themselves uncovered by the spade, the world of antique epic, be it Homeric or biblical, has been revealed for what it was. Although we must turn to Homer or to the Bible for the details, we now have a ready supply of evidence that life as reflected in those ancient books was substantially as it is remembered by them. Heinrich Schliemann discovered to the skeptic's surprise that there was a real Troy. Likewise, the cities of Abraham's migration came to light in substantially the form and at the times expected by the biblical reader. Ancient customs from the sale of a grave to bargaining with the Philistines for iron, were illuminated in the relentless search for ancient mankind.

In this regard, the question is still frequently asked, "Does archaeology prove the Bible?" While the answer must certainly be in the negative (events of history, much less certitudes of faith, are rarely open to the kind of proof archaeology can offer), there is every reason for the believer to take comfort in what archaeology has provided. There may be no way to prove that Abraham heard the voice of the living God in Ur of the Chaldees, but faith is well served by the archaeological recovery of civilizations on both ends of Abraham's migratory pattern which look, for all evidence, remarkably like the background portrayed in Scripture.

The fact, is, we are light-years ahead of our forebears when it comes to knowledge of the ancient world, whether of the Bible or any other antique source. Archaeology may not have "proven" the Bible, whatever that may mean, but it has certainly illuminated virtually every page. From the archaeologist we know of whole lost civilizations like the Hittites. Their labours have given us the lawcodes of Hammurabi, the creation myths of Sumer and Assyria, a picture of the mighty walls of Daniel's Babylon, and wall paintings of Semitic nomads not unlike the family of Joseph.

The people of the Bible now come to life in a context, the context of an ancient history rich with reflection, strong in the arts of civilization, or better yet, a whole series of civilizations, that have provided a cradle for our own Western world.

Our forefathers, whether exegete, pilgrim, or simple Bible reader, knew little of the richness of this heritage. True, they had the essentials; I would rather know right from wrong, and God from the devil, than to know all the secrets of the building of a pyramid. But more fortunate yet are those who have access to both. For this we can only thank those men and women who laboured so long and hard, for so many years, to fill in the details we now easily take for granted.

Conclusion

I may be a failure as an archaeologist, but I hope I have shown that I am not unappreciative. Hardly a day goes by but my research into the Scriptures of Old and New Testament does not benefit from the work of the archaeologist. And while I have chosen to devote myself to biblical studies, I shall always be grateful for that brief year when my friends, the diggers, taught me the secrets of their trade. I learned from them a certain healthy skepticism about unwarranted claims, whether from friends or foes of the Bible. I learned that archaeologists, like other scientists, struggle with truth and work at interpretation. I learned that many archaeologists long, as I do, to know the people whose remains we sometimes callously unearthed. I discovered, in the community of archaeologists, men and women like myself, who above all yearned for that special word from God that would illumine, inspire and teach the wisdom which eluded us in the artifacts. I found that the Bible, in the final analysis, must illumine archaeology more than the reverse.

That, then, is why I remain an appreciative and admiring bystander. Archaeology provides a context for my studies, as for my faith, but the hearts of both remain elsewhere.

This article first appeared in The Navy Chaplain, *Vol. 1, No. 3, Spring, 1987.*

Creation, Covenant and Work

William J. Dumbrell

Vol. XXIV, No. 3 (September 1988):14-24

We will begin with what detail we have about covenant in the Creation narrative of Genesis 1-11. I will suggest that this examination will lead us back naturally to Creation and the detail of Genesis 1-3. That, in its turn will speak to us of man's role and purpose in our world. Since we see man most naturally as the worker, we shall need to note carefully the bearing of the Fall upon this most natural role for mankind. Finally, we shall conclude with brief attention to the question of rest as associated for man with toil, turning our attention at that point to Genesis 2:1-3, in order to ascertain what is the total biblical perspective that the themes of covenant and creation lay before us.

Since biblical eschatology will be progressively associated with a doctrine of a "New Covenant" it will be important for us to note summarily at least, the developing features of the Old Testament covenants. The immediate context of Genesis 6:17-18 is the impending flood but the notion of covenant is before us for the first time biblically. For the first time, we meet the Hebrew word *berit* "covenant" in its some 290 occurrences in the Old Testament. Addressed at Genesis 6:17-18 is Noah, a member of the godly line of Seth, son of Adam, and the context of Genesis 6:17-18 is a promise uttered by God in the very shadow of the impending flood. In the "but I will establish my covenant with you" of Genesis 6:18 several questions are posed for us. What is the precise meaning of the word "establish" here and why is the verb in the future tense? What is the exact meaning of the term "covenant"; why is it used here seemingly without introduction and why further is it "my" covenant? Is the covenant concluded with Noah personally or representatively?

First, the term "covenant." Most naturally the English term "covenant" contains a notion of mutuality. Though some human/human covenants in the Old Testament bear the features of mutuality about them, in the case of Old Testament divine/human covenants there is no element of mutuality. Divine covenants are imposed upon the recipients as the "my" of my covenant here suggests. Thus the actual meaning of b^erit must be determined from within the context in which it is operating, within the general sense of the background of the word which appears in its basic sense to reflect the notion of "bond," "fetter."

Second, the absence of any direct background for the word b^erit in Genesis 6:18 needs to be illuminated from the use of the word within comparable contexts of the period. Instructive here is the use of b^erit in the three secular instances of Genesis 21:22- 32, Genesis 26:26-33, Genesis 31:43-54 concerning Isaac and Jacob in relationship to others. The point in each case of these three covenants is that the covenant in each incident does not initiate the relationship which is already in each case in existence. What the covenant does is to give to the relationship a quasi- legal backing and guarantee its continuance. The point is an important one for Genesis 6:17-18 since it signifies that we must look elsewhere for the origin of the relationship which is referred to by the term "covenant."

Third, the normal term for covenant initiation where the relationship is to be secured in this way is the Hebrew verb *karat,* "cut." In every other case of covenant initiation in the Old Testament the covenant is technically begun by having been "cut." Undoubtedly the idiom "to cut a covenant" goes back to some type of pre-biblical curse ritual enacted by covenant making which confirmed existing relationships but that is not important for our purpose here. Since Genesis 6:17-18 (and the dependent passage in Genesis 9:9-13) is the one Old Testament context where the verb "cut" is absent, the presumption is that we do not have at Genesis 6:17-18 the actual initiation of the covenant with Noah. But is Genesis 6:17-18 merely an anticipation of the more fundamental context in which the same issues are aired, but more widely, Genesis 9:9-13? Genesis 9:9 widens the concept of Genesis 6:18 by including Noah's descendants, making it thus clear that the covenant with Noah was with Noah as representative humanity. Genesis 9:10 takes us further to include the animal species threatened by the flood, (i.e. every living creature— birds, cattle and beasts of the earth). This seems to make it clear that the stress in the Noachian covenant is upon man, but as guarantor of the created order. It becomes apparent that by

Genesis 9:13 the parameters of covenant are even more widely drawn
to include everything that was threatened by the flood, namely the
earth as well and to this covenant with Noah is added in Genesis 9:12
the sign of the rainbow to remind the Creator of his undertaken
obligation to man and his world.

In summary, Genesis 9:9-13 appears to presuppose the context of
6:17-18 but to widen it. Genesis 9:9-13 is not the covenant to which
6:17-18 looks forward but 9:9-13 refers to the covenant of 6:17-18. Noah
is provided with an assurance in the shape of a covenant before the
onset of the flood in 6:17-18 and then at the conclusion of the flood,
9:9-13 the covenant is confirmed and its implications extended. It
seems, then, that we must look for the relationship to which 6:17-18
gives confirmatory point in some act prior to Genesis 6. Here the
precise language of 6:18 helps for the covenant is not "made" with
Noah, but "established." In all other Old Testament contexts in
which the phrase "establish a covenant," *heqîm b^{e}rit*, occurs
(Genesis 17:7,19,21; Exodus 6:4; Leviticus 26:19; Deuteronomy 8:18; 2
Kings 23:3; Jeremiah 34:18 as well as Genesis 9:9,11,17), the initial
institution of a covenant is not referred to, but its perpetuation and
we may thus surmise that the phrase "cause my covenant to stand,"
i.e. "establish my covenant" of Genesis 6:18 also refers to the
perpetuation of some covenant and not to its initiation.

The pledge of divine obligation to creation, as affected by the flood
which is the substance of the covenant with Noah (Genesis 6:18,
9:9-13) seems therefore to refer to a basic commitment to maintain the
structure of creation, given implicitly by the fact of creation itself. It
is important to note that the mandate given to humanity in Genesis
1:26-28 to "be fruitful and multiply and to fill the earth and subdue
it" is virtually repeated to Noah in Genesis 9:1ff, while the further
details of the covenant advanced in 9:9-13 make it clear that what is
being "maintained/established" is some basic arrangement with the
world whereby man, the animal world and the earth itself are
assured of continuance. Since, moreover, the detail of Genesis
1:26-28 (to which the promise given to Noah in 9:1-7 refers) has in
mind a divine purpose to be accomplished by man and his world, it
would seem to suggest that the covenant with Noah has not merely
the fallen world and man in it in view, but also the purpose of
Genesis 1:1-2:3 which will finally be brought into effect. It is in this
latter sense that the covenant with Noah can be called eschatological.
The latter association of the New Covenant with a concept of the
New Creation draws together the two notions of creation and
redemption and thus by redemption of first man and then his world,
by the restitution of all things (Colossians 1:20). As covenant and

creation are associated at the beginning of human experience, so they will be at the end.

Creation

Our review of the use of the term covenant at Genesis 6:18, etc. has led us back to creation itself. For our purposes, what is important for us here will be the definition of man's role in our world and man's reaction to creation as presented in Genesis 2:4- 3:24. We may present the broad outline of Creation in Genesis 1-2 as follows.

Genesis 1:1 - 2:3: Creation in Six Days

Within the parallels of introduction (vv.1-2) and conclusion (2:1, 2:3 which "frame" detail relating to the seventh day) a regular pattern relating to eight acts on six days occurs. The six stages are marked by a conclusion formula (5b, 8b, 13, 19, 23, 31) and the pattern (with some exceptions) is command, execution of command, action of creation and then valuation. The first three stages have to do with progressive separations (light from darkness, water above from waters below, waters from dry land). The next three stages "fill" creation with essential life and there is a general parallelism of form to content in days 1 to 4, 2 to 5, 3 to 6. The narrative proceeds as a series of "begettings" (Hebrew *tôledôt* "generations" 2:4a) and is told in report form. The setting could be the cult (cf. the interest in sabbath 2:2-3) or the royal court (since man in Genesis 1:26-27 is depicted in "royal" terms). The intention is to stress that the origin of all things depended upon God. The use of Hebrew *bara*, "create" in Genesis 1:1 stresses this also.

The structure appears to separate 1:3-31 from 1:1-2 and then to mark off the sabbath in 2:1-3 as important, indeed critical. In these circumstances it seems best to take 1:1 as adverbially dependent upon 1:2 with 1:2 referring in three circumstantial clauses to the primeval unfitness of the earth for human occupation as a first stage of creation (since it was desolate and dark, but even as such completely controlled by the Spirit). Genesis 1:3-31 then deals with the outfitting of creation for human habitation, climaxing in the creation of mankind, while 2:1-3 points to the goal of creation. Genesis 1:2 needs careful attention. The reference to primeval waters covering the earth and the darkness which covered that seems, in view of creation conflict accounts in the later Old Testament (cf. Psalm 74:12-14; Isaiah 51:9-11; Psalm 93; Isaiah 27:1) to point to the threat of disorder. But the Spirit of God which hovers over the waters provides reassurance of divine control. Chapter 1 thus may suggest a knowledge of such ancient Near Eastern creation myths but forms a polemic against them!

The Days of Genesis

There are Three Main Views:

1. They refer to a literal six days. This seems to founder on the scientific evidence available and seems also not to take account of the difficulty that Genesis 2:5 raises.

2. That the days are eras. Apart from the scientific difficulties (sun, moon only created on the 4th day) which are present for chronology on this view, the eras would have to be unequal, at least then weakening the symmetry of six days plus one.

3. The arrangement is logical rather than chronological and the order is an order of interest. This seems to be preferable. The first section in 1:3-13 is of three days, four creative words with a double movement at the climax. The movement is from heavens, to water to earth. The second part, 1:14-31 essentially follows the same scheme, heavens, waters, earth. The eighth action on the sixth day brings us to the creation of man.

Man as the Image

We need first to take up the question of man as the image and relate that to the concept of dominion. The creation account in Genesis 1 indeed climaxes in the account of the creation of man in 1:26-28. True, this is not the climax of the account itself; that comes in the material concerning the Sabbath rest in 2:1-3.

Basic to the account of the creation of man is the nature of the relationship which is conjured up under the term "image." The notion is an important one for the purposes of our discussion of man's role in his world although the phrase "image of God" occurs only twice in Scripture (Genesis 1:26, 9:6). This phrase has been variously handled in the history of Christian thought and we note that Karl Barth (1960) has shown how each age has filled Genesis 1:26 with the philosophical content of its age (i.e., as "soul", etc.)

Selem "image" is an ambiguous word with the possible meanings of "copy" or "representation," always with reference to what is externally presented. Only "representation" fits the theological context of Genesis 1:26 and to weaken further the sense of vagueness imported by "image," *dᵉmût*, "likeness" is added to indicate that man is only an image, only a representation of the deity and nothing more. Indeed, the context goes on to underscore the point: since unlike God, but like the other creatures, man is endowed in v.27b with sexual differentiation. This further distinction anticipates 1:28 but does not directly refer to man as the "image" (Bird, 1981). In regard to the content of the image, we may therefore dismiss earlier Christian internalizations of the term such as rationality, self-consciousness, etc. Of course, Hebrew thought conceived of man as a psychosomatic whole and thus not merely externality is on view in image but that emphasis is predominant.

In the Semitic cognate languages this note of visible representation is plain. So Akkadian *salmu*, "image" refers to a visible symbol, usually representation of the deity set up in a temple as a sign of the authority of the city state deity to whom the image referred. Moreover in Akkadian, when used of the king, "image" referred to the godlike power of the king in his function as ruler. Consistent with this ancient Near Eastern presentation are Egyptian texts where "image" language is found frequently. As the image, Pharaoh was the visible representation of the deity, the god incarnate on earth.

Perhaps the Mesopotamian analogies to which we have appealed throw light also upon the royal connotations which are present in the relationship of man to the deity which Genesis 1 offers. In Mesopotamain royal theology, the king was conceived as a servant of the gods and "image" language used of the king in that context, thus described the king in some relationship to the gods. But the image was clearly conceived of in Mesopotamian thought as being different in character and substance from the god who stood behind it. The designation of the king as the image of the god in Mesopotamia referred to his royal function as having a mandate from the god to rule and thus as one possessing divine power. There is a duality, however, in the Genesis 1-3 account for we are introduced to man in royal terms as the image, consistent with the general ancient Near Eastern picture and yet in creature terms as part of the animate and inanimate creation over which he bears rule.

The nature of this rule now requires attention. The precise word associated with man's rule in Genesis 1:26-28 is Hebrew *radah*. What is signified by the verb *radah* is the exercise of authority by a superior over a positionally inferior. This is not necessarily arbitrary or despotic rule, for where this is indicated in the Old Testament, a further predicate is often supplied (cf. Leviticus 25:43 "with rigour," and vv. 46, 53; Ezekiel 34:4 "with force and with rigour," Isaiah 14:6 "in anger"). The verb is thus appropriately used of the rule of kings (1 Kings 5:4; Ezekiel 34:4; Psalm 72:8, 110:2) and of the rule over fellow Israelites in a way that resembles foreign domination (Leviticus 25:43,46,53). It is thus a peremptory word and by it a state of circumstances normally translated by "subdue," "bring into subjugation" is intended. As has been noted, the use here in Genesis 1 refers to Adam's place and role *vis-à-vis* the created world (Bird, 1981). There is, however, no note within the verb itself of the precise details or type of control or management which dominion in Genesis 1:26 was to assume, but its use is consistent with the extra-biblical royal nuances to which we have referred. They constitute important comments upon Genesis 1, let alone the further fact that Psalm 8:5—in an exposition of man's place in creation—adds that he is "crowned" with glory and honour.

Kabas, "subdue" (Genesis 1:28) which is often taken to be a further predicate of "dominion" relates more narrowly to man's relationship with the ground, and thus to the content of v.28 and blessing (Westermann, 1974).

We may thus sum up our discussion of man's role in Genesis 1 by saying that as the image, man is installed as God's vice-regent over all creation with power to control and regulate it, to harness its clear potential, a tremendous concentration of power in the hands of puny man! What authority he thus possesses to regulate the course of nature, to be a bane or a blessing to his world!

Behold, It was Very Good (Genesis 1:31). Was Creation Perfect?

With man created to exert dominion over the world the account of Genesis 1 comes to a close. We need, however, now to relate more precisely to the world over which man was set in control. God expresses himself in 1:31 as pronouncing the creation which he beheld, "very good." The phrase *kî tôb* appears six times in Genesis 1 with reference to various specifics of creation: light, v.4 on the first day; sea and dry land on the second day; plant life on the third day; celestial bodies, sun, moon and stars on the fourth day; sea creatures and birds on the fifth day; living creatures and beasts on the sixth day, climaxing in *kî tôb me'od* on the sixth day as a final evaluation of the total work.

Each time *kî tôb* is used in Genesis 1, God is the speaker and the form refers to divine approval of some specific act of creation. Traditionally, many different views have been offered as to the meaning of the phrase. Those who interpret the phrase in terms of "perfection" understand the term to mean the complete harmony of creation in its integration with all details. On such views both the parts and the whole of creation emerged perfect from God's hand

(Cassuto, 1944). However, we do not see such perfection obtaining in our world today. Pain, suffering, natural calamities, inevitability of decay, etc. mark the world we know. Such a picture of a perfect creation is also at variance with the biological competition within nature which we know to be clearly our present case.

Hebrew *tôb* has a broad range of meanings: pleasant, pleasing, favourable, useful, suitable, proper, right, beautiful, well- shaped, friendly, cheerful, plentiful, valuable, excellent of its kind, prosperous, benevolent, upright, brave, genuine. Thus the translation of *tôb* will be conditioned by its immediate context. The adjective certainly can mean aesthetic good or ethical good and need not be understood as perfection. Of course to convey absolute perfection the construction which we do have in Genesis 1:31 would serve. Such a concept, however, would be without parallel in the Old Testament, and we agree with Kohler and Baumgartner (1953) that *tôb* in this context is best taken as "efficient." We would therefore see creation as good in its correspondence to divine intention, suitable to fulfil that purpose for which it had been brought into being. We would suggest that the further appeal to ethical nuances in regard to the "good" in Genesis 1 rests upon the general tenor of Scripture as a whole rather than upon the context itself and rests also upon the presuppositions which we generally bring to Genesis 1, namely that a concept of absolute perfection is in view in this narrative.

The Garden—The Ideal World and the Dominion Role of Man Reviewed

We need now to return to the role of man in our world. Genesis 2 treats man in more detail. It is not, as is frequently suggested, a second account of creation. The purpose of the account is to make clear from the perspective of man what was meant to be the relationship of man as exercising dominion to his world under God. The narrative of Genesis 2 indicates that man was created outside of the garden (2:8). This seems confirmed by the progressive movement of the action in Genesis 2-3 from outside of the garden, into the garden, to the centre of the garden and then again finally outside of the garden once more. The garden seems a reserve which has been specially set apart from its world and seems to be completely different from it. The noun *gan* occurs forty-one times in the Old Testament and the feminine noun *gannah* sixteen times. It is derived from *ganan* ("cover," "surround," "defend,") which occurs eight times in the Old Testament. The verb is only used with

Jerusalem or the people of Yahweh as its object. Yahweh is always the subject (Isaiah 31:5, 37:35, 38:6; 2 Kings 20:6,19:34; Zechariah 9:15, 12:8) (Brown, Driver & Briggs, 1972). The use of these nouns indicates that a garden is a plot of ground protected by a wall or a hedge, a concept which the basic meaning of the verb *ganan* with its notes of "protect, defend" would support (*Theological Wordbook of the the Old Testament*, 1980). Walls around royal gardens are specifically mentioned in the Old Testament (2 Kings 25:4; Jeremiah 39:4, 52:7; Nehemiah 3:15). Vineyards also were surrounded by walls (cf. Proverbs 24:30-31; Isaiah 5:5) to protect them from ravage by animals, and we are not surprised that the same precautions would be taken generally concerning gardens (cf. Amos 4:9 where "gardens" and "vineyards" are parallel).

All of this makes the note of a garden as a special place which is spatially separate and different from its world, understandable. It is a valued, fertile, well-watered place which is constantly cared for. These notes are reinforced in the case of Genesis 2 by the Septuagint translation of Hebrew *gan* by *paradeisos*, from Hebrew *pardes*, itself a loan word from Persian. *Pardes* has the basic sense of "what is walled, what is hedged about" and thus "a pleasure garden surrounded by a stone or earthen wall" (Keil & Delitzsch, 1975). The Vulgate translates the phrase "garden of Eden" by *paradisus voluptatis*, "a delightful paradise" (Westermann, 1974).

In the Old Testament, we find that the garden of Eden becomes a symbol for a particularly luxuriant land. In this connection, the proper name Eden is derived from the Hebrew root *cdn* (Jacobs-Hornig, 1978 & 1962) "to delight." So, in Genesis 13:10, the well-watered Jordan valley appeared to Lot "like the garden of the Lord." Later the fertility of the garden of Eden can be contrasted with the desolation which comes upon Judah as a result of the 586 B.C. fall of Jerusalem. Isaiah and Ezekiel can thus predict that Judah, though it is desolate, would become like Eden, the garden of the Lord (Isaiah 51:3; Ezekiel 36:5; cf. Joel 2:3). The existence of gardens and parks as special places in the ancient Near East outside of Israel is abundantly clear from Mesopotamian literature. Kings planted and boasted of extravagant gardens. Sumerian mythology also reveals a paradise myth which speaks of an extremely fertile land, Dilmun, where beasts do not prey upon each other and where sickness and aging are unknown. The Gilgamesh epic also speaks of an island garden with trees bearing precious stones. Egyptian literature and art also describe beautiful gardens as places of love and happiness (Jacobs-Hornig, 1969).

In the light of all this, the garden of Eden in Genesis 2 is best

viewed as a special sanctuary quite unlike the rest of the world.
Genesis 2:5-25 describes the position of man before the Fall, existing
in that openness in the divine presence which the presentation of the
extended seventh day of 2:4a suggests. Some picture of the nature
of man's dominion over nature is thus provided as well.
Paradoxically, man exercises dominion over his world by service and
worship in the divine presence. His service in the garden is denoted
by the verb ^{c}abad (used 290 times in the Old Testament with the basic
meaning of "work" or "serve"). In the context of Genesis 2:15 the
clear meaning of the verb is "till" or "cultivate" but the use of the
verb in the later Old Testament as the customary verb for "worship"
imports into the Genesis 2 context the further nature of man's
response in what is clearly a sanctuary presence. That the garden of
Genesis 2 is a shrine, comes out not only from Chapter 2, but
markedly from the manner in which Ezekiel 28:11-19 describes Eden,
the cosmic focus of the world in the alternate terms of garden/holy
mountain of God (cf. vv. 13, 14). Since after man's expulsion from the
garden, he is described in relationship to the earth by the same verb
^{c}abad (3:23), we may take it that by this verb the very fundamental
character of man's dominion over the earth is being described.
Service which is divine service is thus his role, a dominion which
shows itself first in submission to the Creator is what is required, and
we may refer to Mark 10:45 for a Christian analogy. The note
emphasized for man's role in the garden by Hebrew ^{c}abad is
reinforced by the use of Hebrew samar in the same verse (v. 15). This
verb has the general meaning of "take care of," "to have charge of."
The use of this verb then indicates the nature of the attention devoted
to the garden, within the consciousness of the presence of the
Creator from whom the mandate has been given. Perhaps also there
is latent in the notion of the verb the watchfulness that needs to be
exercised over against the serpent who will appear in Genesis 3.

But we may sum up this section by suggesting that the garden
episode displays, as a paradigm, admittedly under ideal
circumstances, the harmony of created orders that the dominion role
was to secure in the world at large. At the same time Genesis 2
indicates what dominion as such is and how it was to be exercised.
Dominion is the service which takes its motivation from the intimate
relationship with the Lord God on behalf of whom dominion is
exercised. The possibility exists, even within the garden, for man to
exercise his God-given authority independently (Genesis 2:16-17).
We know this will happen in Genesis 3 and expect that it will have
disastrous effects for man's mandate and role. The Fall will deny to
man the further possibility that the garden also holds out to him, that

immortal by relationship to God, he might develop and deepen that relationship by which alone life in God's presence would be retained. We now turn to the Fall account itself.

The Effects of the Fall

The harmony of created orders under man, for which Genesis 2 speaks, is fractured by the Fall, by which the order of Genesis 2 is reversed in Chapter 3. Man's acquisition by the Fall of the knowledge of good and evil is to be understood in terms of the legal background of the ancient Near East which underlies the phrase "good and evil" as W.M. Clark (1969) has made clear. This phrase is not simply a merism for total knowledge. It is legal language denoting the authority to decide an issue (cf. 1 Kings 3:4-28, especially vv. 9,28). In Genesis 3 by eating of the fruit of the tree of the knowledge of good and evil, man claims for himself the moral autonomy and the right to decide for himself apart from God (to whom these decisions properly belong) what is good or non-good.

The consequences which ensue from all this are recorded in 3:14ff. Of primary interest for us in all of this is the curse which is placed upon the ground in v.17 and the description which then follows. What, however, is meant by the fact that in the post-Fall situation, the ground is cursed? In what sense is it cursed, and how are we to understand the prepositional phrase "because of you," "on account of you?" What has changed in all this, the ground or man? Or have both undergone a change as a result of the Fall? Has creation been brought into bondage (cf. Romans 8:20) by man's Fall and if so, in what sense are we to understand Romans 8:18-23 which speaks of creation's bondage and the prospect of its deliverance?

The verb "curse" in 3:17 is Hebrew 'arar. The passive particle Qal which is used here accounts for forty of the sixty-three Old Testament occurrences of the verb. Most curse sayings in the Old Testament are found in declarations of punishment, threat utterances, or accompanying legal proclamations (as in the extended treatment of covenant curses, Deuteronomy 27-28). In each case, they come as a response to the violation of one's relationship with God (*Theological Wordbook of the Old Testament*, 1980). The verb *arar* is an antonym of the Hebrew *barak*, "bless." It is used in opposition to *barak* twelve times (cf. Genesis 9:25-26, 12:3, 27:29). To "bless" means to endow with potential for life, to give the power to succeed, prosper, reproduce, etc. It is always the gift of God, even where a human mediator intervenes. As opposed to bless, to curse is to alienate, to remove from a benign sphere, to subject to deprivation (cf. the Akkadian cognate *araru,* "snare," "bind," [Hamilton, *Theological Wordbook of the Old Testament*]). Thus Joshua's curse upon the Gibeonites means their deprivation of freedom (Joshua 9:23). Contrariwise, when the ground is blessed, it yields an abundance (Genesis 27:27-28; Deuteronomy 28:11) while when cursed, the ground ceases to yield its natural fruit (Deuteronomy 11:17, 28:23-24; Jeremiah 23:10).

The curse of Genesis 3:17 breaks the former natural relationship between man and the earth. What will be involved in man's future relationship with his world is conveyed in v.17 by the noun *cissabon,* "hardship," "pain," "distress." It is derived from the Hebrew root *csb,* "to find fault with, to hurt, to trouble." The root signifies both physical and emotional suffering, i.e., pain and sorrow and these two concepts are reflected in the six nouns derived from the root (*Theological Wordbook of the Old Testament,* 1980). Prior to his sin, Adam was to work; now he must "toil." The same noun is used of Eve's travail in childbirth, v.16 and Lamech's statement where rest from toil over the ground is hoped for (Genesis 5:29). We must see in this the element of pain, sorrow and agonizing effort. This is emphasized by vv. 18-19 by the reference to thorns and thistles which will be reaped when edible plants are desired, and by the note of the sweat on Adam's face as effort is expended. In the garden, however, before the Fall, man's work was evidently free of grief or pain whether physical or psychological.

After the Fall, man will find that his effort to cultivate the ground, and generally to relate to it will be painful and disappointing. But what has changed here? Has the change occurred in man or in the environment, or in both? It is often suggested or implied that the change has occurred both in man and his environment. The Fall, it is suggested, had caused the ground to become recalcitrant in the way which it had not previously been. From this point onwards, pain, suffering, struggle, etc., penetrated the natural order as well as the human order. The lion began to prey on the lamb and the pestiferous entered the human sphere! Yet, scientific opinion indicates that the qualities of suffering and struggle were part of the natural process from the very beginning. Nowhere in the Fall account is it implied that the animal world as well as the ground was cursed. Certainly death now comes upon man as he is identified with the ground from which he came. But death comes explicitly because of man's sin and the expulsion from the garden (Genesis 3:22-24) seems intended as an act of grace. God will not let man live forever (with access in the garden still, it would seem, to the tree of life!) in a fallen state.

It seems therefore preferable to suggest that what is impaired as a result of the Fall is man's control of the ground. In this connection, Hebrew ba^{c}abur^{e}ka (Genesis 3:17, "for your sake") is ambiguous. "For the sake of," the basic meaning of this preposition has the built-in ambiguity of either "on account of" or "for the benefit of." The sense most suited to this Genesis 3:17 context is "because of," i.e., the ground yields a curse because of man's inappropriate use in future of the ground. We may cite here Genesis 8:21 where "for the sake of" seems best rendered as "on account of" since what follows in the postflood world is the preserved stability of nature, in spite of the fact that "the imagination of man's heart is evil from his youth."

We take therefore the meaning of the preposition in Genesis 3:17 to signify that man's use of the ground had become impaired as a result of the Fall. The problem then, after the Fall, and our problem, is man's inability to use natural resources. The Fall has left him "like God," i.e., he has the power to make decisions by which the course of his own life and his world are controlled. He has not the ability, however, to be sure that the decisions taken are right in themselves, nor the assurance that such decisions taken will promote the desired consequences. That is to say, man lives in his world unable to exercise proper dominion over nature. So far from man's dominion over the world producing the ecological problems of our world, *the very opposite is the case.* It has been the *failure* by man to exercise dominion, in the sense in which this concept is understood by Genesis 1-3 which has caused the problem. It has been man's failure to serve his environment, to exercise dominion in this way by proper management, his failure as a worker to understand the nature of his relationship to creation which has furnished our world with its present spate of problems. Man lives out of harmony with nature and himself. In a world after the Fall in which testing difficulties abound, man therefore is found continually deficient and humbled. Unable to administer his charge, his mismanagement and neglect and exploitation only served to accentuate, to increase and to sharpen the inbuilt problems of the natural world, on which it seems that he was charged to expend his energies as steward of creation. Created to rule, man has found that the crown has fallen from his brow.

Work

In view of our exegesis of Genesis 3:17, how does the issue of work in our world relate to all this? Is work simply the monotonous, routine, daily expenditure of energy whose final result is that nothing remains after a lifetime of toil? Is the writer in Ecclesiastes correct and must life be "hated because the work that is wrought under the sun was grievous unto me: for all is vanity and a striving after wind" (Ecclesiastes 2:17)? Should toil and labour, as an accursed thing, commanding the sweat of our brow, be left as Athenians left it to slaves and manual workers as they claimed that the intellectual and the philosopher must give himself to something better, to the *Bios Theoretikos* and not degrade himself by working? Is work therefore beneath the dignity of a gentleman as the Greeks believed?

It is true that the Old Testament generally presupposes the fact of work and the New Testament parables and teachings of Jesus assume for instance that secular labour of all sorts and kinds belong to the lot of man and must be undertaken by him. On the other hand, there is the plain fact that Jesus never called anyone to a particular occupation. Even if Jesus were a carpenter (Mark 6:3), there is no evidence that he continued with his craft after his call to ministry. True again, St. Paul was a tent maker, to take another New Testament example. He worked with Aquila in Corinth at this trade, but this does not provide the type of legitimization for work generally that we need, for Paul was above all a minister of the gospel who happened to be a tent maker and who, for the strategic reasons of his own mission, preferred to keep himself (cf. 2 Thessalonians 3:18; 1 Corinthians 4:12, 9:4; 2 Corinthians 11:7). He tells us that it was his practice to work so as not to be a burden on others and so that his ministry might not be blamed. In several places, he urges Christians to do the same (1 Thessalonians 4:11; 2 Thessalonians 3:10ff.; Ephesians 4:28) but such instructions are peripheral to the thrust of his message. This type of instruction, moreover, is not vigorously pursued by him and it is obvious that while he is concerned with social harmony between classes and the preservation of the *status quo* after Christian conversion, and urges a doctrine of submission to authority (Romans 13), Paul himself has no positive interest in work. We search in vain for the evidence in the Bible generally to support the vigorous way in which the mandate to subdue the earth has been applied since the Reformation with all the vigour of the Protestant work ethic behind it (Brunner, 1957).

While presumably under Greek influence, the monastic movement, which thought it reckoned with work as an able means of self discipline and necessary to support human existence as such, strongly propounded the excellence of the contemplative life as the chief end of man. All this was combatted vigorously at the Protestant Reformation particularly by Martin Luther who attempted to undergird the labours of field and worship, the home and the nursery with the dignity of worship. Luther was therefore a prime mover in generating the Protestant work ethic. Civilization and thus work was recognized as God's will for man. Encounter with the world and not withdrawal from it was henceforth in Protestant circles to mark the Christian man. The Reformation emphasized the truth that it had been the command to subdue the world which had preceded the Fall as man in Genesis 2 had been charged with the care and oversight of the garden with the mandate to till it and to keep it. Man was to control creation and to use it wisely. As Wolff points out, it is important to note that man's charge to till the ground in Genesis 2:5 is the only definition of the way in which man is to relate himself in the world, and the only measure of man's significance (Wolff, 1974). Man as created was removed from the general world outside and given this role in the garden. All the gifts of creation are then made over to man and his duty is now to exercise the innate capacity for toil that God had given him. As the writer continues with his account of the early period, it is of maximum importance to him as the genealogy of Cain is presented to indicate how quickly in the world the ingenuity of man devoted itself to the task of specialization of labour, the tiller of the soil joined by the breeder of the herds, the tent dweller and the musician, the technicians and workers in bronze and iron (Wolff, 1974) came into existence. Man is met by the challenge of his world and by the time we get to Genesis ll, we find that even the construction of a tower whose top may reach to heaven is now not beyond the range of man who has begun at that stage to commit himself to the task of investigation of worlds beyond his own.

In our world, it is the will of God for us that we receive nothing which does not come as a shared blessing. Jesus taught us to pray, "Give us this day our daily bread." Daily bread is the gift of God to us through the service of others. The dignity of labour does not consist of what is done, but in the spirit in which it is done and to this degree Luther was right at the Reformation. But it is in this matter of mutual relationships, in the world of organized labour that the curse of the Fall manifests itself in broken relationships, rivalries, jealousies, sordid self-seeking, cut-throat economic rivalries, and fratricidal quarreling. So far from being the happy workplace where regard is had brother for brother in mutual service, the happy workshop of the commonwealth of man is dis-arranged as a result of man's rebellion (Richardson, 1958). We continue to be fired with the technological illusion that through the ingenuity of man, we can build a better world, the dream which has inspired humanistic thinking since the Fall.

The Bible itself, however, commends industry and conscientiousness in work. The book of Proverbs understands work as an axiomatic claim on man's time and sees success as resulting from application and industry. "A slack hand causes poverty, but the hand of a diligent man makes rich" (Proverbs 10:4). Riches are not seen as part of man's heritage but something which comes to him by the application of ingenuity and diligence. One has only to note the personal experience of the wisdom writer as he relates real life incidents in Proverbs 24:30-34. Laziness is condemned by the book and poverty is one of its expected rewards (cf. Proverbs 13:4), and on the general theme (cf. Proverbs 6:6-11). And yet, for all this, Proverbs sees that there is no automatic connection between industry and success, for the hidden factor in personal blessing is the intervention of God (cf. Proverbs 10:22). The blessing of Yahweh alone makes rich and man's own toil adds nothing to it. Yahweh also intervenes to arbitrate between man's desires and the reality which results so "the plans of the will belong to man, but the answer from the tongue is from Yahweh" (cf. Proverbs 16:1). Riches and success remain ambiguities and thus "Better is a little with the fear of Yahweh than great treasure and trouble with it" (cf. Proverbs 15:16 [Wolff, 1974]).

The Bible thus sees man as one who goes forth to his work and to his labour until the evening (Psalms 104:19-23). Labour is the common lot of man which should be accepted cheerfully. Work is part of the divine ordering for man in this world.

There is nothing to support the Greek or Stoic view, then, according to which the higher class person has to have the leisure to fashion himself physically, intellectually and aesthetically into a harmonious being (Brunner, 1957) with the real working classes existing to provide for the gentleman who is occupied with his own concerns and thus with real living. So the writer of Ecclesiastes, who accepts this under Greek influence, asserted that manual labour and the study of the law were fundamentally incompatible. But the Rabbis of the New Testament period did not accept this view for it was their rule that no Rabbi should accept payment for his teaching or other professional activities. Each must acquire a trade and support himself with honest toil. Happy is thus the man whose labour is blessed by the Lord (Psalm 128:2) and how wretched are those whose toil is not blessed and whose labour is in vain (Isaiah 62:8).

For all this, however, there is no biblical indication that work is a *vocational* call. There is no biblical example of any man being called to a particular trade. Paul thus was *called* to be an apostle and *supported* himself by tent making. The Bible is seemingly uninterested in the various trades and livelihoods and professions in which humans engage. We cannot speak with assurance about God calling a person to be a medical practitioner, a lawyer or a plumber. God calls lawyers and doctors and plumbers to be evangelists, if we are to speak of a biblical calling. First Corinthians is not advice to remain within the secular occupation in which one was engaged prior to conversion; rather it means to be faithful to the spiritual call by which the life changing experience was had. The biblical terms: *klesis, ekklektoi, ekklesia* have nothing at all to do with description of secular occupations. God calls upon us to work honestly in whatever calling we choose and to give good value for our labour (cf. the advice that John the Baptist gave to tax gatherers and soldiers in Luke 3: 13ff). Christians, of course, should be concerned on the score of what occupation is chosen. But work is not an end in itself but the means to an end which is our wider participation in the activities of the Kingdom of God.

Finally, God is at work. God is at work promoting among the lives of individuals at this point in time, the nature and significance of the Kingdom of God. Particularly in John's gospel we see God at work in salvation and grace and Jesus may sum up his ministry in terms of the works that God had given him to do. At the conclusion of his ministry, Jesus could say in John 17:4: "I glorified thee on earth, having accomplished the work which thou hast given me to do," as prospectively he prayed in the shadow of the cross. He prays there for his disciples whom he had sent into the world as God had sent him into the world. This is above all the work that God has committed to us, that of labouring in his field which is the world, or in his vineyard which is the church. No other task is so urgent as the spreading of the gospel on earth.

We turn now to a new and final area for work as part of the divinely ordered structure of the world, the only command relating to our topic in the decalogue and not one related to an admonition to work or a warning against idleness, but one which endorses the need to set aside one day in seven. Though work is presupposed by the Sabbath commandment, what is important for the worker is that the Sabbath be observed and that its nature be understood.

Sabbath

Genesis 2: 1-397 The Sabbath

Structure: Verse 1 is introductory and concludes the creation account while verses 2-3 combine creation with the seven-day scheme. God had completed his work and then rested. This rest is the rest of completion, not of exhaustion. The creation sabbath (the verb, however, and not the noun for sabbath occurs) is meant to provide the context within which man is to operate. After the Fall, the idea of sabbath as "completion" is modelled upon God's action of entering into his rest on the Sabbath day. Genesis 2:1-3 provide the pattern of seven lines which rise to a crescendo in 3a, with 3b emphasizing as a close, the matter of 2b. Verse 2:4a begins what follows. Verse 1 is attached to 2a by a common verb; 2b is attached to 2a because of similar conclusions; 3b provides the reason for 3a but is connected with 2b. No morning or evening is provided for the seventh day, which is thus unending. No light is able to be shed on the origins of the day from extra-biblical sources. Akkadian has the word *shabattu* which perhaps refers to a festival day, but this is uncertain. There is some evidence for the link between the day and the day of the full moon and some biblical support for this but a regular seventh day cannot be obtained from the lunar month. Some suggest that, in the ancient world, there were regularly-occurring market days, but there is no evidence for this in the Old Testament. Others conceive that the day derived from the Kenites who were smiths since firemaking was prohibited on the seventh day. But these and other proposals are too tenuous to be helpful.

The verb *shabat* means "stop" or "cease." Sometimes, it is translated "keep sabbath" but this is a later derived use. The Hebrew root occurs seventy-three times in various themes in the Old Testament and is generally used of persons, habits, customs, coming to an end (*Qal*) or being brought to an end (*Niphal and Hiphil*). In none of these basic usages is the notion of "rest" or desisting from work prominent. The seventh day is that which causes the week to stop and thus completes it. The note of "completion" or "perfection" is thus implicitly there, particular by the sequence of Genesis 2:2-3, and this idea of a creation rest for the creating deity is found in all creation texts of the ancient world.

The seventh day is the goal of creation in Genesis 1-2, and is that for which creation exists. Such a goal cannot be gained by toil or trial but is given. Man's fellowship with God is to be conducted on this "day." There is no question of a rest from a work already done in Genesis 2. The seventh day merely provides the context in which the ongoing relationship is to take place. Man is thus today invited to "rest" from his works and enter God's rest! The Sabbath in Chapter 2 is God's acceptance of his creation and indicates his desire for fellowship with man.

"Sabbath" and "rest" are first brought together as concepts in Exodus 20:8-11 (especially verse 11) in connection with creation. Israel's condition as resident in the promised land is in mind (cf. verse 10). It is important here to note how the meaning of the Hebrew *nuah* ("to rest") is joined with "sabbath." No notion of rest from labour is implied by this verb (cf. Genesis 49:15). Rather, the verb implies movement from an unsettled condition to a fixed or settled condition. There are some few occurrences in the Old Testament meaning of relief from weariness or pain (Proverbs 29:17; Isaiah 28:12) but these seem to be secondary extensions of the verbal idea.

It is important to note that in the early period, the ideas of sabbath and "rest" are quickly brought into close connection with the sanctuary. We note that the promised land, viewed as a sanctuary, is the goal of the Exodus in the old hymnic/creedal statement of Exodus 15:17 and that the sabbath and the sanctuary/tabernacle are brought into close connection in Exodus 31:12-17 and 35:1-3. Indeed, Tabernacle and sabbath are two sides of one reality. The logic seems to be that the building of the sanctuary gives expression to the principle of the Sabbath. Note also that the promised land rest and sanctuary are brought into connection (cf. Deuteronomy 12). The gift of rest makes the building of the sanctuary possible and this, in its turn, documents the promised land as a *promised* land.

So a "rest" of God (Genesis 2:1-3) indicates that creation is now settled and fixed. We note also that in the ancient world, the creation of the world is connected with the building of a temple/sanctuary and that thus man in Genesis 2 is depicted as a king/priest (cf. Ezekiel 28:11-14) offering worship in the sanctuary garden, the centre of the world, which is Eden.

The sabbath was made for man and not man for the sabbath! Man, created to enter in and to enjoy divine rest, still has not enjoyed divine rest! There still remains a rest for the people of God (Hebrews 4:4-11, where Psalms 95, which speaks of Israel's failure to enter that rest, and Genesis 2:2 are brought together). Israel in the Old Testament never possessed its possessions! God's cessation from his work has now become the ceaseless endeavour of Jesus (John 5:19) in providing salvation which brings rest (cf. Matthew 11:28). As a consequence of all this, the shape of the Christian Sunday is given. It is, above all, a time when we reflect upon the blessing of creation and remind ourselves that God's work to bring in the New Creation is unceasing. We further reflect, also, that whatever may be the nature of our secular occupation, God has called us in whatever we do to be faithful to the new light which has shone in our hearts.

Conclusion

The Genesis 6:18 notion of covenant drives us back upon creation and calls upon us to understand the purpose of God for man in Genesis 1-2. Man, as we noted, created to bring harmony into a world which had to be subdued, forfeited his responsibility. As a result, he was expelled from the garden and his basic relationship with God, his fellow creatures and with the soil was broken and has remained so. Yet, for all this, man is aware that there is a dignity still about his relationship with his world and his fellows. Basically, he relates himself to his fellows and to his world by "work." The working week culminates in his use of the seventh day to recall to himself the purpose for which the world was created. In this way, he becomes aware of God's intention through ceaseless endeavour to bring in the new creation to which the misuse of the blessings of this present evil age points.

Bibliography

Barth, K. *Church Dogmatics* III/I. Edinburgh: T&T Clark, 1960.

Bird, P. "Male and Female He Created Them: Genesis 1:27b in the Context of the Priestly Account of Creation," *HTR* 64, 1981, 129-159.

Brown, F. S. R. Driver and C.A. Briggs. *Hebrew and English Lexicon of the Old Testament*. Oxford: Clarendon, 1972 reprint.

Brunner, E. *The Divine Imperative*. Philadelphia: Westminster, 1937.

Cassuto, O. *Commentary on Genesis, Vol. 1.* Jerusalem: Magnes Press, 1944.

Clark, W. M. "A Legal Background to the Yahwist's Use of 'Good and Evil' in Genesis 2-3," *JBL* 88, 1969, 266-278.

Dumbrell, W. J. *Covenant and Creation*. Exeter: Paternoster, 1984.

Jacobs-Hornig, B. *"gan"* in *Theological Dictionary of the Old Testament Vol. III,* ed. G. J. Botterweck and H. Ringgren. Grand Rapids: Eerdmans, 1978.

Keil, C.F. and F. Delitzsch *A Commentary on the Old Testament in Ten Volumes: Vol. 1 The Pentateuch.* Grand Rapids: Eerdmans, 1975 reprint.

Koehler, L. and W. Baumgartner, eds. *Lexicon in Veteris Testament Libros.* Leiden: E.J. Brill, 1953.

Richardson, A. *The Biblical Doctrine of Work.* London: 1958.

Westermann, C. *Genesis 1-11, A Commentary.* Minneapolis: Augsburg, 1974.

Wolff, H.A. *Anthropology of the Old Testament.* Philadelphia: Fortress, 1974.

Laos and Leadership
Under the New Covenant

Gordon D. Fee

Vol. XXV, No. 4 (December 1989):3-13

The New Testament is full of surprises, but perhaps none so much as with its generally relaxed attitude toward church structures and leadership; especially so, when one considers how important this issue became for so much of later church history, beginning as early as Ignatius of Antioch. Indeed, for most people the concept of "church history" refers primarily to its history as a body politic, involving both its evangelism and growth and its intellectual/theological development.

Probably for a variety of reasons,[1] the New Testament documents simply do not carry a concern for church order as an agendum.[2] The thesis of this paper is that the *primary* reason for this stems from their understanding of what it means to be the people of God under a new covenant, as that in turn is related to their common experience of the eschatological Spirit.[3] The burden of the paper is ultimately hermeneutical—how we move from the first century documents to twentieth (twenty-first) century application. But those questions, as always, must first be subject to the exegetical ones—how we understand the texts themselves.

1. The Issue(s)

Historically the church seems to have fallen into[4] a model that eventually developed a sharp distinction between the people themselves (laity) and the professional ministry (clergy), reaching its sharpest expression in the Roman Catholic communion,[5] but finding its way into almost every form of Protestantism as well. The net result has been a church in which the clergy all too often exist apart from the people, for whom there is a different set of rules and different expectations, and a church in which the "gifts" and "ministry," not to mention significance, power structures, and decision-making are the special province of the professionals. Being "ordained" to this profession, the latter tend to like the aura that it provides, and having such ordained professionals allows the laity to pay them to do the work of the ministry and thus excuse themselves from their biblical calling. The rather universal model, with a few exceptions, looks something like this:

The thesis of this paper is that the biblical model looks something more like the following diagram—without clergy at all, but with identifiable leadership, who were simply part of the whole people of God:

The problem for most moderns, of course, in coming to the biblical texts, is that we tend to presuppose our resultant form of church to be theirs; we therefore carry both different agenda and a different experience of the church back to the documents. But history and tradition have had their innings. Even though it is arguable that we have genuine continuity with the New Testament church in many ways—especially our experience of grace and the Spirit—our experience of the church itself is so far different from theirs that seemingly ne'er the twain shall meet.[6]

As I see it, the areas of difficulty are four: (1) the tension between individual and corporate life, where western Christians in particular are trained from birth to value the individual above the group, whereas in the New Testament perspective the community is still the primary reality, and the individual finds identify and meaning as part of the community; (2) the tension between eschatological and institutional existence, most moderns knowing only the latter, whereas the New Testament church existed primarily as an experience of the former; (3) the place of structures as they flow out of these two tensions; and (4) the hermeneutical difficulty created by the nature of data, since the New Testament documents, which teem with reflections and insights, have very little directly intentional instruction on these matters. So how do they apply? Do we seek a biblical norm to follow,[7] or seek to model what fits our situation best, or try rather to approximate the spirit of the biblical pattern in our already existing structures?

I propose in the rest of this paper to take up some of these issues by first examining the biblical data and then by offering some brief hermeneutical observations in light of those data.

2. The People of God in the New Testament

2.1 The Language
By first pursuing the New Testament language for the Christian communities, I hope to demonstrate two realities about them: (a) their strong sense of *continuity* with the people of God under the former covenant, and (b) their basically *corporate* nature.

That the early believers thought in terms of continuity is writ large on nearly every page, in nearly every document.[8] They did not see themselves as the "*new* people of God," but as the "people of God *newly constituted.*" Nowhere is this more clear than in their adopting Old Testament "people of God" language, a language appropriation that is as varied as it is thoroughgoing.

2.1.1 Church (*ekklesia*).
Because this word does not appear in the English Old Testament, and because its usage for the "assembly" of the Greek *polis* is generally well known, the Old Testament background for New Testament usage is frequently overlooked. In the LXX *ekklesia* is regularly used to translate the Hebrew *qahal*, referring most often to the "congregation of Israel," especially when it was gathered for religious purposes.[9] Thus this word in particular was a natural one for the early believers to bridge the gap as they began to spill over into the Gentile world.

Since the concept of a "gathered people" was primary in both Greek and LXX usage, it is arguable that this is what lay behind the earliest Christian usage as well. Thus in its first appearance in the New Testament (1 Thessalonians 1:1) Paul is probably thinking primarily of the Christian community as a gathered people, constituted "in God the Father and the Lord Jesus Christ," who would be listening to the letter as it was read. It is also arguable that its usage throughout the New Testament never gets very far away from this nuance; the *ekklesia* refers first of all to the people in the various cities and towns who gather regularly in the name of the Lord

for worship and instruction.
2.1.2 People (*laos*).

Although not particularly popular with Greek writers, this is the word chosen by the LXX translators[10] to render the Hebrew *'am*, the word that occurs most often (over 2000 times) to express the special relationship Israel had with Yahweh: Above all else they were Yahweh's "people." Although at times the word can distinguish the people (usually non-Israelite) from their leaders (e.g. Genesis 41:40; Exodus 1:22), in most cases it is the collective word that designates the whole people whom God had chosen—people, priests, prophets, and kings together. Thus in Exodus 19:5, in establishing his covenant with them at Sinai, God says (LXX), "You shall be for me a *laos periousios* (special/chosen people) from among the *ethnon* (nations/Gentiles)."

In the New Testament the word occurs most often to refer to the Jewish people of that era.[11] But in several striking passages it is used in its Old Testament sense, especially reflecting the language of Exodus 19:5-6 (cf. 23:22 LXX), to refer to people of the new covenant, usually in contexts that include Gentiles. Thus Luke reports James as saying: "How God at first showed his concern by taking from the *ethnon* a *laos* for his name" (Acts 15:14); in Titus 2:14 the goal of Christ's saving purpose is "that he might purify for himself a *laos periousios*," while 1 Peter 2:9-10 combines "people" language from two Old Testament passages (Isaiah 43:20;Exodus 19:6;Isaiah 43:21), followed by a wordplay on Hosea 2:25 (cf. 1:9), to designate Gentile Christians as "a chosen people, a royal priesthood, a holy nation, a people belonging to God," who were formerly "no people" but now "are the people of God." So also the author of Hebrews transfers several Old Testament "people" passages or concepts to the church (2:17; 4:9; 7:27; 13:12).

2.1.3 Covenant (*diatheke*).

Although this term does not occur often in the New Testament, it is used in ways that are significant to our topic. The author of Hebrews in particular adopts covenantal language to tie the new to the old, seeing Christ as the fulfillment of Jeremiah's "new covenant" in which God says again, as in the Sinaitic covenant, "They shall be for me a people" (Hebrews 8:7-12; citing Jeremiah 31:34). Paul also adopts this language to refer to the "new covenant" of the Spirit (2 Corinthians 3:6; cf. Galatians 4:24). Perhaps even more significantly, as the people joined in common fellowship at the Table of the Lord in the Pauline churches, they did so with these words: "This cup is the new covenant in my blood" (1 Corinthians 11:25; Luke 22:20). It should be noted that both the language "new covenant" and its close tie with the Spirit and the people of God are seen in terms of continuity with the Old Testament (in this case as fulfillment); thus in the church's earliest worship and liturgy there was the constant reminder of their continuity/discontinuity with the past.[12]

2.1.4 Saints (*hoi hagioi*).

Although not frequent in the Old Testament, the designation of Israel as God's "holy people" occurs in the crucial covenantal passage in Exodus 19:5-6, an expression that in later Judaism referred to the elect who were to share in the blessings of the messianic kingdom (Daniel 7:18- 27; Psalms Sol. 17; Qumran). This is Paul's primary term for God's newly formed, eschatological people. He uses it in the salutation of six of the nine letters addressed to congregations, plus Philemon, as well as in several other kinds of settings. Its appearance in Acts 9:41; Hebrews 6:10; 13:24; Jude 3; and Revelation 8:4 makes it clear that this was widespread usage in the early church. In all cases it is a designation for the collective people of God, who are to bear his "holy" character and thus to be "set apart" for his purposes. To put that another way, the New Testament knows nothing about individual "saints," only about Christian communities as a whole who take up the Old Testament calling of Israel to be "God's holy people" in the world.[13]

2.1.5 Chosen (*eklektos* and cognates).

Closely related to the covenant is the concept of Israel as having been chosen by God, by an act of sheer mercy on his part. In the Old Testament this concept is most often found in verb form, with God as the subject. However, the LXX of Isaiah 43:20-21 uses *eklektos* as a designation for the restored people of God. This usage is picked up in several places in the New Testament (e.g. Mark 13:22; 1 Thessalonians 1:4; 2 Thessalonians 2:13; Colossians 3:12; Ephesians 1:4, 11; 1 Peter 1:2; 2:9). As in the Old Testament the term does not refer to individual election, but to a people who have been chosen by God for his purposes; as one has been incorporated into, and thus belongs to, the chosen people of God, one is in that sense also elect. Also as in the Old Testament, this language places the ultimate ground of our being in a sovereign and gracious God, who willed and initiated salvation for his people.

2.1.6 Royal priesthood.

This term, taken directly from Exodus 19:6, is used in 1 Peter 2:9-10 to refer to the church. I include it here not only because it is further demonstration of continuity, but also because as in the Exodus passage it so clearly refers to the people corporately,[14] not to individual priests, nor to the priesthood of individual believers.[15]

2.1.7 The Israel of God.

This unique expression occurs only in Galatians 6:16 in the entire Bible. Nonetheless, in many ways it gathers up much of the New Testament thinking—especially Paul's—on this matter. All those who live by the "rule" that neither circumcision nor uncircumcision counts for anything, these are "the Israel of God" upon whom God's benediction of shalom and mercy now rests.[16] While it is true that Paul does not call the church the "new Israel," such passages as Romans 2:28-29; 9:5; Philippians 3:3, and this one demonstrate that Paul saw the church as the "true Israel," i.e. as in the true succession of the Old Testament people of God. At the same time it emphasizes that those people are now newly-constituted— composed of Jew and Gentile alike, and based solely on faith in Christ and the gift of the Spirit.

This comes through nowhere more forcefully than in the argument of Galatians itself, for which this passage serves as the climax. Paul's concern throughout has been to argue that through Christ and the Spirit Gentiles share with believing Jews full privileges in the promises made to Abraham (indeed are Abraham's true children), without submitting to Torah in the form of Jewish identity symbols (circumcision, food laws, calendar observance).[17] They do *not* need to submit to the regulations of the old covenant in order to be full members of the people of God; indeed in "belonging to Christ," they are "Abraham's seed, and heirs according to the promise" (3:29), which is confirmed for them by the gift the Spirit (4:6-7).

Here especially the primary name for God's ancient people has been taken over in the interests of continuity, but now predicated on new terms. The Israel *of God* includes both Jew and Gentile, who by faith in Christ and "adoption" by the Spirit, have become Abraham's "free children," and through Christ the inheritors of the promises made to Abraham. Gentile believers *as a people* are included in the newly constituted people of God, the Israel of God, which is at the same time also an obviously corporate image.

2.1.8 Further (non-Old Testament) Images.

The essentially corporate nature of the people of God is further demonstrated by the various images for the church found in the New Testament that are *not* from the Old Testament: *family,* where God is Father and his people are brothers and sisters; the related image of *household,* where the people are members of the household (1 Timothy 3:5,15) and their leaders the Master's servants (1 Corinthians 4:1-3); *body,* where the emphasis is simultaneously on their unity and diversity (1 Corinthians 10:17; 12:12-26); God's *temple,* or sanctuary, where by the Spirit they corporately serve as the place of God's dwelling (1 Corinthians 3:16-17; 2 Corinthians 6:16; Ephesians 2:21-22); God's *commonwealth,* where as citizens of heaven Jew and Gentile alike form a *polis* in exile, awaiting their final homeland (Philippians 3:20-21; Ephesians 2:19; 2 Peter 1:1,17).

In sum: By using so much Old Testament language to mark off their own identity, the early church saw themselves not only as in continuity with the Old Testament people of God, but as in the true succession of that people. One of the essential features of this continuity is the corporate nature of the people of God. God chose, and made covenant with, not individuial Israelites but with a people, who would bear his name and be for his purposes. Although individual Israelites could forfeit their position in Israel, this never affected God's design or purposes with the people as a people. This is true even when the majority failed, and the "people" were reduced to a "remnant." That remnant was still Israel—loved, chosen, and redeemed by God.

This is the thoroughgoing perspective of the New Testament as well, but at the same time Christ's coming and the gift of the eschatological Spirit also marked a new way by which they were constituted. The community is now entered individually through faith in Christ and the reception of the Spirit, signalled by baptism. Nonetheless, the church itself is the object of God's saving activity in Christ. God is thus choosing and saving a people for his name.

Perhaps nothing illustrates this quite so vividly as two passages in 1 Corinthians (5:1-13; 6:1-11), where rather flagrant sins on the part of individuals are spoken to. In both cases Paul aims his heaviest artillery not at the individual sinners, but at the church for its failure to deal with the matters. In 5:1-13 the man is not so much as spoken to, and his partner is not mentioned at all; everything is directed at the church—for its arrogance, on the one hand, and its failure to act, on the other. So also in 6:1-11. In this case he does finally speak to the plaintiff (vv.7-8a) and the defendant (vv.8b-11), but only after he has scored the church for its allowing such a thing to happen at all among God's eschatological community, and thus for its failure to act. What is obviously at stake in these cases is the church itself, and its role as God's redeemed and redemptive alternative to Corinth.

2.2 The People and their Leadership.

The sense of continuity with the old, however, does not seem to carry over to the role of leadership as well. Under the old covenant the king and priests in particular, although often included in much of the "people" language, were at the same time recognized as having an existence apart from the people with their own sets of rules and expectations. It is precisely this model of leadership that breaks down altogether in the New Testament. The basic reason for this is the Lordship of Christ himself. As God intended to be himself king over Israel, so Christ has come as God's king over his newly constituted people. As head of his church, all others, including leaders, function as parts of the body both sustained by Christ and growing up into him (Ephesians 4:11-16).

Thus leadership in the New Testament people of God is never seen as outside or above the people themselves, but simply as part of the whole, essential to its well-being, but governed by the same set of "rules." They are not "set apart" by "ordination"; [18] rather their gifts are part of the Spirit's work among the whole people. That this is the basic model (as diagrammed earlier) can be demonstrated in a number of ways, some of which deserve special attention.

2.2.1 The Nature of the Epistles.

One of the more remarkable features of the New Testament Epistles is the twin facts (a) that they are addressed to the church(es) as a whole, not to the church leadership,[19] and (b) that leaders, therefore, are seldom, if ever,[20] singled out either to see to it that the directives of a given letter are carried out or to carry them out themselves.

To the contrary, in every case, the writers address the community as a whole, and the expectation of the letter is that there will be a community response to the directives. In several instances leaders are mentioned (e.g., 1 Thessalonians 5:12-13; 1 Corinthians 16:16; Hebrews 13:17), but basically in order to address the community's attitudes toward them. In 1 Peter 5:1-4 the leaders themselves (apparently) [21] are addressed, in this case with regard to their attitudes and responsibilities toward the rest of the people.

Thus, for example, in 1 Thessalonians 5:12-13 the whole community is called upon, among other things, to respect those who labour among them, care for them,[22] and admonish them; yet in vv. 14-15, when urging that they "admonish the idle, encourage the fainthearted, help the weak, be patient with all," he is once more addressing *the community as a whole*, not its leadership in particular. So also in 2 Thessalonians 3:14 the whole community is to "note that person" who does not conform to Paul's instruction and "have nothing to do with him." Likewise, in all of 1 Corinthians not one of the many directives is spoken to the leadership, and in 14:26 their worship is singularly corporate in nature ("When you [plural] assemble together, *each one of you has...*; let all things be done with an eye to edification"). One receives the distinct impression that people and leaders alike are under the sovereign direction of the Holy Spirit.

This is not to downplay the role of leadership; [23] rather it is to recognize that in the New Testament documents leaders are always seen as *part of the whole people of God,* never as a group unto themselves. Hence they "labour among" you, Paul repeatedly says, and their task in Ephesians 4:11-16 is especially "to prepare God's people ['the saints'] for works of service ['ministry'], so that the body of Christ may be built up." Thus the model that emerges in the New Testament is not that of clergy and laity, but of the whole people of God, among whom the leaders function in service of the rest.

All of this is quite in keeping with Jesus' word that they are to call no one "rabbi," "father," or "master," for "you have one teacher and you are all brothers and sisters" (Matthew 23:8-12), and with his word that "those who are supposed to rule over the Gentiles lord it over them, and their great men exercise authority over them. But it shall not be so among you; but whoever would be great among you must be your servant, and whoever would be first among you must be slave of all" (Mark 10:42-44).

2.2.2 The New Testament Imperatives.

Closely related to this is another reality that is easily missed in an individualistic culture, namely that the imperatives in the Epistles are primarily corporate in nature, and have to do first of all with the community and its life together; they address individuals only as they are part of the community. In the early church everything was done *allelon* ("one another"). They were members of one another (Romans 12:5; Ephesians 4:25),[24] who were to build up one another (1 Thessalonians 5:11; Romans 14:19), care for one another (1 Corinthians 12:25), love one another (1 Thessalonians 3:12; 4:9; Romans 13:8; 1 John *passim*), bear with one another in love (Ephesians 4:2), bear one another's burdens (Galatians 6:2), be kind and compassionate to one another, forgiving one another (Ephesians 4:32), submit to one another (Ephesians 5:21), consider one another better than themselves (Philippians 2:3), be devoted to one another in love (Romans 12:10), and live in harmony with one another (Romans 12:16).

All of the New Testament imperatives are to be understood within this framework. Unfortunately, many texts which Paul intended for the community as a whole have been regularly individualized, thus losing much of their force and impact. For example, in 1 Corinthians 3:10-15 Paul is not talking of believers building their individual lives on Christ; rather the admonition in v.10 ("let each one take care how he/she builds") is intended precisely for those in Corinth responsible for building the church, that they do it with the imperishable materials compatible with the foundation (a crucified Messiah), not with "wisdom" and division. Likewise vv. 16-17 are a warning to those who would "demolish" God's temple, the church in Corinth, by their divisions and fascination with "wisdom." And on it goes. "Work out your own salvation with fear and trembling, for God is at work in you both to will and to work for his good pleasure" (Philippians 2:12-13) is not a word to the individuals in the community to work harder at their Christian lives, but is spoken to a community that is out of sync with one another (as vv. 1-5 make clear) and needs to work out its common salvation with God's help. In the same vein, it is impossible to compute the misunderstandings that have arisen over 1 Corinthians 12-14 because the text has been looked at outside the context of the community at worship.

All of this, then, to say that the people of God in the New Testament are still thought of corporately, and individually only as they are members of the community. And leadership is always seen as part of the whole complex. Leaders do not exercise authority over God's people—although the community is to respect them and submit to their leadership; rather they are the "servants of the farm" (1 Corinthians 3:5-9), or "household" (1 Corinthians 4:1-3). The New Testament is not concerned with their place in the governance structures (hence as we will note below, we know very little about these), but with their attitudes and servant nature. They do not rule,[25] but serve and care for— and that within the circle, as it were.

3. The Theological Basis for the New Testament People of God

Before turning our attention to some observations about the nature of structures and ministry in the New Testament, it is time now to suggest the theological/experiential basis for the New Testament church's *discontinuity* with the old, and thus for their being a newly constituted people, which in turn accounts for their relaxed attitude toward governance structures as such. This basis, I suggest, is a combination of three realities:[26] the work of Christ, the gift of the Spirit, and the eschatological framework within which both of these were understood.

3.1 The work of Christ.

We need not belabour this point. The single, central reality of the New Testament is that "God has made him both Lord and Christ, this Jesus whom you crucified" (Acts 2:36); and that changes everything. On the one hand, he "fulfills" all manner of hopes and expectations, thus functioning as both continuity and discontinuity with the old: he is the "seed" of Abraham, inheritor of the promises to Abraham, through whom both Jew and Gentile alike are now "heirs according to promise" (Galatians 3:16,29); he is the great high priest, whose singular sacrifice of himself eliminates all other priests and offerings, through whom we all now have direct access to the Father (Hebrews); he is the rejected stone now become the chief cornerstone by whom we have become living stones in God's new "spiritual house" (1 Peter 2:4- 8).

On the other hand, the death and resurrection of Christ bring an *end* to the old and begin the new. His death ratified a new covenant, so that the people of God are newly constituted—based on faith in Christ and including Gentile as well as Jew.[27] His resurrection set the future in motion in such a way that this newly constituted people are "raised with him" and enter an entirely new mode of existence—so much so that a radically new understanding of that existence also emerged.

This is obviously the focus of New Testament theology, and the primary reason for discontinuity with the former people of God (in the sense that they must now come through Christ in order to belong). But such focus does not in itself account for the people of God sensing themselves to be a *newly constituted people* as well.[28] This can only be accounted for on the basis of the eschatological framework of their self-understanding and the role of the Spirit within that understanding.

3.2 The Gift of the Spirit.

Although the New Testament people of God were constituted on the basis of Christ's death and resurrection, the Spirit, who appropriated that work to their lives, was the key to their *present* existence as that people. The Spirit is both the *evidence* that God's eschatological future had dawned (Acts 2:16- 21) and the *guarantee* of their own inheritance at its consummation (Ephesians 1:13-14).[29]

The Spirit is that which marks off God's people from the rest, whereby they understand the wisdom of the cross, which the world counts as foolishness (1 Corinthians 2:6-16). Their common experience of Spirit, both Jew and Gentile, plus their continuing experience of the Spirit's activities among them, is that to which Paul appeals in Galatia as evidence of the new expression of being God's people (Galatians 3:2-5); and the Spirit by whom they walk, in whom they live, and by whom they are led is the reason they no longer need Torah (5:16-28). Not only has Christ brought an end to Torah but by belonging to him believers have also crucified the flesh (Galatians 5:24) that was aroused by Torah (Romans 7:5). Through the Spirit they fulfill the whole Torah as well as the law of Christ by loving one another (Galatians 5:13-14; 6:2).

Moreover, the Spirit is the key to their existence as a people. Through Christ both Jew and Gentile together "have access in one

Spirit to the Father" (Ephesians 2:18). By their common, lavish experience of Spirit the many of them in Corinth, with all their differences and diversity, became the one body of Christ (1 Corinthians 12:13); by the Spirit's abiding in/among them they form God's temple, holy unto him—set apart for his purposes as his alternative to Corinth (1 Corinthians 3:16-17).

Finally, the Spirit serves as the key to their new view of ministry. Ministry lies not in individuals with inherited offices, nor even in individuals with newly created offices. Ministry lies with the gifting of the Spirit. God through his Spirit has placed ministries in the church; and since the Spirit is the eschatological Spirit of Joel's prophecy, all of God's people are potential prophets—Jew/Gentile, male/female, home owner/slave. The Spirit is unconscious of race, sex, or rank. He gifts whom he wills for the common good (1 Corinthians 12:7-11).

Thus the Spirit, as available to all, and gifting various people in diverse ways as he wills, is the crucial ingredient of their new self-understanding—and thus of their discontinuity with the old.

3.3 The eschatological framework.

The net result of Jesus' death and resurrection followed by the advent of the Spirit was that the early church understood itself to be an eschatological community, "upon whom the end of the ages has come" (1 Corinthians 10:11). Their citizenship was already in heaven, from whence they were awaiting Christ's return to bring the final consummation (Philippians 3:20-21). With the resurrection of Christ God set the future inexorably in motion (1 Corinthians 15:20-28), so that the form of this present world is passing away (1 Corinthians 7:31).

Thus the early church understood the future as "already" but "not yet"[30] and its own existence as "between the times." At the Lord's Table they celebrated "the Lord's death until he comes" (1 Corinthians 11:26). By the resurrection and the gift of the Spirit they had been stamped with eternity. They had been "born anew to a living hope...to an imperishable inheritance preserved in heaven for them" (1 Peter 1:3-5). They already "sat in the heavenlies" through Christ (Ephesians 1:4). In their present existence, therefore, they were living the life of the future, the way things were eventually to be, as they awaited the consummation. It is thus in light of the eschatological realities of their existence that Paul tries to shame the Corinthians by trivializing both the need to redress one's grievances and the secular courts in which such litigation took place; in light of eschatological realities such things count for nothing (1 Corinthians 6:1-6).

As much as anything, it is this sense that Christ's death and resurrection marked the turning of the ages, and that the Spirit in/among them was God's down payment and guarantee of their future, that marked the crucial point of discontinuity with what had gone before. With Christ and the Spirit they had *already begun their existence as the future people of God.* And it is precisely this new, eschatological existence that transforms their understanding of being his people. The future has already begun; the Spirit has come upon all of the people alike, so that the only differences between/among them reflect the diversity of the Spirit's gifts, not a hierarchy of persons or offices. There can be no "kings" or "priests" in this new order, precisely because this future kingdom, which was inaugurated by Jesus and the Spirit, is the kingdom *of God,* and thus a return in an even grander way to the theocracy that was God's first order for Israel.

4. Structure and Ministry in the New Testament

As already noted, one of the truly perplexing questions in New Testament studies is to determine the shape that leadership and structures took within the earliest congregations of God's new covenant people. The difficulties here stem from the lack of explicit, intentional instruction, noted at the beginning of this paper. The reasons for it are related both to the twofold reality of their eschatological existence and their experience of the Spirit, not to mention the simple fact that one seldom instructs on something that is generally a given.

What I hope to do here is to offer some reflections on the data as they come to us in the documents. Several things seem quite certain:

4.1 Leadership was of two kinds.[31]

On the one hand, there were itinerants, such as the apostle Paul and others, who founded churches and exercised obvious authority over the churches they had founded. On the other hand, when the itinerant founder or his delegate was not present, leadership on the local scene seems to have been left in the hands of "elders,"[32] all expressions of which in the New Testament are plural. Thus Paul founded the church in Corinth, and it is to him that they owe their allegiance—so much so that he rather strongly denounces other "apostles" who teach foreign doctrines on his turf (cf. 2 Corinthians 10:12-18).

In the same vein Paul delegates Timothy, and apparently later Tychicus, to straighten out the mess in Ephesus created by some false teachers, who in my view were elders who had gone astray.[33] Timothy is not the "pastor"; he is there in Paul's place, exercising

Paul's authority. But he is to replace the fallen elders with new ones, who will care for the church and teach when Timothy is gone (1 Timothy 5:17-22; 2 Timothy 2:2; 4:9). The elders in the local churches seem to have been composed of both *episkopoi* (overseers) and *diakonoi* (deacons), who probably had different tasks; but from this distance there is little certainty as to what they were (except that the *episkopoi* were to be "capable teachers," 1 Timothy 3:2).

Unless Revelation 2-3 provides an exception, there is no evidence in the New Testament of a single leader at the local level who was not at the same time an itinerant. The status of James in Jerusalem is at once a more vexed and complex issue. In an earlier time, as evidenced by both Luke and Paul, he appears to have been one among equals. But as the others moved on and he stayed, he apparently emerged eventually as the predominant leader, but in what capacity one is hardpressed to determine. In any case, he was not native to Jerusalem—a kind of "permanent itinerant?"—and probably exercised the kind of leadership there that Paul did over his churches.

4.2

Because of the authority vested in the apostle as founder of churches—either by the apostle himself or as in the case of Epaphras one of the apostle's co-workers—there does not seem to be any other outside authority for the local churches. That is, apostles apparently did not assume authority in churches they had not founded. Paul's considerably more restrained approach to the church in Rome in contrast to his other letters serves as evidence.

Moreover, even though there is a form of collegiality among the "apostles" and "elders," Paul at least did not consider any one of them to have authority over him, although he felt a kind of urgency that they all be in this thing together. Thus, there appears to have been a kind of loose plurality at the top level, with recognition of each other's spheres and ministries as given by God (Galatians 2:6-10).

4.3

Apart from the authority of the apostles over the churches they had founded, there seems to be very little interest in the question of "authority" at the local level. To be sure, the people are directed to respect, and submit to, those who laboured among them and served them in the Lord (1 Corinthians 16:16; Hebrews 13:17). But the interest is not in their authority as such, but in their role as those who care for the others.

The concern for governance and roles within church structures emerges at a *later* time. Nonetheless, the twofold questions of laity and women in ministry are almost always tied to this question in the contemporary evangelical debate. The great urgency always is, Who's in charge around here? which is precisely what puts that debate outside New Testament concerns.

4.4

One of the difficulties in the Pauline letters is to determine the relationship between certain gifts, especially prophecy and teaching (as e.g., in 1 Corinthians 14:6,26), and people who are designated as prophets and teachers. The clear implication of 1 Corinthians 14:6 and 26-33 is that teaching, for example, is a gift that might be exercised by anyone in the community; yet in 12:28 he sets prophets and teachers after apostles as God's gifts to the community. Most likely both of these phenomena existed side by side; that is, prophesying and teaching, as well as other gifts, were regularly exercised in a more spontaneous way by any and all within the community, whereas some who exercised these gifts on a regular basis were recognized as "prophets" and "teachers." The former would be ministry for the upbuilding of the community; the latter would naturally emerge in roles of spiritual leadership within the community.

4.5

Thus, in the final analysis we know very little about the governance of either the local or larger church. That structures of some kind existed can be taken for granted; but what form these took is simply not an interest in our documents themselves. It is arguable that at least part of the reason for this is their sense of corporate life as the people of God, among whom the leaders themselves did not consider themselves "ordained" to lead the people, but "gifted" to do so as one gift among others.[34]

5. Some Hermeneutical Observations.

How, then, does all—or any—of this apply to us? Here our difficulties are a mixture of several realities. First, how does one handle biblical revelation that comes to us less by direct instruction and more by our observations as to what can be gleaned from a whole variety of texts? Second, if we do think in terms of "modeling" after the New Testament church, which of the various models do we opt for, and why? Third, since we are already set in various traditions, and since so much water has gone under the bridge in any case, what difference does any of this make on our very real personal and corporate histories? I have no illusions that I can resolve these matters; indeed, they merely raise some of the deep hermeneutical issues that have long divided the people of God. For most of us, there is comfort in the known, and structures we are used to are easily seen as biblical. Nonetheless, I want to conclude this paper with a few observations.

5.1

We should probably all yield to the reality that there are no explicitly revealed church structures that serve as the divine order for all times and in all places. Even so, I think there are *ideals* toward which we might strive—although we may very well keep present structures in place. In this regard, I would put at a top level of priority our need to model the church as an eschatological community of the Spirit, in which we think of the church as a whole people among whom leaders serve as one among many other gifts, and that one of the basic priorities of leadership is to equip and enable others for the larger ministry of the church. Despite years of ingrained "division of labour," I am convinced that a more biblical model can be effected within almost any present structure. But it will take a genuine renewal of the Holy Spirit, so that the "clergy" cease being threatened by shared gifts and ministries, and the people cease "paying the preacher to do it."

5.2

As to structures themselves, it is my guess that the model that emerged was the result of a transference of roles, in which there arose at the local level a more *permanent, single* leader, but now based on the model of the *itinerant apostle*. This bothers me none, as long as the model of a single pastor wielding great authority in the local church is not argued for as something biblical in itself. The danger with this model, of course, is that it tends to focus both authority and ministry in the hands of one or a few persons, who cannot possibly be so gifted as to fill all the needs of the local community. Furthermore, leadership, especially of the more visible kind, can be heady business. For me the great problem with single leadership is its threefold tendency to pride of place, love of authority, and lack of accountability. Whatever else, leadership in the church needs forms that will minimize these tendencies and maximize servanthood.

5.3

Thus I would urge the movement toward a more biblical view of church and leadership in which we do not eliminate "clergy"—except for all the wrong connotations that that word often brings with it—but look for a renewed leadership and people, in which ordination is not so much to an office as the recognition of the Spirit's prior gifting, and the role of leadership is more often that of Ephesians 4:11-16, preparing the whole church for its ministry to itself and to the world.

5.4

If the structures of the New Testament church themselves are not necessarily our proper goal, I would urge that the recapturing of the New Testament view of the church itself is. If the church is going to be God's genuine alternative to the world, a people truly for his name, then we must once again become an eschatological people, people who are citizens of another homeland, whose life in the Spirit is less creedal and cerebral and more fully biblical and experiential, and a people whose sense of corporate existence is so dynamic and genuine that once again it may be said of us, "How those Christians love one another."

Endnotes

This paper was originally prepared for discussion at a Regent College faculty retreat. Rather than a research paper that tries to take account of the vast array of secondary literature (on church order and laity), I have attempted something more modest: an essay that offers one New Testament scholar's reading of the biblical texts on specific issues related to the church as the people of God, namely, the interrelationships between people, clergy, ministry, and church order. Although what I do here is akin to re-inventing the wheel, hopefully some items will be fresh—although on others I can be easily scored for not having consulted the literature.

I am grateful to my Regent colleagues for a vigorous discussion of the paper, from which I have made a few small revisions and added a few footnotes for greater clarity.

1. One reason not otherwise noted in this paper is the especially *ad hoc* nature of our documents. Even the so-called Pastoral Epistles show little interest in church leadership or governance as such. Rather Paul is concerned with the character and qualifications of those who assume positions of leadership. See G. D. Fee, *1 and 2 Timothy, Titus* (Peabody, MA: Hendrickson, 1988): 19-23, 78-79.

2. As I have noted elsewhere, the very fact that such diverse groups as Roman Catholics, Plymouth Brethren, and Presbyterians all use the Pastoral Epistles to support their ecclesiastical structures should give us good reason to pause as to what the New Testament "clearly teaches" on these matters. See "Reflections on Church Order in the Pastoral Epistles, with Further Reflection on the Hermeneutics of Ad Hoc Documents," *Journal of the Evangelical Theological Society* 28.(1985): 141-51.

This is one of the things that make Acts such a different kind of "church history" from its successors. There is scarcely a hint of church organization or structures (1:15-26 and 6:1-6 play quite different roles). At some point, for example, leadership in Jerusalem passed from the Twelve to James (cf. 6:2 and 8:14 with 11:2; 12:17; and 15:13), without so much as a word as to how or why. At the local level, in 13:1-3, those who appear to be in leadership are "prophets and teachers," while in 14:23 elders are appointed for each congregation. This is hardly the stuff from which one can argue with confidence as to how the early church was "organized"—or whether it was!

3. By this I mean something quite technical, namely the outpouring of the promised Holy Spirit as the primary reality indicating that Jewish eschatological hopes had been fulfilled, or realized. For the early church "this is that which was spoken by the prophet Joel" (Acts 2:16), the sure evidence that the End (*Eschaton*) had begun and the time of the Future had dawned.

4. In contrast to having come by such order through purposeful, intentional action on its part.

5. I mean *de jure*, of course. One of my colleagues pointed out that *de facto* there is nothing more severe in this regard than some independent churches (baptist, pentecostal/charismatic).

6. For me this is always brought home as a living reality in teaching New Testament Theology. Although my emphases and packaging of the biblical data frequently stimulates rousing discussion (debate?), nothing does so quite as much as the section in Pauline theology on the nature of the church as the eschatological people of God, presently living out the life of the future as they await the consummation. Not only do I have great difficulty in helping students to catch the New Testament perspective, but even when it happens, there is difficulty in assimilating it—because this touches them right where they live.

7. Whether we should try to model the New Testament church, of course, is yet another hermeneutical question in its own right. On the place of "historical precedent" in Christian hermeneutics, see some programmatic suggestions in G. D. Fee and D. Stuart, *How to Read the Bible for All Its Worth* (Grand Rapids: Zondervan, 1982): 87-102.

8. This is no more than we should expect, given Jesus as the fulfillment of Jewish messianic expectations, his own announcement of the kingdom as "fulfilling the time," and the Jewish complexion of the earliest believers. Continuity is thus found in a whole variety of ways in the Gospels: e.g. in direct statements reflecting the motif of promise and fulfillment, in symbols and images of various kinds (Jesus' choice of the Twelve is scarely accidental!), in the hymns in Luke's birth narrative.

9. Thus, e.g., Deuteronomy 31:30: "And Moses recited the words

of this song from beginning to end in the hearing of the whole *ekklesia* of Israel."

10. Probably because the more common word *ethnos* was used by Greek writers to refer to themselves as a people in the same way the Hebrews used *'am*. Thus for the Jews *ethnos* came to = "gentiles," and was so used by the LXX translators. Hence the need for a different word to distinguish themselves.

11. Luke uses it most often (84 of 142); Matthew 14; Hebrews 13; Paul 12; Revelation 9. In many of these it occurs in citations of the Old Testament.

12. Just as the Table, through its symbol of the bread (1 Corinthians 10:16-17), should serve for us as a reminder of our continuity with centuries of believers.

13. See G. D. Fee, *The First Epistle to the Corinthians* (Grand Rapids: Eerdmans, 1987): 32-33, for the difficulties in rendering this term into English; the option which seems best to capture its inherent nuances is "God's holy people."

14. Cf. B. Childs on Exodus 19:6: "Israel as a people is also dedicated to God's service among the nations as priests function with a society" (*The Book of Exodus* [Philadelphia: Westminster, 1974]: 367).

15. The New Testament knows nothing of the "priesthood of the believer" as it is popularly conceived, with each person's being his or her own priest with God, without need of an external priesthood. To the contrary, the New Testament teaches that the church has a priestly function for the world (1 Peter 2:9-10); and our role of ministering to one another makes us priests one for another.

16. Although it is grammatically possible that this phrase refers to Jewish people, and is so argued by many (see esp. P. Richardson, *Israel in the Apostolic Church* [Society for New Testament Studies Monograph Series 10: Cambridge University Press, 1969]: 74-102), both the unusual nature of the qualifier "of God" and the context of the whole argument argue for the position taken here.

17. The issue in Galatians is not first of all justification by faith (i.e. entrance requirements), but whether Gentiles, who have already been justified by faith in Christ and given the Spirit must also submit to Jewish boundary markers (i.e. maintenance requirements) in order to share in the covenant with Abraham (as Genesis 17:1-14 makes so clear). For arguments presenting this perspective see T. David Gordon, "The Problem in Galatia," *Interpretation* 41 (1987): 32-43; and J. D. G. Dunn, "The Theology of Galatians," *Society of Biblical Literature 1988 Seminar Papers* (Atlanta: Scholars Press, 1988): 1-16.

18. That is, they are not "set apart" to an office; rather hands are laid upon them in recognition of the Spirit's prior activity. Cf. Acts 13:1-2; 1 Timothy 4:4.

19. The one exception to this is Philippians, where Paul writes to the church "together with the overseers and deacons." One might also include Philemon, where Paul includes Archippus in the salutation, but since the letter is addressed to Philemon, Paul continues by mentioning two further individuals before including the church. Some, of course, would argue that 1 Timothy and Titus are such documents; however, both of these younger colleagues serve as Paul's own apostolic delegates in Ephesus and Crete. They are both itinerants, whose stay is temporary. Thus they are not church leaders in the local sense.

20. The one exception to this might be Philippians 4:3, where Paul asks a trusted fellow-worker to mediate the differences between Euodia and Syntyche. But more likely, since these two women are also designated as his fellow-workers, he is asking for help not so much from a church leader as such, but from one who has been a co-labourer with both Paul and these women. As in the preceding note, Timothy and Titus are "leaders" of a different kind. They are in their respective situations in Paul's place; they are not local leaders "in charge" of the church.

21. This seems almost certainly to be the case, despite the corresponding "younger men" that follows in v.5.

22. The verb in this case is ambiguous in Greek, meaning either to "govern" or to "care for." Apart from 1 Timothy 3:4-5, elsewhere in the New Testament, as here, it is used absolutely so that one cannot determine which nuance is intended. But in the Timothy passage the synonym that is substituted for it in v.5 means unambiguously to "care for." This seems most likely what Paul ordinarily had in mind. Cf. E. Best, *The First and Second Epistles to the Thessalonians* (San Francisco: Harper, 1972): 224-25.

23. Indeed, despite some New Testament scholarship to the contrary, it is highly unlikely that the early communities ever existed long without local leadership. The picture Luke gives in Acts 14:23 is an altogether plausible one historically, given the clear evidence of leadership in the earliest of the Pauline letters (1 Thessalonians 5:12-13)—a community where he had not stayed for a long time, whose leadership must have been in place when he was suddenly taken from them (Acts 17:10; 1 Thessalonians 2:17).

24. This is an obvious reference to the imagery of the church as the body of Christ, another corporate image used by Paul, which I have not dealt with in this paper because it is both so obvious and lacking

Old Testament roots.

25. Language of "rulership" and "authority" is altogether missing in the New Testament passages which speak about leadership, except as Paul refers to his apostolic authority in his own churches.

26. To be complete and more precise, of course, one should start with their absolutely primary theological presupposition: That the one God—holy, sovereign, and gracious—had purposed their salvation, which he effected in Christ and made available for all through the Spirit (see e.g., Galatians 4:4-7).

27. The classic illustration of Paul's own struggle with continuity and discontinuity between the new and the old— expressed in terms of Gentile and Jew—is Romans 11, where Gentiles have been grafted onto the olive tree "and now share in the nourishing sap from the olive root" (v. 17, NIV). Yet Israel itself must be regrafted in order to be saved.

28. After all, in the early going, as Luke portrays things in Acts 1-6, the early believers lived within Judaism—and surely expected that all Jewry would acknowledge Jesus as Messiah, Saviour, and Lord.

29. Cf. the powerful eschatological metaphors of the Spirit in Paul that especially make these double points: "seal" (2 Corinthians 1:21-22; Ephesians 1:13; 4:30); "earnest/first installment" (2 Corinthians 1:21-22; 5:5; Ephesians 1:14); "firstfruits" (Romans 8:23). This latter metaphor in particular helps us to see how Paul views life in the Spirit as lived in the eschatological tension of the "already" and the "not yet"; while at the same time the Spirit is the guarantee of our certain future. The larger context of Romans 8:12-27 is especially noteworthy. With the Spirit playing the leading role, Paul in vv. 15-17 has struck the dual themes (1) of our present position as children, who are thus joint-heirs with Christ of the Father's glory, and (2) of our present existence as one of weakness and suffering, as we await that glory. These are the two themes taken up in vv. 18-27. By the Spirit we have already received our "adoption" as God's children, but what is "already" is also "not yet"; therefore, by the same Spirit, who functions for us as firstfruits, we await our final "adoption as children," "the redemption of our bodies." The first sheaf is God's pledge to us of the final harvest.

30. Cf. 1 John 3:2: "Beloved, we are God's children *now*; it does *not yet* appear what we shall be, but we know that when he appears we shall be like him, for we shall see him as he is."

31. But not of the two kinds most often noted in the literature: charismatic and regular. Rather, it is itinerant and local. Authority lies with the itinerant, whether he is on the local scene or otherwise.

32. Since the earliest congregations grew out of Judaism, the (chiefly lay) elders of the Jewish synagogues almost certainly served as the model for the early Christian communities.

33. See Fee, *1 and 2 Timothy, Titus*, pp. 7-10.

34. In this regard see especially how the participle for leaders "those who care for the church" is found nestled between "contributing to the needs of others" and "showing mercy" in Romans 12:8.

Church and State in Socialist China, 1949-1987

Jonathan Chao

Vol. XXV, No. 2 (June 1989):8-20

Introduction

Church-state relations may seem to be a settled question in Western, Christianized countries. But in socialist countries like mainland China and in other Third World countries where revolutions are still going on, the relationship between church and state is usually the most important issue affecting the life and witness of the church.

In Hong Kong today, as the British colony makes its transition to Chinese sovereignty, church-state relations have become a matter of primary concern for the Christian church, both Catholic and Protestant. Recently a writer using the pseudonym Hsin Wei-Su (a Chinese pun for Hsin hua-she, or New China News Agency) wrote two articles suggesting that the principle of separation of church and state should be incorporated into the Basic Law, the constitution of the Hong Kong Special Administrative Region under the People's Republic of the China after 1997.[1] Hsin's definition of the separation of church and the state is essentially the separation of religion from politics, and so he suggested that neither the church nor the clergy should become involved in politics and that the Basic Law should only guarantee "normal religious activities." Religion, he argued, belongs to the realm of the mind (thinking, the noumenal world), and politics deals with political power. Since their purposes and spheres are different, the clergy should confine themselves to religious matters and should not comment on, or participate in, politics.

Hsin's articles elicited a lively response from Christians which appeared in Hong Kong Chinese-language newspapers. This debate on the separation of religion from politics has yielded over twenty articles and is still going on. Many who disagreed with Hsin could not understand his logic, and thought his demands rather absurd. However, if one reads Hsin's articles from the perspective of the Chinese Communists' attitude toward religion, one can see almost at once that his position is none other than a reflection of standard Chinese Communist religious policy.[2]

The people of Hong Kong already feel pressure from Beijing as their future is being shaped by the Basic Law Drafting Committee. The churches and their leaders are beginning to sense the coming of a new reality: that Hong Kong will soon come under Chinese Communist rule and that a new relationship between the churches and the new Hong Kong government will eventually emerge. What is it going to be like? How much of the current religious freedom will extend beyond 1997, and for how long? These are questions of existential interest to the Christian community in Hong Kong. The issue of church and state has arrived at our door steps!

The churches in Hong Kong, therefore, are looking at the experience of the church in mainland China for some insights into how to prepare themselves for life and ministry beyond 1997, especially in the matter of church-state relations.

Churches in other parts of the world are becoming increasingly interested in mainland China, in the story of the church there, and in the future prospects for missions. To understand all these questions correctly, one must deal with the basic issue of church and state in Mainland China as a socialist country.

To deal with this subject, we must first understand Chinese Communist religious policy. Second, we must analyze the main ideological sources contributing to the development of that policy. Third, we have to trace the historical development of the church-state relationship since 1949. We shall confine ourselves to the Protestant experience.

The Nature of Chinese Communist Religious Policy

In socialist China, the Communist Party's religious policy forms the framework within which church-state relations take place. The policy is that "citizens of the People's Republic of China [PRC] enjoy freedom of religious belief," as stated in article 36 of the 1982 Constitution.[3] This policy is more fully expounded in Document No. 19 of the Chinese Communist Party (CCP) Central Committee issued on March 31, 1982. However, "freedom of religious belief" is defined essentially in terms of freedom of inward faith: the right to believe or not to believe in one's heart.[4] It does not include freedom of propagation or freedom to conduct church life as prescribed in the Scriptures, or according to the wishes of religious bodies. Nor does freedom of religious belief include the social expressions of one's faith: religion must not interfere with politics, education, marriage and family life, etc.[5] Religion is to be kept as a private matter and is not allowed to exert any influence on society. Religious activities may be conducted so long as they are done under control of the state and are carried out under the supervision of the patriotic religious organizations. These are called "normal religious activities," which are to be conducted in "designated places" by designated religious personnel (clergy approved by the patriotic organizations such as the Three-self Patriotic Movement), and even approved clergy must work only in designated areas.[6] This is called the "three-designates" policy.[7]

All religious activities conducted by believers themselves outside the control of the state and its patriotic religious organizations are considered "abnormal religious activities," and hence are regarded as illegal and anti-revolutionary. Such activities, like independent home meetings and itinerant preaching, are not considered as religious activities, but as political violations of state policy, and violators are dealt with as political criminals.[8]

With this kind of definition of normal and abnormal religious activities, there is no legal provision for a direct relationship between mainland Chinese believers and believers or churches in foreign countries as religious people. Foreign religious bodies are forbidden to develop a direct working relationship with churches in mainland China.[9] The independence of the mainland Chinese church is stressed by the state and its patriotic organizations in the name of the former Protestant missionary goals of the "three-self": self-support, self-government, and self-propagation.[10]

However, the united front theory dictates that religion be used as an avenue for winning international goodwill in order that mainland China's national program might be advanced. For this purpose, patriotic organizations, such as the Three-self Patriotic Movement (TSPM) and the Chinese Catholic Patriotic Association, are encouraged to receive foreign religious groups as well as to send delegations to other countries.[11] Domestically, united front thinking also directs government officials and patriotic church leaders to win the support of the religious masses to contribute toward the national program of modernization.

These religious policies are formulated by the United Front Work Department of the CCP Central Committee in consultation with the Institute of Research on World Religions under the Academy of Social Sciences, the State Council Religious Affairs Bureau (RAB), and the national leaders of the patriotic religious organizations.[12]

Religious policies are implemented by the Religious Affairs Bureau, which has a national office that directs the provincial and municipal bureaus, which in turn direct the numerous county level bureaus.[13] According to the directives of the RAB, policies are carried out by the major patriotic religious organizations, namely: (1) the Buddhist Association of China; (2) the China Taoist Association; (3) the China Islamic Association; (4) the Three-self Patriotic Movement Committee of Protestant Churches of China (1954), which established the Christian Council of China (1980); and (5) the China Patriotic Catholic Association (1957), which in turn formed the Chinese Catholic Bishops College and the National Administrative Commission of the Chinese Catholic Church.[14]

These Patriotic associations report to the RAB, which is usually a part of the local united front office under the Party branch, and which works closely with the local Public Security Bureau (PSB). Religious policies are enforced by the Public Security Bureau. Without this enforcement, the policies and the patriotic organizations are powerless. Suspected violators of the policy are warned and interrogated by officials of the RAB. Sometimes, they are arrested by the Public Security Bureau and kept at its "detention centres." Often, officials of the TSPM act as informants.[15] Arrested suspects are further interrogated by the Public Security Bureau, and then the case is investigated by the Bureau of Investigation which turns the case over to the court. The district court would then either sentence the accused or release him.[16] This process, from arrest to sentencing, could take anywhere from six months to two years or even longer. Those sentenced are then transferred from the Public Security Bureau's detention centre to prison.

There is an interlocking relationship between the United Front Work Department, the Religious Affairs Bureau, the patriotic religious organizations (such as the TSPM), and the Public Security Bureau at national, provincial, and county levels.

How, then, did these religious policies and practices develop? We must now turn to the historical factors contributing to their formation.

Historical Sources of Chinese Communist
Religious Policy and Practice

There are four major sources contributing to the formation of Chinese Communist religious policy. These interacted with each other, producing a blend of traditional and modern Chinese totalitarian state control, the essential nature of church-state relations in socialist China.

First, there is the tradition of state control of religions in traditional China. In imperial China, the state assumed a right of sovereignty over all aspects of its subjects' lives. There was no separation of church and state as understood in the West, neither in theory nor in practice, and the Chinese people have never established their right to question such overall sovereignty of the state. Since the late Han Dynasty and definitely after the mid-T'ang Dynasty, Confucianism enjoyed the status of "official orthodoxy," not only as a system of political philosophy, but also as a way of life.[17] With this affirmation of Confucian orthodoxy, all systems of belief were considered "heterodox." However, major institutional religions were tolerated so long as they were brought under the control of the state. Through law codes and government control, the state reduced the influence of religious groups to a level of sociopolitical insignificance. At the same time, the state developed a system of control whereby religious expansion was contained, and the activities of religious groups were strictly controlled by the government, which used religious leaders who worked for the Board of Rites.[18] All other sectarian groups were not only considered heterodox, but also viewed as potential rebels, and hence were outlawed and often suppressed by force. Catholic Christianity suffered nearly 150 years of suppression as a foreign heterodox sect before it was tolerated in 1844.[19] Protestant and Catholic Christianity enjoyed freedom of propagation primarily on account of the toleration clause included in the Treaty of Tientsin (1858).

This tradition of the state control, official orthodoxy, state toleration, and the suppression of heterodox sects, is illustrated by the diagram above.

The second source is the anti-religious thinking which arose from the New Culture Movement of 1920-21. As a result of the debate on religion, Chinese intellectuals of the May Fourth era adopted the position that all realities must be tested by science and, in the process, rejected all religions as having no value for the building of a modern China. Religious beliefs were considered a hindrance to the development of a young, modern China.[20] This anti-religious sentiment influenced many of the intellectuals and students from whom the Chinese Communist Party drew its first recruits.

Some intellectuals tried to make room for religion by relegating it to the realm of subjectivity, acknowledging that science is the test for objective realities. This is why even today, Chinese Communist theoreticians still relegate religion to the private sphere, denying it any objective social value.[21]

The revolutionary view of religion that prevailed in the nineteenth century West greatly influenced Chinese intellectuals of the May Fourth era. Religion was seen as a historical phenomenon in the evolution of human society, which had its own process of rise, development, and disappearance. Religion, it was claimed, arose as a result of primitive man not understanding the natural forces around him. Religions began to develop when man entered into class society and could not free himself from its system of exploitation; and they will disappear when man enters into a socialist society, and the social basis for their existence has been removed.[22]

The third source is Lenin's anti-imperialist attitude toward religion. Lenin believed that religion is an opium which imperialists give to the people to dull their will to resist exploitation. Therefore, to fight against imperialism, one must oppose religion. Lenin's view was imported into China, and propagated widely by the Socialist Youth League under the leadership of the Chinese Communist Party during 1922-23.[23] Later, during the Chinese Communists' first period of collaboration with the Kuomintang (1924-27), Lenin's anti-religious views were popularized by the anti-Christian movements which the CCP and KMT sponsored as part of their anti-imperialist campaign. Since then, Christianity has been regarded by the Chinese Communists as the vanguard of foreign imperialism, and missionaries and Chinese pastors have been seen as the agents of cultural aggression.[24] This view was so widely propagated, and for so long, that even today many Chinese people are still influenced by it.

The fourth source is Mao Tse-tung's theory of contradictions and the united front policy. Mao asserted that there are antagonistic contradictions, such as political and ideological contradictions and nonantagonistic contradictions, such as religious differences among the people. Mao also differentiated primary contradictions from secondary contradictions, and he stressed the mobility of these contradictions according to changing historical situations. Under this system, religion was considered a nonantagonistic and secondary contradiction.[25]

When this system of contradictions is applied to the united front policy, the task of the Party is to unite with, or befriend, secondary contradictions in order to oppose primary contradictions. For example, since 1969, mainland China has been befriending the United States in order to oppose the Soviet threat, which has become Peking's primary contradiction. Similarly, the religious masses must be won over to fight against backwardness in the pursuit of modernization. While uniting or befriending secondary contradictions, religious people must also be educated so that they will gradually abandon their subjective worldview, and take on an "objective" materialistic worldview, abandoning their religious superstitions. They will then be won over to the Party's side. These are the positive dimensions of the united front policy.

But the united front policy also has its negative dimension, namely, those who refuse to accept the Party's lenient educational persuasion and persist in their own views must be dealt with in a more aggressive manner, by criticism, threats and, if necessary force, so that in the end the recalcitrant person will be isolated and his influence minimized. But who is to determine what is the primary contradiction (which should be attacked) and what is a secondary contradiction (to which a policy of friendly persuasion should be applied)? Historically, this has been determined by whoever holds power in the party in relation to what kind of national program he desires to implement. The historical context, therefore, determines how the united front policy is to be implemented in the realm of religion and in other areas.

The Development of Church and State Relations as seen from the Protestant Experience, 1949-1987

How has the Chinese Communist Party dealt with the Protestant church which it has all along regarded as an instrument of cultural imperialism? What procedures did the Party take to bring the pluralistic Protestant church in mainland China under its control? How did church leaders respond to government pressures? What kind of changes in the relationships have occurred during the long historical process since 1949? We shall now examine these questions in a historical manner.[26]

A. During the initial stage (1949-50), the State sought to establish a patriotic agency to give direction to the Protestant church: the rise of the Three-self Movement.

During the initial months after the Communist takeover of China (October 1949 to July 1950), the new government was too busy establishing economic and political order to bother with religious affairs; the churches were left alone to "do their own thing" without much interference. Church activities, such as revival meetings, were carried on as usual. Many missionaries stayed with their Chinese colleagues. However, a small nucleus of pro-government church leaders were already being formed when these churchmen were invited to attend the Chinese People's Political Consultative Conference held in Peking from September 23-30, 1949.[27] At that Conference the new government was born, and on October 1, Mao Tse-tung declared the formal beginning of the People's Republic of China. After the Conference, the Protestant participants, headed by Y.T. Wu (the former Y.M.C.A. publications secretary), formed a "Christian Visitation Team," to visit the Protestant leaders in a few major cities, and to explain to them the new government's "Common Program" and its policy of freedom of religious belief.[28]

During May 2, 6, 13-21, 1950, when this group of leaders were visiting the churches in Peking, Premier Chou En-lai summoned its members to discuss the future course of Christianity in mainland China. The end result of three nocturnal visits was the publication of a document called "The Path of Endeavour for the Chinese Protestant Church during the Course of China's Construction," known in the West as the "Christian Manifesto."[29] Published on July 28, 1950, this document was immediately circulated among church leaders throughout mainland China for signature. The document basically called for Christians to oppose imperialism and to accept the leadership of the Chinese Communist Party. It also called upon Protestant churches to become self-supporting, self-governing, and self-propagating, and hence it became the founding charter of the "Three-self Movement." The signature movement differentiated the "patriotic" church leaders who signed it from those who refused to sign it.

Prior to Chou En-lai's summons, the National Christian Council (NCC) of China (formed in 1922) had already made plans on January 26, 1950, to hold a National Christian Conference from August 19-27 to study an appropriate Christian response to the new situation, but this plan was aborted soon after the May meeting between Chou and Y.T. Wu and his associates.[30] The new body, which took on the name "Three-self Reform Movement," soon replaced the NCC as the national coordinating body representing Protestant Christianity in mainland China.

The church-state relationship at this initial stage may be illustrated by the following charts.

During this stage, individual churches still retained their autonomy. They could continue to conduct their regular religious activities. The state did not exercise its control directly over the churches, nor did it use existing Protestant channels, such as the

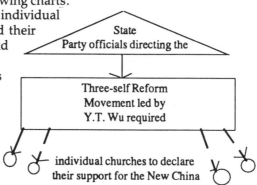

NCC, to influence them, but created a new informal body made up of pro-government clergy and assisted by Party secretaries. Through this body the state made its position known to the churches, and required their loyalty. This informal body, known as the "Three-self Reform Movement," was not an ecclesiastical organization, but a "political movement" which published the "Christian Manifesto" mentioned above, and which was signed by forty prominent church leaders.[31] This movement, headed by Y.T. Wu, began to give political direction to the Chinese Protestant church on behalf of the new government, and church leaders had to deal with it accordingly.

B. During the 1951-54 period, the state controlled the churches through the formation of the Chinese Protestant Anti-America and Aid Korea Three-self Reform Movement.

After the outbreak of the Korean War, especially after the Chinese Communist People's Liberation Army crossed the Yalu River, the United States became an antagonistic contradiction in relation to Communist China. On December 29, 1950, the United States froze Chinese assets in America, and Peking froze American assets in mainland China. This change in Sino-American relations seriously affected the Chinese Communist government's attitude toward the

Christian church, both Protestant and Catholic. All churches which had received, or were receiving, financial subsidies from the United States immediately became suspect, and were required to register themselves with the appropriate local authorities, to which they had to make regular financial reports.

From April 16-20, 1951, the Religious Affairs Bureau of the Ministry of Education and Culture summoned 151 Chinese Protestant leaders from churches which were receiving foreign subsidies to come to Peking. At this conference, these church leaders were told to sever their relations with U.S. imperialism. They were also taught how to conduct accusation meetings against "reactionary" missionaries and Chinese pastors who had at one time or another collaborated with Chiang Kai-shek or who had failed to pledge their support for the new government. Furthermore, at this meeting the "Preparatory Committee of the Chinese Protestant Anti-American and Aid-Korea Three-self Reform Movement Committee" was formally organized.[32]

After the Peking conference, the 151 delegates were told to carry out anti-imperialist accusation meetings in their own churches.[33] Those who had successfully conducted such meetings were urged to join the Three-self Reform Movement. Simultaneously, this movement also began to organize provincial and local committees. These committees were made up of church leaders who had declared their allegiance to the government. Meanwhile, the movement for signing the "Christian Manifesto" continued. By 1953 nearly 400,000 out of a total of 840,000 Chinese Protestants had signed this document.

Church-state relations during this stage may be illustrated as follows:

Some of the ways in which the state exercised control over Protestant churches included the following: (1) Churches were required to fly the five-star flag and/or display Mao's picture; failure to do so could be used as evidence of reaction, and reactionary

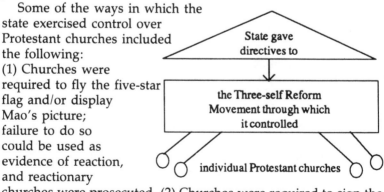

State gave directives to

the Three-self Reform Movement through which it controlled

individual Protestant churches

churches were prosecuted. (2) Churches were required to sign the

"Christian Manifesto," and to conduct anti-imperialist accusation meetings. (3) Christian educational and medical institutions founded by foreign missions were taken over by the state, and church boards were disbanded by 1952. (4) Theological schools in the north were amalgamated into the Yen-ching School of Theology, and those in the south into the Nanking Theological Seminary. (5) Christian publishers were told to comply with the policies of the new regime and most of them were closed down before 1954.

By 1953, all Protestant churches founded by foreign missions were brought under the control of the state through the agency of the Three-self Reform Movement.

C. During 1954-58 the state reformed the church through political education.

In July 1954, Peking promulgated its first constitution, and the churches were called upon to support it. The Korean War was over by 1953, and a new name was needed for the Anti-American Aid-Korea Three-self Reform Movement. This movement, therefore, held the first "National Christian Conference" in July 1954 in Peking. At that conference, the name of the body was changed to the "Three-self Patriotic Movement" and a TSPM constitution was adopted.[34]

After the first National Christian Conference, further efforts were made to organize local committees of the TSPM, and all churches were required to join the body, the symbol of anti-imperialist patriotism. Whereas the earlier Three-self Reform Movement had led or directed the churches as an *ad hoc* patriotic movement, now the TSPM had become an organization which delineated the sphere of patriotic religious existence.

Churches which refused to join the TSPM *ipso facto* declared themselves "non-patriotic." Furthermore, whereas in the earlier period, mainline churches founded by foreign missions were the main targets of attack, after 1954 indigenous Chinese churches came under pressure. In 1955, those church leaders who resisted the TSPM, such as Wang Ming-tao in Peking and Lam Hin-ko in Canton, were arrested.[35] Similarly, Chinese Catholic clergy who refused to cooperate also came under scrutiny. Bishop Kung Pin-mei was also arrested in 1955.

The relationship between church and state during this period is seen in the following illustration.

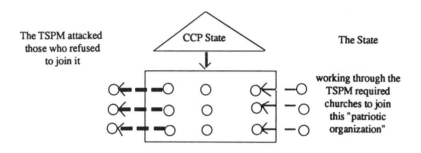

However, even at this stage, individual churches remained intact in that each church could still make its own ecclesiastical decisions, including whether to join the TSPM or not. Within the framework of the TSPM, the state conducted political education classes for pastors, hoping that they would come to the viewpoint of the Party on the place of Christianity in socialist China.

D. During 1956-66, a union of church and state took place in the formation of Three-self (state) churches.

Starting in the summer of 1957, the CCP began to conduct a "Socialist Education Movement," which was further intensified after the beginning of the Great Leap Forward Movement in 1958. In the fall of 1958 in Shanghai, pastors who had already joined the TSPM were told to attend political study sessions away from home. These sessions lasted for six months. A second series of sessions was conducted during the first half of 1959.[36] During the course of study, the question of the class nature of preachers came up. Are preachers exploiters or exploited? Those who realized that they were exploiters "volunteered" to join the proletarian class by becoming factory workers.[37] Those who were less "enlightened" were sent to manual labour anyway.

The prolonged absence of these pastors from their churches and their subsequent departure from the ministry left most churches half empty and without pastors. The TSPM then called for a "church union" movement. Some of the congregations "offered" their church buildings to the state; others united themselves with neighbouring congregations. The result was a remarkable reduction in the number of churches. For example, the two hundred plus churches in Shanghai were reduced to eight, and the sixty-six churches in Peking to four.

The few churches that remained after the amalgamation movement were led by men appointed by the TSPM, and since then have been called "Three-self churches." A team of pastors from several denominations who did well in their political studies or

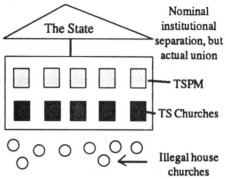

whose respected names were still useful to the TSPM, worked in these three-self churches.

The relationship between the church and the state during this period may be illustrated as a union of church and state (as shown above).

Individual congregations in the TSPM no longer had autonomy; the congregations could no longer make decisions on the election of church officers or the appointment of pastors. After 1958, country churches were closed down by the government, and independent church meetings were considered illegal, and their leaders were subject to arrest. House churches had to meet in secret.[38]

E. During the Cultural Revolution (1966-76), the state sought to destroy the church.

When the Cultural Revolution broke out in August 1966, the Red Guards stormed party headquarters, closed down the United Front and the Religious Affairs offices, and closed all existing Three-self churches. In their attempt to destroy the "four olds," they sought to do away with all organized religion along with Chinese folk religion, all of which they considered to be superstition. Their attacks represented a drastic shift from the soft-line, united front-oriented religious policy that was operative during 1958-66, to a hard-line policy which left no room for religion in the new revolutionary society.[39] Although no documents on religious policy were published during the latter part of the Cultural Revolution (1969-76), the actual practice of the state as carried out by its local revolutionary committees may be described as a policy of relegating religion to a position of illegality and suppressing its re-emergence. The state no longer tolerated some religious practices; it simply outlawed them all. The state had become a monolithic institution.[40]

However, Chinese Christians continued to meet secretly in their homes, especially in the countryside. Such meetings were illegal and were subject to closure, and their leaders subject to arrest. Nevertheless, because of the people's need for the comfort, community, and hope, needs which house church Christianity fulfilled, these house churches began to grow in size and in number.[41] They sustained no formal relations with the state, but existed as illegal groups and were often suppressed by the local authorities. The church-state relationship may be illustrated as follows:

Even after the death of Mao Tse-tung and the arrest of the Gang of Four in 1976, this state of affairs continued to exist. It was a totalitarian state which left no room for religion. The more open policy adopted by Ten Hsiao-p'ing after his return to power in 1977

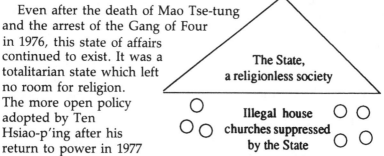

The State, a religionless society

Illegal house churches suppressed by the State

necessitated a reduction in the degree of religious suppression, but there was no change in the hard-line policy until April 1979.

F. During 1979-82 the state began to restore its soft-line religious policy and revive the patriotic organizations.

With Teng Hsiao-p'ing's return to power, as evidenced by the reform policies of the Third Plenum of the CCP's Eleventh Party Congress (December 1978), the Central Committee's United Front Work Department was re-established in March 1979.[42] This was followed by the re-establishment of the Religious Affairs Bureau in April of the same year. Simultaneously, the Chinese Communists began to restore their pre-Cultural Revolution soft-line policy of freedom of religious belief.[43] The Protestant church in Peking has allowed Chinese worshippers since April 1979.

In August 1979 the Shanghai Committee of the Three-self Patriotic Movement was reorganized. Former TSPM churches in larger cities, which had been closed down since 1966, started to reopen in September 1979. In February 1980, the Executive Committee of the TSPM National Committee held an "extended meeting" in Shanghai—the first since 1961. In October 1980, the TSPM held its third National Christian Conference in Nanking, and thereby formally reconstituted the defunct Protestant patriotic organization, the Three-self Patriotic Movement.[44]

However, at the Nanking conference another organization called the Christian Council of China (CCC) was formed. The TSPM has been described by its officials as a "mass political organization" whose function is to assist the government in implementing its religious policy and to educate the church to become patriotic. The role of the new council is to take care of ecclesiastical matters in the TSPM churches, such as Bible printing, theological education, Christian publications, and conducting fraternal visits with churches in other lands. In reality, however, the staffs of these two organizations are almost identical and they almost always meet jointly.

To the Peking government, the TSPM is a patriotic religious organization, but to church councils abroad, the CCC is a church body representing the church in China, and so the name Christian Council of China is used when TSPM leaders go abroad on goodwill trips.

As the TSPM and the CCC began organizing themselves at the provincial level in 1981 and at county level during 1982, they ran into conflicts with the numerous house churches that had been flourishing since 1970.[45] But in the countryside, house churches continued to grow in strength and number, though they had to operate as illegal entities, with their leaders subject to arrest. Yet they maintained their autonomy as Christian groups independent of state control.

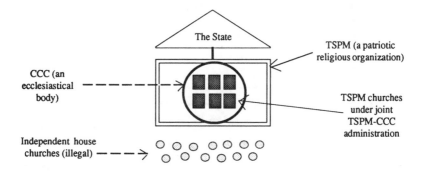

The situation of church-state relations during this period is illustrated by the diagram above.

G. During 1982-87, the state consolidated its control over all churches.

As stated earlier, the Party has worked out a comprehensive religious policy for the current transitional state of socialism, namely, the policy of "freedom of religious belief" as contained in Central Committee Document No. 19 of 1982 which was circulated to county level Party secretaries. To study this policy, the TSPM held an extended Executive Committee meeting in Peking in September 1982. Thereafter, the TSPM and the CCC, in concert with the local RAB offices, began to implement the "three designates" by urging existing house churches to join the TSPM/CCC.[46] A few of them joined, but the remaining majority refused to do so, preferring to preserve their own ecclesiastical autonomy in order to conduct their ministries according to the teachings of Scripture. Those who refused to comply came under pressure beginning in August 1982, and they experienced severe persecution from the latter part of 1983 until the end of 1984.[47] On the other hand, in those areas where there were no open churches, the local authorities complied with the believers' requests to restore their former churches.

In October 1984, the Party passed a "Decision on Reform of the Economic Structure."[48] This became the basis of a national program for economic reform, which included toleration of the urban market economy. As a result of this general relaxation of controls, the suppression of house churches was softened and eased off somewhat during 1985-86, and quite a few house church leaders who had been arrested during 1982-84 were released or had their sentences reduced. During this period, a number of independent house churches in the countryside joined the TSPM county committees, paid their annual dues, but continued to conduct their religious activities as before, keeping their ecclesiastical autonomy while submitting themselves to TSPM policies.

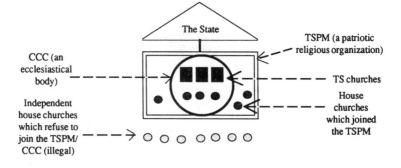

Still, the majority of house churches remained outside the TSPM. Hence, the church-state relationship during this period may be illustrated as in the previous illustration.

Concluding Observations

Church-state relations in socialist China since the founding of the PRC have been determined by the Chinese Communist Party. The Party took the initiative and dictated the terms for the existence of religions. Religious bodies, such as the Protestant church, were never given an opportunity to negotiate development of a mutually satisfactory church-state relationship. From the very beginning, independent Christian bodies representing the Protestant church, such as the National Christian Council of China, were gently pushed aside and later forced to dissolve themselves. The control of the state over Protestant Christianity was supreme and unquestioned.

From the very beginning, the Party set up its own body, the Three-self Reform (later Patriotic) Movement, to lead and direct Chinese Protestant churches, and designated it the spokesman for the Protestant churches. This control has never been relaxed. The TSPM may be seen both as the arm of the state controlling the church and the limit of state toleration of church affairs. The realm of the TSPM is the realm of legality, and that realm also defines the limits of religious freedom. Within that realm there is also socialist education for the clergy. The TSPM is more of a representative of the socialist state to the church than a representative of the church to the state. But in their propaganda, the TSPM and CCC claim to represent the Protestant church in mainland China. Perhaps they do represent the four thousand churches and the three million members under their administration; they certainly do not represent the more than fifty million believers who meet in at least two hundred thousand locations outside their control.

The relation of church and state in socialist China basically follows the pattern of state control of religions in traditional China. The parallel between the two is very obvious. (See diagram below.)

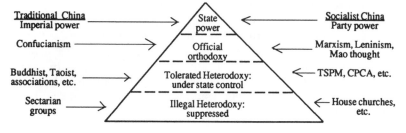

In the matter of state control of religion the present totalitarian socialist state inherited the position of the former feudalistic, imperial state. Hence, it may be said that current Chinese Communist religious policy is both totalitarian and feudalistic. If mainland China is to make any significant progress toward modernization and to develop any kind of authentic "spiritual civilization," its leaders will have to re-examine their current theories and practice regarding religion and make changes appropriate to a modern, developing and democratic society.

The response of the Chinese Protestant church to state initiatives may generally be described as passive. During the 1950-58 period, the majority of the nearly ten thousand Christian workers gave in under pressure; they signed the "Manifesto," accused their former co-workers, and joined the TSPM. Only a few chose the prophetic role of demonstrating their loyalty to Christ and they suffered for this. After 1958, those who remained in the Three-self churches accepted the leadership of the government in church affairs, but a number of faithful lay leaders began to develop underground meetings, accepting the consequences of civil disobedience for the sake of conscience.

During the Cultural Revolution, Christians were forced to confess Christ, and such pressure and concomitant suffering trained many believers for faithful witness in subsequent years. They learned from experience to be "gentle as doves and shrewd as serpents." They sought to witness Christ by living exemplary lives, to avoid confrontation with a hostile state, and to conduct an active program of evangelism and church building secretly. These principles have now become standing policies for the house church movement even after the death of Mao. There is no apparent conflict between TSPM pastors and the state. They have already accepted the leadership of the state in church affairs. Some do experience inner conflicts, but in order to conduct their ministries within the realm of legality, they have to confine themselves within the limits determined by the state. The house church leaders who choose not to join the TSPM, do so in order to express their singular loyalty to Christ in church affairs and to have the freedom to conduct evangelistic work.[49]

From the Christians' viewpoint, the basic issues in church-state relations in a socialist country like China are essentially three: (1) the question of leadership over the church: who leads the church, Christ or the state? (2) the question of evangelism: to evangelize or not to evangelize? (3) the universal character of the church: should a national church cut off its fellowship with the international body of Christ or not?

For mainland China, the above conflicts cannot be resolved until Peking abandons the view that its own ideology is orthodox while that of its competitors is heterodox. Second, until there is a genuine separation between the Party and the state according to law, the pattern of state control of religion can hardly be changed. Finally, until mainland China adopts a policy of ideological pluralism, Christianity cannot enjoy genuine freedom under the law. These, therefore, are future challenges for those who pray for China and who wish China well.

Endnotes

1. "Tsung-chiao tzu-you yu chi-pen-fa" [Religious Freedom and the Basic Law], *Ming-pao*, Dec. 5, 1986; Feb. 3, 4, 1987.

2. See Chao T'ien-end, "Tsung chung-kung Tsung-chiao cheng-ch'e k'an chi-pan-fa yu tsung-chiao tzu-you" [The Basic Law and Religious Freedom as seen from the Perspective of Chinese Communist Religious Policy], *Chiu-shih nien-tai* [The Nineties], No.206 (March 1987), pp.46-48.

3. The full text of Article 36 reads: "Citizens of the People's Republic of China enjoy freedom of religious belief. No state organ, public organization, or individual may compel citizens to believe in, or not to believe in any religion: nor may they discriminate against any citizens who believe in, or do not believe in, any religion. The state protects normal religious activities. No one may make use of religion to engage in activities that disrupt public order, impair the health of citizens, or interfere with the educational system of the state. Religious bodies and religious affairs are not subject to any foreign domination." For the Chinese text of the 1982 constitution, see *Chung-kuo shuo-ch'e* 1984 (Hong Kong: *Ta Kung Pao* [Oct. 1, 1984], p.4.)

4. For the full text of Document No. 19 in Chinese, see *San-chung-ch'uan-hui i-lai chung-yao wen-hsien hsuan-pien* [Selected Important Documents Since the Third Plenum] (Tientsin: *Jen-min Jih-pao Ch'u-pan-she*, 1982), pp. 1218-1240.

5. *Ibid.*, p.1226.

6. *Ibid.*, p.1230.

7. This term, "*san-ting*," is used in the various local Three- self Patriotic Covenants (*Ai-kuo kung-yueh*). See, for example, "Kuan-yu wei-hu cheng-ch'ang tsung-chiao huo-tung ti chueh- ting" [Resolutions on Maintaining Normal Religious Activities], published by the Yunnan Three-self Patriotic Movement Committee and the Yunnan Christian Council, March 29, 1982 (Circulated

locally).

8. Section 10 of Document 19 reads: "While we resolutely protect all normal religious activities, we must resolutely attack illegal criminal activites and anti-revolutionary destructive activites under the cloak of religion, as well as various superstitious activities which do not fall into the realm of religion, but which are harmful to the national interest and to lives and property of the people" *ibid.*, p.1235. Section 11 reads: "We must intensify our awareness, paying close attention to hostile foreign religious forces attempting to establish underground churches and other illegal organizations. Institutions where espionage activities are carried out under the cloak of religion must be resolutely attached" *ibid.*, p.1237.

9. Part of Section 11 of Document 19 reads: "International reactionary forces, especially imperialist religious forces, including the Vatican and Protestant missions will attempt to use all kinds of opportunities to conduct infiltration activities, seeking to return to mainland China. Our policy is to positively expand friendly international religious relations and, at the same time resolutely resist the infiltration of all hostile foreign religious forces" *ibid.*, p.1236.

10. See Ting-Kuang-Shun, "San-Chih tsai jen-shih" [Reunderstanding Three-Self], *Tien-feng*, new series, No. 14 (Feb. 1983), pp. 2-9.

11. The TSPM sent delegations to Hong Kong (March 1981), Canada and the U.S. (October 1981), Scandinavia (1982), Australia and New Zealand (March 1984), Japan (Sept., 1984), W. Germany, Hungary and Switzerland (November 1983), and India (February 1985).

12. This process can be observed in the consolidation of religious policy between December 1981, when consultation with TSPM leaders began, and December 1982, when the constitution was promulgated.

13. For a description of the inner workings of the RAB, see Chapter I of George Patterson's book, *Christianity in Communist China* (Waco, 1970) and Holmes Welche's *Buddhism Under Mao* (Cambridge, 1971), Chapter I. The source for both appears to be the same person.

14. For the Chinese original, see Section 7 of Document No. 19, *ibid.*, p.1231: "The task of these patriotic organizations is to assist the party and the government in carrying out the policy of freedom of religious belief, to help the broad mass of believers and religious personages to continuously raise their patriotic and socialist consciousness, to represent the legal rights and interests of the religions, to organize normal religious activities and deal with religious affairs. All patriotic religious organizations should accept

the leadership of the Party and the government, and Party and government cadres should become adept at supporting and assisting religious organizations in solving their own problems, and should not try to take over themselves."

15. This working relationship between the TSPM, the RAB and the Public Security Bureau is commonly known by Christians in mainland China who have gone through the experience of interrogation, but it is little known outside the mainland.

16. In a recent case, a woman evangelist was arrested by the Public Security Bureau on December 14, 1984 and charged with conducting anti-revolutionary activities. Her criminal activities were described as joining an illegal Christian organization (house church), participating in an evangelistic team to Szechwan, engaging in itinerant preaching, and developing churches, etc., activities which "deceived the masses and seriously disturbed social order." On December 14, 1985, the Bureau of Investigation moved her case to the district court. In the Letter of Prosecution, the investigator stated that the accused "by conducting illegal missionary activities and seriously influencing social order, and production order, has violated Article 158 of the Criminal Code of the PRC and so is guilty of the crime of disturbing social order." On January 28, 1986, the district court released her, citing sections 1 and 2 of Article 158 of the Criminal Code. These facts are taken from the certificate of court decisions given to the accused.

17. For studies on official Confucian orthodoxy, see Paul A. Cohen, *China and Christianity, The Missionary Movement and U.S. Growth of Chinese Anti-Foreignism, 1860-1870* (Cambridge, 1961), pp.3-60. See also Arthur Wright, *Buddhism in Chinese History* (Stanford, 1959), especially his section on the Sui period, pp.65-85.

18. For a description of the history of this control, see C. K. Yang, *Religion in Chinese Society* (Berkeley, 1961), pp.180-217.

19. See Searle M. Bates' unpublished paper on "Church and State in Traditional China," seminar on Modern China, Columbia University, November 1967, p.13.

20. For a fuller analysis of this debate on religion and anti-religious sentiment in the May Fourth era, see chapter III of my thesis, "The Chinese Indigenous Church Movement: Protestant Response to Anti-Christian Movements in Modern China, 1919-1927," Ph.D. thesis in Oriental Studies, University of Pennsylvania, 1986. See also Yu-ming Shaw, "Reaction of Chinese Intellectuals towards Religion and Christianity in Early Twentieth Century," in *China and Christianity* (Notre Dame Conference book, 1979), pp.154-183.

21. See the various responses of religious leaders to the article on religion in the Constitution, "Kuo-chia pao-hu cheng-ch'ang ti tsung-chiao huo-tung," *People's Daily*, July 3, 1982, p.4.

22. See Hsiao Hsien-fa [former director of RAB], "Cheng-ch'ueh li-chieh ho kuan-ch'e tangti tsung-chiao hsin-yang tzu-yu cheng-ts'e" [Correctly Understanding and Implementing the Party's Policy of Freedom of Religious Belief], *People's Daily*, June 14, 1980. This interpretation was repeated in a similar article in *Kuangming Daily*, February 18, 1985, the latest document on religious policy, which simply repeated what Hsiao said in 1980 and what was published in Document No. 19 of 1982.

23. For an account of the anti-imperialist propaganda in China by the CCP and the Socialist Youth League, see Jonathan Chao, *op. cit.*, pp.169-195. For original sources, see *Chung-kuo ch'ing-nien* (1924-1927 period); *Hsueh-sheng tsa-chih* (1923-1926); *Chueh-wu* (1924-1926); *Chung-kuo kuo-min-tang chou-k'an* (1924-25). For studies on the anti-Christian movement during this period, see Ka-che Yip, "The Anti-Christian Movement in China, 1922- 1927, with Special Reference to the Experience of the Protestant Missions," Ph.D. dissertation, Columbia University, 1970 (later published as a book).

24. See Ch'en Tu-hsiu's denunciation of missions in *Hsiang-tao*, No. 22 April 1923), p.160, and the Socialist Youth League instructions to the students to struggle against the church in *Chung-kuo Ch'ing-nien*, No. 34 (June 7, 1924), p.12.

25. See Mao Tse-tung, "Mao-tun-lun" [On Contradiction] (1937), *Collected Works of Mao* (Chinese text), I, pp.279-283. For a recent application of the united front theory, see Li Wei-han, "Mao Tse-tung ssu-hsiang chih-tao hsia ti Chung-kuo t'ung-i-chan-hsien" [Chinese United Front under the Direction of the Thought of Mao Tse-tung], *People's Daily*, December 17, 1983, pp.4-5.

26. For a fuller historical study on how the Chinese Communists sought to control the Protestant church, see George Patterson, *Christianity in Communist China* (Waco, 1970), Richard Bush, *Religion in Communist China* (Nashville, 1969), and Jonathan Chao, ed., *Chung-kung tui-Chi-tu-chiao ti cheng-ts'e* (Chinese Communist Policy towards Christianity) (Hong Kong: Chinese Church Research Center, 1983).

27. Protestant participants in the first CPPCC were: Wu Yao-tsung, Teng Yu-tzu, Chao Tsu-chen, Chang Hsueh-yen, and Liu Liang-mou; see "Wuo-men tsan-chia jen-min cheng hsieh hui-i ti ching-kuo" [The process by which we joined the People's political Consultative Conference], *T'ien-feng* No. 128 (Oct. 1, 1949), pp.1-4.

28. For a brief study of this initial period, the beginnings of the

Three-self Movement, see Yang Yang, "San'tsu' yun-tung wei-yuan-hui ch'an-sheng ti Ching-Kuo" [The Process by which the 'Three-self' Movement Committee was Born], *Chung-kuo yu chiao-hui*, No. 28 (May - June 1983), pp.2-10. Original sources from *T'ien-feng* are listed in the notes.

29. For the original text, see "Chung'kuo Chi-tu-chiao tsai hsim Chung-kuo mu-li ti t'u-ching," *T'ien-feng*, Nos. 233-234 (September 30, 1950), p.2. For a recent reprint of the document, see Jonathan Chao, *op. cit.*, pp.271-272. For the English translation of this document, see Wallace Merwin and Francis P. Jones, eds., *Documents of the Three-self Movement* (New York, 1963), pp.19-20.

30. On April 15, 1950, *T'ien-feng* reported that the National Conference was postponed, and on August 5 it was reported that the conference was cancelled.

31. For a list of the original forty signatories, see *T'ien-feng*, Nos. 233-234, p.3.

32. On the formation of the Preparation Committee of the Anti-America, Aid-Korea Three-self Reform Movement, see *T'ien-feng*, Nos.262-263 (May 8, 1951), pp.30-31. For an analysis of the events of this period, see Yang Yang, "Cheng-fu tao-yen-hsia ch'an-sheng ti k'ung-su yun-tung" [The Accusation Movement Produced under the Directorship of the Government], *Chung-kuo yu chiao-hui* No. 30 (Sept.-Oct. 1983), pp.1-10.

33. For articles and reports on local accusation meetings conducted in Shanghai, see *T'ien-feng*, No.264 (May 19, 1951). pp.1-5.

34. Yang Yang, "San-tsu-hui ti fa-chang ho kung-ku" [The Development and Consolidation of the Three-self Movement], *Chung- kuo yu chiao-hui*, No.31 (Nov.-Dec., 1983), pp.11-20.

35. On the accusation of Wang Ming-tao, *T'ien-feng*, Nos. 471-495 (July-Dec. 1955), see also Richard Bush, *Religion in Communist China*, Nashville, 1970, pp.214-215.

36. See Yang Yang, "Ta-lu chiao-hui lien-ho ting-hsing" [Mainland Churches Unite and consolidate the Form], *Chung-kuo yu chiao-hui*, No. 32 (Jan.-Feb. 1984), pp.7-14. Original sources are cited from *T'ien-feng*.

37. On the discussion of the class nature of preachers, see *T'ien-feng*, No. 559 (Aug. 25, 1958), pp.27-30. See also Shen I- fan, "kai-tsao tsu-chi, tso lao-tung jen-min ti yi-yuan" [Reforming Myself and Becoming One of the Labouring People]. *T'ien-feng*, No. 556 (July 14, 1958), p.10. In Shanghai, for example, after the first political study session, the TSPM had church leaders write a "Self-reform Covenant." See *T'ien-feng*, No. 557 (July 28, 1958), p.15.

38. See "Chiangsu sheng Chi-tu-chiao san-shih ai-kuo tai-piao

hui-i kuan-yu hsiao-mieh hun-luan hsien-hsiang ho i-ch'ieh fei-fa-huo-tung ti ch'aug-i-shu" [A proposal by the conference of the Three-self Patriotic Movement of Chiangsu Province concerning eliminating the phenomenon of confusion and illegal activities] *T'ien-feng,* No. 553 (June 2, 1958), p.12.

39. For an analysis of religion during the Cultural Revolution period, see Wan Wai-yao, "Wen-ko shih-nieh" [Ten Years of the Cultural Revolution], *Chung-kuo Yu chiao-hui,* No. 12 (Sept.-Oct. 1980), pp.13-14. For a Protestant believer's description of what Christians went through in those days, see *ibid.,* pp.2-4.

40. See Fr. L. Ladany "Religion," *China News Analysis,* No. 935 (Oct. 5, 1973), pp.1-3.

41. See Jonathan Chao, "The Witness of a Suffering Church," *China and the Church Today* 5:5 (Sept.-Oct. 1983), pp.8-11. See also David Adeney, *China: the Church's Long March* (Ventura, 1985).

42. The CCP Central announced the restoration of the United Front Work Department, Ethnic Work and Religious Affairs Bureau on March 16, 1979. See *People's Daily,* March 19, 1979.

43. The initial announcement was made in an editorial "response to questions from readers" which appeared in the *People's Daily,* March 15, 1979.

44. See J. Chao, "An Analysis: Christian Conference Meets," *China and the Church Today,* 2:6-3:1 (1981), pp.1-2.

45. See "TSPM Wants You, But Do You Want Them? Apparently Dong Yang House Churches Say No," *China and the Church Today* 4:4-5 (1982), pp.3-4.

46. On the decisions made at the Peking Conference, see the report of the Second Meeting of the Third Conference of the Three-self Patriotic Movement Committee in *T'ien-feng,* New series, No. 13 (Jan. 30, 1983), p.1. See also the speech by Ch'iao Lien-sheng, Director of the Religious Affairs Bureau, given at the September Peking TSPM conference. There he urged the implementation of the "three-designates" policy. *Ibid.,* p.13.

47. See the "Chart on Political and Church Developments in 1983," in *Chung-kuo yu chiao-hui,* No. 32 (Jan.-Feb. 1980), pp.21-22.

48. See "Chung-kung chung-yang kuan-yu ching-chi ti-chih kai-ke ti chueh-ting" [Decision on the reform of economic structure by the Central Committee of the Chinese Communist Party], *People's Daily,* Oct. 21, 1984.

49. See Jonathan Chao, "Christianity in the Totalitarian State," *China and the Church Today,* 5:1 (Jan.-Feb. 1983), pp.7-11.

The Promise of Adolf Schlatter

W. Ward Gasque

Vol. XV, No. 2 (June 1979):5-9

The work of Adolf Schlatter (1852-1938) is not well known in the English-speaking world, although he authored scores of books, including commentaries on every book in the New Testament and hundreds of essays, rivaling both Ferdinand Christian Baur and Rudolf Bultmann for bulk and erudition. Only one of his books and one essay have been translated into English.

In his day, Schlatter made a profound impression on the life of the church in Germany and German-speaking Switzerland. During my sabbatical year in Europe in 1975-76, I met a number of elderly German and Swiss pastors who had studied under Schlatter. It soon became clear that the sometimes North American impression of the German church as totally controlled by very liberal theology is a caricature. There are many exceptions, and no one has outdone Schlatter in leading at least a segment of the church in a much more positive direction. His popular commentary on the New Testament, for example, still in print, is widely read by both lay people and pastors. His major commentaries have also been kept in print or recently reprinted.

Academic Neglect of Schlatter

In the academic theological community, his impact has not been as profound as upon the church, for until very recently, his work had generally been neglected by academia. Possible reasons for this have been suggested:

(1) He was somewhat isolated, generally eschewing controversy, and refusing to get directly involved in the current heated debates, to stoop to name-calling or to become embroiled in polemics. Rather,

he went about his scholarly research and taught in a quiet manner, attempting to offer a positive alternative to the radical theology of his day. Even in his writings, he is somewhat aloof from the controversies, though the content often speaks very appropriately to key theological issues of the time.

(2) Schlatter was overshadowed by the developing dialectical theology of the 1920's and 30's, which divided into the two very diverse but extremely influential streams of German-speaking theology, one led by Karl Barth and the other by Rudolf Bultmann. In a sense, the dialectical theologians stole much of Schlatter's thunder since in some ways he is similar to Barth—at least manifesting some of the same theological concerns—but ultimately Schlatter was overshadowed by him.

(3) The school of Bultmann has dominated German academic theology in the past several decades, being generally hostile to the attempt to combine the most rigorous New Testament historical criticism with an equally profound commitment to the church's faith. Rather than separating between faith and history as the Bultmannians insisted, Schlatter sought to bring the two together very intimately.

(4) There may be a fourth reason. Various German writers have indicated that his style was quite difficult to understand. Personally, I find most German theologians difficult to understand! Someone whose mother-tongue is German would be better judge of whether Schlatter is any more difficult than normal.

Recent Interest in His Work

There is, however, a good deal of evidence to suggest that this academic neglect of Schlatter is coming to an end. First, in 1972, Robert Morgan, a young British scholar, published a monograph entitled *The Nature of New Testament Theology,* which included two essays thought to sum up the key issues in the scholarly debate about the essence of New Testament—one by Wilhelm Wrede and the other by Schlatter. Morgan's introduction was a lengthy, programatic essay bringing Schlatter's name to the attention of the English-speaking world and underlining his significance by including him with Wilhelm Wrede whose theological importance had been universally recognized.

Second, Peter Stuhlmacher of Tübingen, the successor to Ernest Käsemann one of the last of the influential generation of Bultmann disciples to hold a New Testament chair in Germany, has regularly drawn attention to the significance of Schlatter (See, for example, his *Historical Criticism and the Theological Interpretation of Scripture* 1977).

More recently, in *New Testament Studies* (24 1978, 433-46), he contributed an essay on Adolf Schlatter's interpretation of Scripture. Although one cannot simply push the clock back, repeating Schlatter's interpretation of Scripture as though it were fully adequate for the contemporary situation, one can find a basic rapprochement to the current hermeneutical impasse in which the historical-critical method seems to have broken down and become of very little value in the task of constructive theology.

This year Stuhlmacher has led his students in an in-depth seminar study of Schlatter's work. Doubtlessly there will result from this seminar many other papers, and possibly monographs, giving further indication of a revival of interest in Schlatter.

As for the English-speaking world, the time seems ripe for the translation of the more significant Schlatter commentaries. More importantly, some young aspiring biblical scholar or systematic theologian should write a major work on Schlatter, introducing him and his thoughts to English-speaking readers. Here is a Ph. D. thesis which is bound to find a publisher!

According to Stuhlmacher, Schlatter was "theologically the most important figure in the faculty of Protestant Theology at Tübingen in the first third of this century." In the opinion of Morgan (who finds a greater spiritual kinship with Wrede than with Schlatter) he was "the greatest conservative of the generation before Bultmann...perhaps the only 'conservative' New Testament scholar since Bengel who can be rated in the same class as Baur, Wrede, Bousset and Bultmann." Bishop Stephen Neill says: "There are certain writers of the past—Augustine, Calvin, Bengel, Westcott, Schlatter—to whom we shall always turn with gratitude for the timeless insights that are to be found in their writings." In view of these comments, it seems high time for the Christian community at large to wake up and take notice of Adolf Schlatter.

Schlatter's Life

What about the man? Schlatter was born in St. Gallen, in German- speaking Switzerland in 1852. His father was a pharmacist and Baptist lay preacher. His mother remained a member of the local Reformed Church in Switzerland, though she was united with her husband in a common commitment to Christ and involvement in the revival movement of the time. This dual home background gave Schlatter an ecumenical attitude in his relationship with Christians and in his concern for the church. In school, he first was interested in natural science and philosophy. Through the influence of his sister, he decided to study theology but not without a great struggle, for to him it represented a challenge to his own faith. Could he maintain a positive, evangelical faith while at the same time studying academic theology? Looking around him in many of the university settings of the day, it did not seem very likely. His sister managed to convince him that he might not lose his faith if he studied theology. It was this desire to go into theology that he later regarded as the time of his conversion to Christ.

From 1871 to 1875, Schlatter studied theology in the Universities of Basel and Tübingen. From 1875 to 1880, he was a pastor. At the request of Swiss revival leaders, in 1880 he qualified himself as a lecturer in the Theological Faculty in Berne and taught there for eight years. He first taught Old Testament, then New Testament, and then Dogmatics. From the time of his work in Berne, he was attacked on two sides. On the one hand, some revivalist friends labelled certain of his views concerning the historical nature of the New Testament as too critical and really incompatible with his commitment to supernatural religion and to the Christ of faith. On the other hand, his liberal colleagues in the Berne Faculty of Theology thought he was what we would call today "an unreconstructed fundamentalist." This early battle on two fronts set the pattern for his future work. Besides pointing out the inadequacy of liberal theology, Schlatter constantly had to defend to fellow conservative Christians the idea of New Testament study as a historical discipline.

In 1888, Schlatter accepted a call to Greifswald, Germany, where he joined Hermann Cremer, Lutheran theologian and author of the New Testament theological dictionary that became the prototype of the later monumental project founded by Gerhard Kittel. In 1894, he took a newly established chair of theology at Berlin, a call attempted to appease church leaders outraged by Adolf Harnack's denials of basic Christian doctrine, for Harnack had publicly denied the truth of the Apostles' Creed. Schlatter lectured here for four years, but reading between the lines one senses he was unhappy at Berlin, having been placed in the awkward situation of championing orthodoxy in a university where this view was by no means popular.

In 1897, Schlatter was called to Tübingen University to fill a similarly created chair, which he himself named "Chair of New Testament." It presumably was flexible; before accepting the job, he got the authorities to agree that he could teach Dogmatics as well as New Testament. He spent the rest of his academic life here in Tübingen, becoming professor emeritus in 1922, though he continued to give lectures for eight more years since he did not have great confidence in his successor.

Schlatter's writings are voluminous. They include, *inter alia: A thorough-going examination of the concept of Faith in the New Testament* (1885); a two volume *Theology of the New Testament* (which first appeared in 1909); major works on Christian dogma and Christian ethics; a history of the primitive church (E.T., *The Church in the New Testament Period*); elementary commentaries on the whole New Testament (*Erlaevterungen zum Neuen Testament*); and a series of very learned commentaries on Matthew (1929), John (1930), Luke (1931), James (1932), Corinthian Epistles (1934), Mark (1935), Romans (1935), Timothy - Titus (1936), and I Peter (1937). His two greatest commentaries are his works on Matthew and Romans (entitled *Gottes Gerichtigkeit.* "The Righteousness of God"). He also wrote many other historical, theological and devotional books and essays. Schlatter died on 19 May 1938, shortly after the end of his 86th year.

Schlatter's Theology

When one considers Schlatter's interpretation of Scripture, one is impressed by the difference between him and many of his contemporary theologians. Schlatter makes an interesting comparison to B.F. Westcott and J.B. Lightfoot in nineteenth century England, who were successful in opposing the radical views of New Testament criticism then being expounded in Germany. (See my essay, "Nineteenth Century Roots of Contemporary New Testament Criticism," in *Scripture, Tradition and Interpretation*, ed. W.W. Gasque and W.S. LaSor, 1978, 146-56.) In Schlatter's day the dominant tide of academic theology was certainly not orthodox or what we know as evangelical.

Schlatter stands in contrast to many of his contemporaries in a variety of ways. First, he was preeminently a "self-conscious Christian theologian" (Morgan, p.27). He approached his study of the Bible as a theologian, a *Christian* theologian. For him, as Stuhlmacher points out, "his Christian faith, his biblical and historical work, and his theological effort towards an understanding of Christ and faith appropriate to the present day are quite inseparable." He was unwilling to agree that one should, or could, radically separate the biblical historian's work from that of the preacher, or the two from the theologian's. A temporary methodological distinction may be made between these three tasks: The basic, foundational work of biblical-historical is methodologically different from the task of systematic theology and from preaching in that you step back and look at the text, conscious of your own presuppositions and refusing to impose them upon the text; but it is only a temporary stepping back. Ultimately one must lead to the next; historical criticism must lead ultimately to proclamation and theologizing upon the basis of the text, each informs the other in its responsibility. In a celebrated essay, Schlatter passionately rejected the methodological atheism of the historical criticism represented by Troeltsch and others of his day. The assumption of totally objective historical research is, he argued, false. Those who think they are most free from presuppositions in their biblical study are in fact the most determined by them. It is only when we recognize our own presuppositions that we are set free and are able to do a careful "objective" examination of the text. This does not mean, of course, that Schlatter suggested one should allow one's theological presuppositions to determine one's exegesis. That is, he did not simply look at the text and decide that it meant what he already believed it would mean. No, on the contrary, careful exegesis which is based on a historical observation should always provide the foundation for dogmatics. However, neither dogmatics nor historical exegesis are independent of one another; rather, they mutually inform one another.

Schlatter comes to the text as a Christian theologian. He is aware of his own presuppositions, yet he looks at the text objectively and historically to see what is really there, aware that his discoveries may cause a readjustment in his previous theological position. So he turns from the text back to his theology to revise it in the text's light and then again from his theology back to the text in an attempt to carefully examine it. Scripture and theology are thus organically inter-related. One does not determine the other totally; his theology in particular does not determine the historical exegesis but instead the results of his careful historical examination of Scripture is the foundation for his developing theological system. As he works Schlatter is quite conscious of being a theologian with a definite faith commitment. He refuses to feign some sort of independent, objective approach that is quite apart from theology.

Second, Schlatter focused on the Bible as a whole. He was not a *Neutestamentler*, a New Testament specialist in a narrow sense; though he was in another sense. Even though his most important work was done on the New Testament, he did not ignore the Old Testament. Early in his life he wrote a Bible introduction which he constantly revised until his death. In his commentaries there is something strikingly different from other technical commentaries for there is only occasional, rather than detailed, reference to secondary literature. Instead, the pages are filled with appeals to the biblical text. He compares Scripture with Scripture, very carefully and thoroughly, observing parallels and showing how one passage illuminates another. He is essentially a biblical theologian and in both his theological work and his exegetical work he emphasizes the unity of Scripture.

Schlatter recognized and gave due weight to the diversity of Scripture. He insisted on historical interpretation, and it is this historical dimension that lays adequate stress on the real theological diversity in Scripture. However, in spite of diversity among various writings and traditions, there is an over-riding unity, a common view of Christ which links the whole together. Therefore, Schlatter did not limit himself to biblical studies, he also moved into the areas of Christian ethics and systematic theology.

Third, Schlatter was one of the earliest German scholars to recognize the distinctive Jewish character of the New Testament, i.e. that the New Testament documents found their home in Palestinian Judaism and also, when Paul moved out into the Roman world, in the synagogue of the Hellenistic world. It is easy to discern a latent anti-Semitism in German theology from the Enlightenment onward, particularly behind some of the critical biblical work from the period immediately preceding Schlatter and continuing to the present. For example, we can see that F.C. Baur generally regards Judaic things in a very negative fashion. Also, Wellhausen, the influential Old Testament critic, has recently been scored for his not only implicit but very explicit anti-Semitism, running straight through his writings as well as his personal life. In my understanding, there is not a trace of this in Schlatter. Quite the contrary, he stresses very positively the Jewish setting of the Gospels. He is the perfectly at home not only in Josephus and inter-testamental literature but also in the Rabbinic writings, and he applies his research results to his New Testament study. Being at the beginning of his discipline he does not sift his materials as critically as more recent scholars do in terms of dating and the historical origin of Rabbinic ideas, but he is certainly moving in the right direction. He pioneered the approach, later taken up by Dahlman, Jeremias and a host of contemporary New Testament scholars, which fills out New Testament historical background and brings to bear on the text not only Old Testament material but also first-century and subsequent Jewish literature as it carried down traditions already present in Jesus' time.

Fourth, Schlatter placed primary emphasis on the biblical text rather than on hypotheses about it. He was very skeptical of "fantasies," as he called them, which sought to recreate the historical background on the basis of very little historical data and no very definite textual reference. This concern for the primacy of the text is clear in his historical/exegetical work and in his theologizing.

He warned both conservative and liberal students of Scripture against attempting to force the biblical teaching into their own mold. On the one hand, the liberals attempted to rule out the basic message of the New Testament by definition and therefore were unable to hear its authentic voice because of this "methodological atheism." The orthodox, on the other hand, often appropriated Scripture's teaching too quickly into the confines of received theological categories without attempting serious historical study and careful exegesis. Schlatter was really arguing with both, trying to gently nudge them into more positive directions. As a result, of course, he was misunderstood to some degree by both, yet he did have a profound influence on many conservatives. In liberal theology, he saw an antipathy to the fundamental ethos of the New Testament teaching. As a result, rather than observing carefully what was in the text, the historical criticism had to develop fantastic hypotheses to explain away biblical data, such as the elaborate and unlikely theories to "explain" the doctrine of the resurrection. On the other hand, he saw conservatives frequently assuming they already understood the biblical text without having taken the pains to carefully consider it.

In his writings, Schlatter constantly calls the reader to look at "the facts" of Scripture in terms of the historical connections. The fundamental obligation of the theologian- exegete is observation of the text, an obligation Schlatter contrasts to observation with "imagination" or "fantasy." An anecdote often told of Schlatter in connection with his appointment in Berlin is that he was asked by a churchman on the committee, "Herr Schlatter, do you stand on the Bible?" He responded, "Nein, I stand *under* the Bible." This ancedote characterized the perspective of Schlatter in regard to Scripture.

In contrast to the fundamentalists who stood, in a sense, *on* the Bible, Schlatter always gave primacy to the data of Scripture not prejudging but standing *under* the Bible, allowing it to shape his views. This was also in contrast to the liberals, who tended to stand *over* Scripture, judging it from the perspective of "modern" and "enlightened" thinking.

Fifth, Schlatter was conscious of doing this New Testament work in the context of the church and, as an exegete, of being a servant of Jesus Christ. This does not mean he allowed the church or its dogmas to dictate the terms of his historical and exegetical work, much less to dictate the results. Rather, he realized he had a pastoral responsibility, that he was not an independent historian simply concerned with historical data, but a servant of Christ entrusted with a sacred calling to study and teach the Word of God.

Schlatter's Pastoral Concern

His pastoral concern for his students is possibly his greatest legacy. He influenced these students not only in the classroom but also outside it by giving regular systematic InterVarsity-type Bible readings. Stuhlmacher writes, "With regard to Schlatter's theological and pastoral work, it seems to me particularly worthy of note that to my knowledge he never brought his students, or his other hearers and readers, to contempt of their faith or their loyalty to the church. Rather, he continually encouraged them to abide by their faith and in their love for the church." This does not mean he failed to raise questions. The reaction of some conservative brethren makes it clear that he often raised awkward questions. But he raised them from within the Christian community, and they were intended to strengthen one's faith through looking at Scripture deeply and asking questions so as to hear the Word of God authentically. He had a profound understanding of the importance of both academic theology and the potential pastoral role of the academic theologian.

We see his pastoral concern also in his ministry to the laity. He never wrote exclusively for the world of scholarship, though he certainly wrote books that were quite technical. He always wrote with the ordinary believer in mind, and he wrote many articles and books primarily for the lay man or woman who was concerned with Scripture study. He was concerned to use his great learning in the service of Christ for the building up of Christ's body.

Finally, his stance as a servant of Christ, studying Scripture in the context of the church, gave to his work a devotional quality, even in his most technical commentaries. Today, we tend to make a very strong dichotomy between the academic and the devotional. This has not been the church's historical view of theology until relatively modern times. Great theologians have not normally distinguished between their intellectual work and their spiritual work, between rigorous theology and devotion to God. That is as it should be, and certainly that is what one finds in the work of Adolf Schlatter.

A Key to Biblical Interpretation

Was there a theological key to Schlatter's biblical interpretation? Was it the Creed? A particular brand of Christianity—reformed theology, revival Christianity or pietism? Was it a doctrine of verbal inspiration or inerrancy? It was not any of these. Not that he did not affirm the Creed, or cannot be theologically pegged in some degree, or did not have a theory, or at least a doctrine, of inspiration. Rather, the focal point of his theology was simply the conviction that Jesus was "the Christ of God," a phrase that he uses frequently, and that Christ himself is the heart of the New Testament, indeed, of the Bible. A very simple conviction: that Jesus is the Christ of God and that he is the heart of the Scripture. He was committed to the belief that Jesus was already in his earthly life Son of God and Messiah. This was not (as Wrede had argued) something assigned to him at a later date. The Jesus of the New Testament was not the product of the church's faith but, rather, a historical given. To put it in other words, the church's faith was the product of Jesus, who himself was the Christ of God. This conviction was not merely an inheritance from his pious parents or from a revivalistic faith. Rather, it was a conclusion he continued to hold because it did the best justice to the historical data of Scripture in its first-century setting. He did not, of course, hold this because he became a Christian through historical research. Rather, as a historian he found convincing evidence for Jesus being the Christ and the reality of the resurrection in Scripture.

It is this, Schlatter was convinced, which gives the certainty that God is speaking to us in the Bible, not a theory of inspiration or detailed doctrinal statement. We see the reality of God in the fact of Jesus. This principle was the centre and determining factor in Schlatter's approach to Scripture. Stuhlmacher has noted the end of the Bultmannian school's domination over contemporary New Testament scholarship as marking the end of an era. With the later Bultmannians, biblical research, which had lost its moorings in the church and its faith, tended to run aground. There are many signs today, however, of a new vitality in biblical studies. Particularly evident is the renewed concern for a theological understanding of Scripture and a return of Schlatter's view that Jesus was in fact the Christ of God and is himself the hermeneutical key to the New Testament. There are definite signs of this in Germany, and I think I see a few signs of this in other parts of the world.

In the past decade there has been a spate of writings from a variety of perspectives pointing to the current impasse in the historical-critical task. Historical criticism is supposed to give assured results, yet the results obtained are so very diverse, and there seems to be such a gap between the results of historical research and the church's faith. How can this be overcome? Stuhlmacher is representative of various scholars who seek to bridge this gap by taking cues from Schlatter. It may be that in rediscovering Adolf Schlatter, New Testament scholarship will begin to recover its true faith—faith in Jesus and faith in its true task, the service of the church through the elucidation of the text.

The Literary Apologetic of Flannery O'Connor

Julie Lane Gay

Vol. XIX, No. 4 (December 1983):27-32

The fiction of Flannery O'Connor has been appreciated in the literary world since the publication of her first novel *Wise Blood* in 1949.[1] This appreciation culminated in O'Connor's being awarded, posthumously, the National Book Award in 1971 for *The Complete Stories*.[2] Today she is widely recognized as being a modern master of the short story. Among Christian readers, however, appreciation of O'Connor's fiction has been much slower in coming. Although O'Connor was far more explicit about the apologetic intention of her fiction than were other twentieth century Christian writers such as C. S. Lewis and J. R. R. Tolkien, evangelical Christians in particular have generally been reluctant to accept her work as genuinely Christian.

Why this reluctance? It is undoubtedly due to the confusing nature of the stories. Their dark and shocking events make it difficult to see that they were indeed written from a Christian perspective. Many readers, in fact, insist that unless they already knew, from other sources, that O'Connor was a Christian, they would never figure it out from the stories themselves. O'Connor's essays, as published in *Mystery and Manners*[3], and her letters, collected in *The Habit of Being*[4], make the point quite clearly that she is a Christian, and writing with a Christian view of the world. Nevertheless, many readers sense an inexcusable discrepancy between O'Connor's intentions and the actual effect of her stories on the reader. Such readers, for example, feel that O'Connor's story "The River" is simply a parody of fundamentalism, and her story "Good Country People" merely an attempt to mock the naively Christian clientele of sharpster Bible salesmen. Understandably, these readers find themselves wondering what would prompt a Christian to write such stories.

This discrepancy between O'Connor's intentions as a Christian writer and the effect of the stories on their readers is the subject of this essay. My purpose is not to convince O'Connor's doubtful readers that there is no discrepancy; it is rather to shed enough light on O'Connor's work so that her intention, the value of her work, and the nature of the "discrepancy" may be more clearly seen. I hope to provide this insight by looking at three facts about O'Connor's intention and her personal life, and by considering as well three additional aspects of O'Connor's work within the realm of fiction in general and "Christian fiction" in particular. Before explaining these factors, however, it is important first to give a brief introduction to O'Connor's work.

O'Connor had no special blueprint for "writing Christianly." She wanted not only to entertain but to stimulate. O'Connor wanted to make her readers reevaluate both their perception of the world and their sense of control over it. "My audience is the one who thinks God is dead," she wrote to a friend: and it was this Godlessness she wanted to attack.[5] Though her plots vary, her stories tend to take place in the deep South, usually among lower-class rural people. Her stories are typical fiction in that they build gradually to a climactic event which is followed by a resolution; but O'Connor, as a Christian, attempts to shape that climax and resolution so that it provides spiritual insight. Furthermore, O'Connor's fiction often teeters between comedy and tragedy. For example, when Hulga Hopewell in "Good Country People" gets her wooden leg stolen after being duped by a phony Bible salesman, the reader wants both to laugh, and to cringe at the situation.

O'Connor's stories are upheld by two pillars, the first and most striking of which is shocking or terrible events. Polish immigrants are run over by tractors, little girls are murdered by their grandfathers, and women are gored by bulls. As O'Connor explains:

> ...In my own stories I have found that violence is strangely capable of returning my characters to reality and preparing them to accept their moment of grace. Their heads are so hard that almost nothing else will work. This idea, that reality is something to which we must be returned at a considerable cost, is one which is seldom understood by the casual reader but it is one which is implicit in the Christian view of the world.[6]

O'Connor uses shock and violence to grab the attention of her characters and to undermine their world-view—and she hopes to have the same effect on the reader. By using violence and shock to make her characters vulnerable, she makes them look at spiritual realities in a new light. As she insists, "Some kind of loss is usually necessary to turn the mind toward faith. If you're satisfied with what you've got, you're hardly going to look for anything better."[7]

The second pillar of O'Connor's stories is the offer of grace that is extended to the protagonist, usually immediately after the climactic moment. O'Connor understands this offer of grace as an action of God, inviting men and women back to himself and into his love for them, despite their previous rejection. Within the story, the offer of grace is the resolution to the climax; it is not simply "stuck in" to make a point. O'Connor assumes that once the character is left vulnerable and in need of help he will be able to recognize this offer of grace, this ever-pursuing love of God. Some characters accept it, while others reject it. As O'Connor explains:

> Storywriters are always talking about what makes a story "work." From my own experience in trying to make stories "work," I have discovered that what is needed is an action that is totally unexpected yet totally believable, and I have found that for me, this is always an action that indicates that grace has been offered...My subject in fiction is the action of grace in a territory held largely by the Devil.[8]

The phrase "offer of grace" sounds abstract and ethereal, but O'Connor makes such offers bluntly down to earth. In "A Good Man is Hard to Find," for example, the offer of grace comes shortly after a grandmother watches her family being murdered and realizes that her death will probably be next. Only in the face of the shocking immediacy of death does she realize that she is unable to control her circumstances, and, more important, does she realize her sinful state and her need for God. "Why, you're one of my babies!" she says to the murderer, reaching out to him in a gesture which both acknowledges their similar sinful state, and prompts him to shoot her.[9]

Unfortunately, as most of O'Connor's readers are well aware, the climactic, violent events usually seem to overshadow the offer of grace. In stories such as "A Good Man is Hard to Find" readers are likely to be so overwhelmed by the violence that they miss the offer of grace, but bold in her use of violence, and herein lies much of the confusion over her work. One critic, Carol Schloss, comments on this ambiguity:

> For as talented as O'Connor is at rendering the violent or profound moment, she is unable or unwilling to dramatize

states of consciousness, to take her readers inside the mind
of the perceiving characters and show them what exactly has
been experienced...For whatever reasons, O'Connor was
manifestly hesitant to "tell" enough to make textual
meanings unambiguous to the nonreligious...Her readers
did not "get" the theological overtones—her method of
indirection often prohibited inferring the intended
theological meaning of the fiction.[10]

O'Connor was so hesitant to move out of her stories' naturalistic
confines, and so steeped in her Catholic theology, that she
sometimes doesn't seem to present grace with enough gusto to move
the readers' focus *past* the violence onto the subsequent offer of
grace. Addison Leitch, a theologian, once wrote "Flannery
O'Connor insists that there is grace at work at some crucial point in
all her stories. I must confess that sometimes the grace is very hard
to find."[11]

With this background of O'Connor's work, and the apparent
discrepancy between her intention and her effect, it is possible to
proceed to the factors that may shed light on the difficulties. The first
set of factors revolves specifically around O'Connor and her
intentions. For gaining insight into O'Connor herself gives the
reader a better vantage point from which to critique her work.

One factor crucial to understanding O'Connor is her desire to
write about the supernatural Presence in human life without writing
sermons or fantasy. She wants to make grace and mercy be present
without making her readers leave the realm of everyday life.
Unfortunately, this is not easy to accomplish. As O'Connor writes,

The problem with the novelist who wishes to write about
man's encounter with God is how he shall make the
experience—which is both natural and supernatural—
understandable and credible to his reader. In any age this
would be a problem, but in our own it is a well-nigh insur-
mountable one. Today's audience is one in which religious
feeling has become if not atrophied, at least vaporous and
sentimental.[12]

O'Connor wrestles with this problem and avoids both fantasy and
sermonizing. But one result of her avoidance is that she is
sometimes too subtle for some readers. A few stories, such as "The
Artificial Nigger," make the supernatural meanings of the story
quite explicit. But for the most part, O'Connor's Christian readers
must remember that a story is not a sermon, and O'Connor is
primarily committed to telling a good story. They should remember
also that it is not Christians, but "the Godless" who are the intended

audience for her work.

A second characteristic of O'Connor is that she cares immensely about vivifying the fallen state of man: she sees "fallenness" as something the modern world has increasingly succeeded in forgetting about. But perhaps O'Connor is too successful. She sometimes presents fallenness so vividly that the reader fails to relate to it. O'Connor sometimes does not enable her readers to identify with her characters with enough depth, so that when the sin or the violence has occurred, the reader thinks, "That could have been me." When a woman allows a tractor to run over a Polish farm worker whom she has not had the guts to fire, the reader is too able to distance himself, to become judgmental rather than empathetic. (It is an open question whether this problem is due to O'Connor's vividness or her readers' squeamishness.)

O'Connor usually uses terrible events to shock both the character and the reader, and while she often succeeds in waking the character into spiritual awareness, she sometimes shocks the readers to the extent that she alienates them from the character. Of course there are exceptions: some readers see—or at least *sense*—exactly what O'Connor is trying to elucidate. And from a Christian perspective, O'Connor's efforts are honourable: partial success is adequate: for genuine portrayal of the fallen state of man can be an unpopular subject, and understandably results in unpopular fiction.

The third aspect of O'Connor to be understood is personal—her southern environment, and her Catholic faith. These two factors are vital to understanding her writing; in fact for the reader who does understand them, the discrepancy between purpose and effect will be greatly minimized. In "The River," for example, the reader acquainted with the southern, rural way of life will know that O'Connor is not parodying fundamentalism or the backwoods preacher, but instead writing a story about the seriousness of baptism, using as raw material unexaggerated pictures of Southern Protestantism. Similarly, in "A Temple of the Holy Ghost," there is a great deal that simply reflects the southern way of life. The Wilkie brothers, the county fair, the depressing heat, and Alonzo Myers aren't objects of ridicule, as some readers might think; they are simply what O'Connor saw living around her.

In a similar way, O'Connor's Catholic view of grace manifests itself in the stories, for O'Connor was as comfortable a resident of Catholicism as she was of Georgia. O'Connor believed (in her words), that "Grace, to the Catholic way of thinking, can and does use as its medium the imperfect, purely human, and even hypocritical."[13] She saw it as perfectly natural that grace came through the most mundane and sinful experiences. To O'Connor, the offer of grace that comes to Thomas in "The Comforts of Home" immediately after he has shot his mother is just right; without the experience of being so horrified at what he has done, Thomas would never have known how rotten he was and how much he needed God's grace. Yet to the Protestant way of thinking this sacramental view, in which God's love comes through the elements of everyday life, is very confusing. Protestants tend to look for grace to be offered to men in their moments of greatest virtue and deserving, not in their moments of greatest sin. As a result, they aren't as likely to recognize the appearance of grace in O'Connor's stories.

With these three factors about O'Connor in mind—her desire to write about the action of God within the realm of everyday life; her desire to stress the fallen nature of man, and her use of both southern and Catholic ways of thinking—it becomes possible to understand why she wrote the way she did. Some readers might ask how O'Connor defends the confusing impact of her stories. To such questions she gave different responses in different circumstances, but the following is one particularly eloquent response to the question, "Why write that way?"

He [the novelist] may find in the end that instead of reflecting the image at the heart of things, he has only reflected our broken condition and through it, the face of the Devil we are possessed by. This is a modest achievement, but perhaps a necessary one.[14]

While I agree in theory that this is a danger, I don't think it adequately characterizes O'Connor's fiction. In general, the devil in her stories is too unspecific to be recognized as the same powerful spirit who is in opposition to the Almighty triune God. There are simply not enough clues for us to make such a deduction from the stories themselves.

The second way of gaining an understanding into the discrepancy that seems to colour O'Connor's work is to step back and look at that work within the realm of fiction in general and "Christian fiction" in particular. While all three of the following considerations are fairly applicable to other works of fiction written from the Christian perspective, they are especially pertinent to a consideration of O'Connor.

The first consideration is the fact that to understand O'Connor's work as she intended might demand both literary and theological sophistication. This is of course true of many other works: *Ulysses*, *Paradise Lost* and *The Brothers Karamazov* are not any less significant because of their complexity, or because of the theological or literary knowledge assumed by the writer as a prerequisite to their understanding. Not all literature is accessible to everybody, even if it is Christian literature. Similarly, understanding O'Connor may demand some knowledge of how to respond to work that is prophetic in nature. O'Connor explains why some fiction demands a prophetic response:

> Prophecy, which is dependent on the imaginative and not the moral faculty, need not be a matter of predicting the future. The prophet is a realist of distances and it is this kind of realism that goes into great novels. It is this realism that does not hesitate to distort appearances in order to show a hidden truth.[15]

Like the word of the Old Testament prophets, O'Connor's message of man's fallenness and desperate need for God is not a popular one. Many readers undoubtedly *want* to misunderstand it. Readers, especially in this age of instant communications, are used to being spoon-fed. Christian readers especially must remind themselves of the value of learning, and more importantly, of thinking. It is inexcusable to limit ourselves to works which don't require thought.

Second, from a Christian perspective there is a great deal of value in O'Connor's work even though it is not of evangelistic value. O'Connor has the rare capacity to flesh out spiritual mysteries that are difficult to conceptualize. The very fact that she goes to such extremes to emphasize that man will not recognize his need for God until he has first recognized his own fallenness is a testimony to O'Connor's spiritual wisdom. Richard Lovelace, the church historian, suggests that "Among contemporary fiction her work gets closer to the Augustinian Calvinistic sense of the grandeur of God and the depravity of man and the glory of God than anyone else.'[16] Becky Pippert, the author of a popular book on evangelism, *Out of the Salt Shaker*, values O'Connor's ability to show spiritual mysteries for still other reasons:

> O'Connor shows the stupidity in thinking we've gotten so good that you don't have to believe in evil, especially in *Wise Blood*...she also has the message of hope, that you can't flee the love of God; it's always pursuing us up till the moment we die, as we see in her stories so often. She also shows the absurdity of fleeing the God-image in us.....[17]

O'Connor is of value for what she says about Christianity, even if she does not always draw unbelieving readers to faith. People like Richard Lovelace and Becky Pippert frequently draw upon O'Connor's stories to elucidate points in their lectures and writings.

A story like "Revelation," for example, is a classic example of
illustrating a basic but confusing fact of the Christian faith: the
totally fallen but totally cleaned status of a Christian. In Mrs. Turpin
we see the living embodiment of this paradox when she stands in her
garden and yells to God:

> "What do you send me a message like that for?...How am
> I a hog and me both? How am I saved and from Hell too?"[48]

Last, and most important, readers need to reevaluate what they
expect of fiction writers who are Christians. Fiction should never be
a disguise for a tract. Fiction writers who write from a Christian
viewpoint may have an evangelistic effect, but if their primary intent
is evangelistic, the author has lost sight of the main purpose of
fiction. It is, of course, advantageous if fiction written from a
Christian perspective confirms a Christian view of the world, but
such confirmation is not fiction's primary intention. Throughout
history, as well as now, Christians have sometimes tried to isolate
themselves from various works of literature, including some works
which are of great value despite their secular author. For example,
O'Connor has often been excluded from the reading lists of Christian
schools because of the violence of her stories. This is most
unfortunate. O'Connor's stories are great literature regardless of
their explicit Christian content. Readers, especially Christian
readers, need to read good literature in order to understand their
culture, and they need to understand their culture in order to bring
Christ to it. Deane Downey, chairman of the division of humanities
at Trinity Western College, wrote in a recent issue of *Christianity
Today* words which are particularly applicable to the work of
Flannery O'Connor:

> Good literature engages us as whole beings, directing our
> attention to both the awesomeness and the awefulness of
> the human condition. It is not limited to nice stories about
> people who inevitably find God, always overcome evil and
> selfishness in themselves and others and live happily ever
> after...Therefore, the believer who desires to be informed
> about society cannot outrightly reject an exposure to its
> literature.[19]

O'Connor may not write what some people want to read, but both
as a storyteller and as a Christian she has important things to say.
The discrepancy between her Christian faith and the harshness of
her stories may be confusing to some. But if one understands her
intentions and her southern, Catholic background, one can gain a
great deal from O'Connor's fiction. Critics of society and prophets
are rarely popular: but someday most people will wish they had

understood and heeded the words of such prophets.

Endnotes
1. *Wise Blood,* New York: Farrar, Straus and Giroux, 1949.

2. *The Complete Short Stories of Flannery O'Connor,* New York: Farrar, Straus and Giroux, 1971.

3. *Mystery and Manners,* New York: Farrar, Straus and Giroux, 1971.

4. *The Habit of Being,* New York: Farrar, Straus and Giroux, 1979.

5. *The Habit of Being,* p. 92.

6. *Mystery and Manners,* p. 112.

7. *Ibid.,* p. 159.

8. *Ibid.,* p. 118.

9. *The Complete Stories,* p. 132

10. Carol Schloss, *The Dark Comedies of Flannery O'Connor,* Baton Rouge: Louisiana State University Press, 1980, p.101.

11. Addison Leitch, "The Christian Novelist," in *The Christian Imagination,* ed. by Leland Ryken, Grand Rapids: Baker Book House, 1981, pp. 195-196.

12. *Mystery and Manners,* p. 161.

13. *Habit of Being,* p. 389.

14. *Mystery and Manners,* p. 168.

15. *Ibid.,* p. 179

16. Interview with Richard Lovelace, April 16, 1983.

17. Interview with Becky Pippert, April 14, 1983.

18. *The Complete Stories,* p. 56.

19. "Refiner's Fire"in *Christianity Today,* April 8, 1983, pp. 61-62.

The Reconciliation of Parties in Conflict: The Theory and Application of a Model of Last Resort

Preston Manning

Vol. XXI, No. 1 (March 1985):10-18

The subject of this paper is "peacemaking"—in particular the reconciliation of parties estranged and alienated from one another by seemingly irreconcilable differences.

The need for more effective approaches to the resolution of deep-seated conflicts is painfully evident when one considers such situations as the following:

1. The increasing number of homes and families being pulled apart by the conflicting interests of husbands and wives, parents and children.

2. The declining productivity and social utility of industrial sectors and economies torn by labour/management strife and warring special interests.

3. The increasing difficulty of establishing and maintaining political unity in nation states such as Canada due to conflicting interests—in Canada's case, the conflicting interests of federalists and provincialists, nationalists and continentalists, easterners and westerners, southerners and northerners, socialists and free enterprisers, anglophones and francophones.

4. The pain, suffering, and hopelessness produced by the seemingly intractable conflicts and between Protestants and Catholics in Northern Ireland, Arabs and Israelis in the Middle East, blacks and whites in South Africa, and warring tribal groups in the majority of black African states.

5. The great gulf between rich nations and poor nations, and between the rich and the poor within particular nations, regions, and communities.

6. The threat to world peace and the personal well-being of millions of human beings posed by the seemingly irreconcilable differences between the great powers—alienated from one another by profound ideological differences and armed to the teeth with nuclear weapons.

A variety of strategies or "models" are available to guide disputants and peacemakers who want to achieve reconciliation, or at least a reduction of tensions, in such situations. These include:

1. "Separation" models, in which disputants go their separate ways, and conflict is reduced or eliminated by absence of contact. The "peace" of the parties is achieved at the price of the relationship.

2. "War" models or "self-assertive" approaches in which disputants "fight" until the strongest, or smartest, or most persistent, prevails. The conflict is "resolved" (temporarily, and usually with much bitterness) when one party is able to impose its will on the other.

3. "Super-power" models characterized by authoritative interventions whereby an authority superior in strength to the disputants enforces settlements. The "peace and harmony" of totalitarian states (where "peace" has been achieved at the expense of freedom) is a variant of this approach, as is the concept that world peace can be achieved by establishing a supranational authority with "clout" (e.g. a strengthened United Nations with military capability).

4. "Transactional" models, which may be economic (e.g., bargaining in the market place), or interpersonal ("You're OK, I'm OK"). Where the transactional approach is utilized, conflict resolution is achieved through mutually advantageous trade-offs and compromises.

5. "Jurisprudential" models in which disputants submit differences to judicial authority or independent third parties for binding arbitration.

6. "Educational" models in which disputants, with the aid of a sympathetic counsellor, are urged to seek accommodation through improved "understanding" of their own interests and those of the other side.

7. "Surrender" models in which interests and positions are surrendered by one or the other of the disputants "for the sake of peace" or in the hope of "surviving to fight another day."

The theory and application of the above models to conflict

resolution is the subject of a considerable body of literature. Some of these models have demonstrated their usefulness and effectiveness to the point where they have become part of the "standard tool-kit" and conventional wisdom of peacemaking in our time.

Most of us are aware, however, of conflict situations where the alienation of the parties is so profound, or where the conflict has become so institutionalized and self-perpetuating, that the conventional strategies for peacemaking are simply inadequate. Unfortunately, many of the most serious conflicts fall into this category.

In such circumstances, the gulf between the ideal of peacemaking and the adequacy of the strategies available for achieving peace becomes so great and so self-evident, that the ideal is often abandoned as impractical and unattainable.

The purpose of this paper is to outline a "model of last resort" for the resolution of deep-seated conflicts—a model which is especially applicable to conflict situations where previous peacemaking attempts have failed, and where the achievement of peace is still important enough to satisfy one more effort at high cost.

This "model of last resort" is based on generalizations drawn from an empirical exercise in reconciliation which has been part of human knowledge and experience for almost twenty centuries.

The author's personal experience with alternative approaches to conflict resolution has been gained primarily from the conduct of studies and assignments as a management consultant to energy companies, government agencies, and interest groups in the Province of Alberta. These studies and assignments have included:

- Attempts to reconcile energy company interests with those of public policy makers.
- Attempts to reconcile electric utility company interests (Alberta has four major electric utilities) in the context of long range inter-utility planning.
- Attempts to reconcile the interests of resource developers, local communities and native people in relation to mega-projects (in particular heavy oil plants, highways, and pipelines).
- Attempts to reconcile certain ideals of democratic socialism with those of "free enterprise" political ideology, under the label of "social conservatism."
- Exploration of alternative ways of reconciling federal and provincial interests through the development of a transactional model for predicting the outcomes of federal-provincial conferences.
- Attempts to ascertain "the public interest" in certain regulatory contexts and public policy issues, where the public interest is defined as "that course of action which best reconciles a number of legitimate

but conflicting private and societal interests."

Like many others involved in conflict resolution, the author has long been familiar with the general thesis and historical context of the "model of last resort" described hereafter. This model, however, is usually presented in a context and in language having no direct and strategic connection with the conflict situations in which the author is most frequently engaged. The discovery that this ancient model is not only relevant to such conflict situations but offers new hope of achieving peace in situations where conventional strategies have failed, has proven to be a source of both encouragement and practical guidance.

The Model of Last Resort

I. The Situation

In this empirical situation there are two parties, the second a creation of the first, who originally enjoy a harmonious, productive, and mutually satisfactory relationship. Their relationship rests on certain commonalities despite the fact that they differ significantly in origins, character, power and resources.

Under the influence of a third party hostile to both, the second party commits an act which breaks the relationship with the first party at a vital point.

The reactions of the first party, and subsequent actions by the second party, reinforce the original separation until the alienation becomes complete, and self-perpetuating.

Reconciliation under these circumstances requires that certain wrongs be righted. But the second party, who initiated the alienation, finds himself incapable of righting these wrongs by reason of their impact on himself (his nature) and his resources.

As the situation deteriorates, it is the first party which consistently attempts to restore the original relationship and initiates a variety of actions to effect a reconciliation. These are largely unsuccessful, due to the absence of a positive response to these initiatives by the second party.

The second party also attempts in his own way to take steps to renew a relationship with the first party, but the approaches taken always fall short of what is required and only deepen the alienation.

The most substantive of the reconciliation attempts made by the first party is jurisprudential in character, involving the use of law as the primary instrument of reconciliation. After a lengthy and involved attempt to effect reconciliation by this approach it becomes evident that the effort will not be successful. (This aspect of the case is instructive regarding the limits to the use of law as an instrument of reconciliation.)

Finally the first party initiates a "strategy of last resort." The strategy is extremely costly. Since it recognizes the freedom of the second party, this strategy of last resort cannot "guarantee" reconciliation of the two parties. What it does achieve, however, is the establishment of a channel whereby complete and lasting reconciliation can be effected if the second party chooses to utilize it.

While the "model of last resort" does not guarantee peace in every instance, it does guarantee the possibility of peace.

II. The Players

The key players involved in the application of the "model of the last resort" are briefly described hereafter. They include:

1. The Initiator (the first party)
2. The Alienated Community and Its Members (the second party)
3. The Mediator
4. The Agent of the Initiator
5. The Advance Man
6. The New Order and Its Members
7. The Opposition
8. The Agents of the Opposition
9. The Traitor
10. The Organizer

The objective of the model of last resort is not merely to arbitrate the differences of the two parties, in the hope of finding some mutually agreeable compromise. Rather the objective is far more ambitious—i.e., to truly reconcile the two parties—to restore the relationship to its original wholeness—by dealing conclusively with the root causes of their alienation. Indeed, the objective goes beyond the restoration of the original relationship, to the establishment of a new relationship superior to the original.

The first of the two parties may be referred to as the *Initiator* because it is this party who initiates the reconciliation effort. In the empirical situation from which the model of last resort is derived, the Initiator is singleminded in interests and purpose and is by far the stronger of the two parties.

Despite the fact that it is the second party who has initiated the breakdown of the relationship, it is the first party (the "offended" rather than the "offending" party) who initiates the reconciliation process.

The motive of the Initiator in launching the reconciliation effort is difficult to describe in technical terms. The Initiator's motivation has its roots in an exalted vision of the potential of the second party, a great longing for a restored relationship, and a preparedness to make enormous sacrifices in order to realize that vision and achieve the desired relationship.

The second of the two parties may be referred to as the *Alienated Community and Its Members.* In the empirical situation from which the model of last resort is derived, the alienated community is the weaker of the two parties. The alienated community is heterogeneous in its composition and interests so that if reconciliation is to be achieved with the Initiator it must be achieved by dealing with the relationship of each member of the alienated community to the Initiator on an individual as well as a collective basis.

To effect the reconciliation process defined by the model of last resort, four additional players or instrumentalities are required. These may be referred to as *the Mediator, the Agent of the Initiator, the Advance Man, and the New Order and Its Members.* It should be noted that each of these instrumentalities is drawn from or related to one or the other of the principal parties; none are "independent" of the principal parties to the dispute.

The *Mediator* is without question the central figure in the reconciliation process defined by the model of last resort. This Mediator is not a distant or impartial "judicial" mediator. Rather, he embodies or integrates in his person certain key characteristics and interests of *both* parties, and is so positioned as to be able to communicate effectively with both. There is no doubt, however, that the Mediator is ultimately accountable to the Initiator and acts on his instructions.

The Mediator is positioned, encouraged, supported and assisted in his mediating role and activities by the *Agent of the Initiator.* During the early phase of the mediation process, the Agent is virtually invisible to the Alienated Community and its Members. His meetings with the Mediator are held in secret. Later, when the Mediator's work is finished, the Mediator introduces the Agent to the New Order and its Members, and the supportive work of the Agent becomes more visible.

The transition of the Mediator from a position of obscurity as a member of the Alienated Community to his position as Mediator is facilitated by the work of the *Advance Man.* The Advance Man, also supported by the Agent of the Mediator, "prepares the way" for the Mediator and introduces him as Mediator to the Alienated Community.

Initially the work of the Advance Man and that of the Mediator are very similar, so that there is the possibility of one being mistaken for the other. This confusion is avoided by the termination of the

Advance Man's activities shortly after the work of the Mediator begins.

The work of the Mediator is educational, organizational and substitutional (this will be elaborated upon in considerable detail in the next section). As the Mediator's work proceeds, he is successful in establishing a new and positive relationship between individual members of the Alienated Community and himself, which in turn facilitates the establishment of a new and positive relationship between individual members of the Alienated Community and the Initiator.

These individuals become members of a *New Order*. This New Order is in effect a community of reconciled individuals within the Alienated Community. An increasing proportion of the Mediator's time and effort is devoted to the strengthening and training of the New Order and its members.

The reconciling initiative of the Initiator, and the reconciling activity of the Advance Man, the Mediator, the Agent of the Initiator, and the New Order are systematically and inexorably opposed by a personage who may be referred to as *the Opposition*.

The Opposition is a contemporary of the Initiator who is implacably opposed to the Initiator and his approach to reconciliation. The Initiator and the Opposition are competing for the allegiance of members of the Alienated Community, the Opposition hoping to prevent any reconciliation of members of the Alienated Community to the Initiator.

The *Agents of the Opposition* include instrumentalities similar to the Agent of the Initiator, as well as members of the Alienated Community who are inspired and encouraged by the Opposition to oppose the whole reconciliation process, in particular the work of the Mediator.

In the empirical situation from which the model of last resort is derived, the most vigorous Agents of the Opposition are recruited from those members of the Alienated Community who favour alternative approaches to the reconciliation process represented by the Mediator, rather than from those who are simply indifferent to reconciliation or hostile to the Initiator. The Opposition is also successful in recruiting a disillusioned member of the New Order, *the Traitor*, to assist his Agents in attempting to bring the work of the Mediator to a halt.

The members of the Alienated Community are only dimly aware, if at all aware, of the larger designs and interests of the Initiator and the Opposition. For the members of the Alienated Community, it is the claims and activity of the Mediator which constitute the immediate reality and which they must decide to accept or reject.

The work of the Mediator culminates in an act which is accepted by both the Initiator and the members of the New Order as fulfilling the pre-established terms and conditions for the reconciliation of the parties.

The Mediator then departs the Alienated Community, and it is the members of the New Order, in association with the Agent of the Initiator, who continue the process of reconciliation "in the name of," "in the spirit of," and "after the example of" the Mediator.

The New Order's understanding of the work of the Mediator, and the further development and expansion of the New Order, is greatly facilitated by the emergence of *the Organizer*—a former Agent of the Opposition who becomes a member of the New Order and one of its most effective leaders.

III. The Process

Figure I is generalized flow diagram[1] of the reconciliation process employed by the model of last resort.

Figure I shows the key functions performed in the empirical case from which the model of last resort is derived, in order to achieve the objective of reconciliation. These key functions include:

1. Prior efforts to achieve reconciliation.
2. The establishment by the Initiator of terms and conditions for

Figure I: Simplified Version of the Model of Last Resort

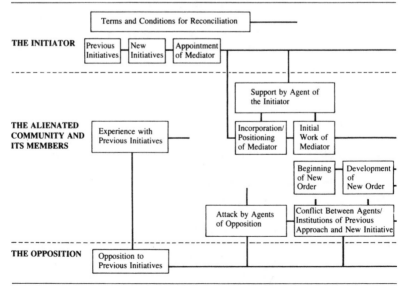

an "effort of last resort."
3. The decision to initiate action.
4. The appointment and incorporation of the Mediator.
5. The positioning of the Advance Man and Mediator in the Alienated Community.
6. The public disclosure of the Mediator ("going public" with the mediation process).
7. The initial work of the Mediator, including:
   (a) Announcement of the prospects for a new relationship.
   (b) Involvement in specific situations.
   (c) Presentation of credentials.
   (d) Maintenance of communications with the Initiator.
   (e) Description of the New Order.
   (f) Recruitment of the initial members of the New Order.
8. Continuous but discreet relations between the Mediator and the Agent of the Initiator.
9. Development of the New Order and its Members, including:
   (a) Listening and observing.
   (b) Lessons in communications.
   (c) Liberation from past practices.
   (d) Organizing for action.
   (e) Lessons in self-sacrifice.
   (f) Closer relations with the Mediator and one another.

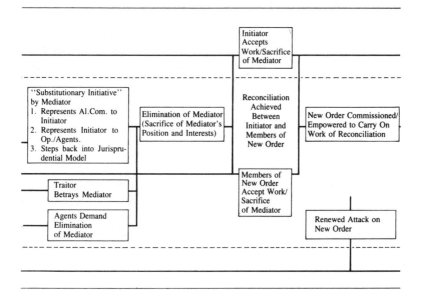

(g) Promises for the future, including introduction to the Agent.
10. Increasing contact with, and resistance from, the Agents of the Opposition.
11. Final positioning of the Mediator to achieve reconciliation.
   (a) Positioning relative to the Initiator (requires a "substitutionary initiative").
   (b) Positioning relative to the Opposition and his Agents (requires a "substitutionary initiative").
12. Elimination of the Mediator.
13. Return of the Mediator to the Initiator.
14. Temporary return of the Mediator to the New Order.
   (a) Commissioning of the New Order to carry on the work of reconciliation.
   (b) Provision for members of the New Order to meet directly with the Agent of the Initiator.
15. Departure of the Mediator.
16. Public disclosure of the Agent of the Initiator, and empowering of New Order to carry on work of reconciliation.
17. The reconciliation of the parties.
18. Further development and expansion of the New Order.

IV. The Principles (A Summary)

The following principles or guidelines for reconciliation efforts based on the model of last resort are obtained by generalizing from the empirical situation.

1. Model is applicable where there have been previous reconciliation attempts (especially jurisprudential actions) and these have failed. In fact, the model requires a prior reconciliation attempt in order to be operationalized.

2. Objective is to create a new relationship between the parties superior to the original relationship, rather than merely to arbitrate or achieve a compromise.

3. Reconciling action is initiated by the "offended party" rather than the "offending party" and must be properly motivated (see previous discussion).

4. The Initiator establishes terms and conditions which the reconciliation effort must satisfy. The Mediator is not free to "do whatever must be done to achieve reconciliation."

5. The reconciliation action must be consistent with the character of the Initiator and previous approaches to reconciliation taken by the Initiator.

6. The reconciliation approach is persuasive but non-coercive, respecting the freedom of the members of the Alienated Community

to accept or reject the reconciliation initiative.

7. The reconciliation approach must be capable of being employed and continued by reconciled members of the Alienated Community.

8. Terms and conditions of reconciliation include a requirement that the "root causes" of the alienation of the parties be dealt with

9. Mediator is *not* independent of the parties to the dispute but is intimately related to both and "internalizes" the conflict between them. Mediator has a "conflict of interest."

10. Incorporation and positioning of the Mediator is the most time-consuming aspect of the reconciliation process.

11. The most direct and vicious attacks of the Opposition occur during the incorporation and positioning period when the Mediator is most vulnerable, and when the Mediator deliberately renders himself vulnerable by taking his "substitutionary initiative."

12. The most dangerous Agents of the Opposition are those drawn from, and loyal to, the institutions established by the previous reconciliation attempt.

13. The Initiator generally presents only "one face, one voice" to the Alienated Community. The Advance Man leaves the scene shortly after the Mediator is disclosed, and the Mediator departs before the Agent becomes visible.

14. Mediator intervenes in certain situations to demonstrate the character of the Initiator and his desire for the reconciliation, according to the dictum, "As the Initiator would act in this situation, so acts the Mediator."

15. The Mediator is willing to sacrifice his own position and interests in order to create a New Order (set of relations) which will continue and complete the reconciliation process.

16. The support and guidance of the Agent of the Initiator is essential to the survival and work of the Mediator and the New Order.

17. The principal point of entry into the New Order is an invitation to interested members of the Alienated Community to put their confidence in the Mediator and his work.

18. Members of the Alienated Community first enter into a positive personal relationship with the Mediator and this leads to membership in the New Order and a restored relationship with the Initiator.

19. Members of the New Order are carefully prepared for the departure of the Mediator and the acceptance of personal responsibility for carrying on his reconciling activity in direct association with the Agent.

20. The relation of the Opposition to the Initiator is characterized

by a "perverse dialectic" whereby the Opposition strives to twist the positive initiatives of the Initiator to negative ends, and the Initiator strives to convert the negative attacks of the Opposition into positive means. The Opposition and its Agents have an essential (even though negative) role to play in the reconciliation process.

21. The final positioning of the Mediator requires a "substitutionary initiative" whereby the Mediator represents the Alienated Community (in its offending characteristics) to the Initiator, and represents the Initiator to the Opposition on the vulnerable ground of the previous reconciliation attempt.

22. The Mediator positions himself with respect to the Initiator and the Agents of the Opposition in such a way as to produce reactions which satisfy the terms and conditions for reconciliation.

23. The model of last resort calls for the elimination of the Mediator (sacrifice of the Mediator's position and interests).

24. The elimination of the Mediator (the sacrifice of the Mediator's position and interests) is voluntary but opposition-induced, and satisfies the terms and conditions of reconciliation established by the Initiator.

25. The reconciliation of the parties is achieved when the Initiator and the members of the New Order both accept the claim that the work and sacrifice of the Mediator has satisfied the terms and conditions of reconciliation.

26. In order for the members of the New Order to be convinced that the work and sacrifice of the Mediator has been effective and acceptable to the Initiator, evidence is required to demonstrate that this is in fact the case. This evidence is provided in the temporary return of the Mediator to the New Order after his elimination, and the sending of the Agent of the Initiator to the New Order.

27. The work of reconciliation among the remainder of the Alienated Community by the members of the New Order is carried on "in the name of," "in the spirit of," and "after the example of" the Mediator.

28. Members of the New Order become Mediators themselves— willing to sacrifice their own positions and interests, at the direction of the Agent and after the example of the Mediator, for the sake of achieving the reconciliation of others to the Initiator and harmonious relations among themselves.

29. The implementation of the reconciliation strategy employed by the model of last resort is extremely costly. The costs are not equally distributed among the parties, but are borne primarily by the Initiator and the Mediator.

V. The Constraints
The reconciliation process embodied in the model of last resort is subject to certain limitations.
1. Scope.
While the process is profound in its strategic dimension and particularly applicable to intractable situations which have defied treatment by other approaches, it is not unlimited in scope. For example, this model does not achieve reconciliation of the Initiator and the Opposition.
2. Voluntary Nature.
As previously mentioned, this model respects the freedom of the participants. It does not require the Initiator to violate his own character for the sake of peace. The Mediator is a volunteer, not a conscript. And the process does not compel compliance nor impose reconciliation on members of the Alienated Community, who remain free to accept or reject the work of the Mediator and the New Order.
3. Costliness.
Reconciliation achieved by the model of last resort is extremely costly both to the Initiator and the Mediator. The model is only applicable therefore to situations where the Initiator values reconciliation very highly and where a Mediator can be found who is prepared to sacrifice his own interests and standing for the sake of reconciling the parties in conflict.
4. Susceptibility of the Model of Last Resort to Perversion.
In the model of last resort, the *modus operandi* of the Opposition is to utilize the instrumentalities of the previous reconciliation attempt to frustrate the new initiative.

Even after the new initiative is successfully launched, the Opposition continues to attack it—seeking to twist and pervert the instrumentalities of the new initiative toward negative ends just as he was able to twist and pervert the previous reconciliation attempt.

The history of the empirical case indicates that the model is indeed susceptible to a wide range of such perversions—the Opposition enjoying frequent success in corrupting the New Order and misdirecting its reconciling activities.
5. Inapplicability of Model to Situations Which Are Not Completely Analogous to the Empirical Situation.
There is evidence that the original members of the New Order believed the reconciliation process of the model of last resort was in some way relevant and applicable to relations between husbands and wives, economic classes, and racial groups (in particular, Jews and Greeks).

One obvious objection to the applicability of the reconciliation process of the model of last resort to conflict situations in such cases is the contention that the positions of the two parties in the empirical case were unique. In particular, it would appear that "all the right" was on the side of the Initiator, and "all the wrong" was on the side of the Alienated Community. In real life disputes, however, it is rarely the case that all the right or all the wrong is exclusively on one side. It may be argued therefore that the model of last resort, in its empirical form, is of limited relevance to most contemporary conflict situations.

The allegation is a serious one, which in fact may severely limit the application of the model. However, in most contemporary conflict situations, one or both of the parties *contend* that most of the right is on their side and that most of the wrong is on the other side. It is suggested that where this situation prevails, the model of last resort is indeed applicable, with the onus of "initiating" reconciliatory action resting upon that party which *considers* itself to be primarily in the right.

VI. Strengths and Potentials of the Model of Last Resort.

Notwithstanding these constraints, the model of last resort is an extremely powerful model.

The fact that the literature embodying its premises has appealed to people of every class, educational background, nationality, and generation over a period of twenty centuries is at least one measure of its capacity to command attention. The model of last resort has a cultural base in much of the Western world.

Another source of strength and potential of the model lies in the fact that its implementation does not require the prior consent of both parties. The strategy of the model can be set in motion by one party to the dispute, provided that party is prepared and able to play the role of Initiator.

A third source of strength and potential of the model is its unconventionality. The key players—in particular the Initiator, Agent of the Initiator, Mediator, and New Order—do not behave in the conventional manner of participants in a dispute. The strategy followed by these players is unanticipated by the other side—its unpredictability being a key element in its success.

A fourth source of strength and potential for application is the fact that the model "feeds on" past failures. It is particularly fitted to "hopeless disputes" where reconciliation has been previously attempted but not achieved.

Finally, there remains the question as to whether or not some yet imperfectly understood explanation of reality exists which posits a "process" for the reconciliation of conflicting interests in the same way that the models of nuclear physics suggest a process for unleashing atomic energy or the models of the life sciences suggest processes for accomplishing "healing" in living organisms.

The original members of the New Order came to believe that the "model of last resort" as understood and experienced by them was in fact *the fundamental process* whereby the author of the universe accomplishes the ultimate reconciliation of all things. From this perspective, the strength and potential of the model of last resort may be regarded as "infinite."

Endnote

1. In the author's field of expertise, functional flow diagrams such as this are often utilized to describe and analyze historical events and processes, or to guide the implementation of strategic plans. In the latter case, an objective (such as the reconciliation of parties A and B) is first specified. All the tasks or "functions" which must be performed in order to achieve the objective are then identified, assigned, and related (for example, in series or in parallel) one to the other. The requisite functions are ultimately organized and discharged in such a fashion as to achieve the objective, subject to given time, cost, and other resource constraints.

To Fight a Losing Battle Victoriously—A Personal Comment

Philip G. Ney

Vol. XVI, No. 4 (December 1980):5-8

Introduction

Today Christians are being forcefully faced with the old, yet ever-present issue of how to fight a losing battle victoriously. There are so many critical social issues that conscientious Christians must confront. Wanting to win, but knowing that the tide is against them, they become desperate in their efforts, often forgetting that in fighting the issue so strenuously, they are wounding people. Christ, when he died, demonstrated that it is possible to fight a losing battle and be victorious.

Experience

At two recent international Christian conventions, I found the format depressingly similar to any other medical convention. At the Continental Congress of the Family, the message was clearly "the ship of family life is sinking," yet the behaviour was that of people serenely travelling on smooth water. Why is there such expression of tremendous concern, which results in so little effective action? Whenever an action was suggested, it was to provide another major program or institution, effectively eliminating any real personal responsibility or any interpersonal contact.

At the International Congress of Christian Physicians in Singapore, I was distressed by the apparent crass indifference of the North American doctors to the desperate needs of the people. While most shook their heads in horror at the poverty and desperation, some went on buying expensive gems and even making fun of the tour guide's inability to communicate clearly in English. We visited

Bangkok, which has all the signs of morally defeated Saigon. People there are desperately trying to find the greatest pleasure in the little time remaining them. Is it possible the Christian physicians aren't disturbed, or are they so disturbed they cannot put their intentions into useful action?

Working with the pro-life movement, I became aware that the national executive is embarrassed by the very right-wing members. These rightists want to fight and win regardless of what they do to their opposition. Many of them have insulted honorable citizens and politicians.

I am continually saddened by the many friends who are struggling with tottering marriages. It appears that they can't or won't fight this growing trend where forty-eight percent of American marriages will end in divorce. Among Christians also there is the growing tendency to give up and go their own separate hedonistic ways, then justify it by saying it is best for the children.

Conviction

These experiences are related to each other; I am convinced that, as world moral values rapidly decay, there will come an apathy which allows any kind of interpersonal injustice. When it is possible and even easy for Christians to accept a break-up of built-in guiding principles that counter worldliness, then the salt has gone from the earth. When they shake their heads piously and either do nothing or fight to win by wounding, then they have lost the courage to die.

One of the best indications of social decay is the increasing acceptance of transgressing basic social taboos. Once taboo and instinct were able to restrain man in his most suicidal and homicidal rages. Man's God-given instincts have kept him from totally destroying his own species. Now we have socially sanctioned feticide, there is a growing rate of infanticide. The killing of small children by parents is now one of the leading causes of infant death.

Evidence indicates there is a correlation between infanticide and feticide. Parents have, for many generations, threatened children with "I'll kill you, you little so-and-so" or "if you don't stop that, I'll wring your bloody neck." But that has been restrained by built-in taboos. Now these taboos are weakened. Once society has socially sanctioned feticide, it is small wonder that the taboo which restrains parents from carrying out their destructive rages against little children is weakened. Added to this, society is convincing itself that children are an inconvenience and an irritation.

In some Asian countries, it appears that abortion is looked upon as a device for population control. In poor and crowded cities, I saw waifs wandering about, apparently orphaned, but well-fed and clothed. I have a growing suspicion that, once people in these countries are convinced that abortion is good family planning and is the best way to obtain a "high standard of living"—materialism—then those waifs will no longer have the same kind care and consideration.

While there is no convincing evidence that abortion is therapeutic for anyone, it is encouraged by politicians and physicians. When it's obviously necessary for those who would take a fetal life to demonstrate that beyond any reasonable doubt, feticide has value, they don't seem to feel that obligation. Those whom I have debated with agree that they have little argument for abortion and yet they will continue the practice. What is happening in a world where the behaviour of people is no longer determined by rational, logical, or scientific argument?

Sexual relationships are becoming increasingly abnormal. Face to face interpersonal relationships are no longer popular but front to back "dog position" sex is portrayed as more exciting. Although more sex education and less guilt are supposed to solve sex problems, there is growing impotence, homosexuality, rape, and sado-masochistic relationships. While good people protest all of these, they sense their helplessness in correcting the increasingly rapid moral slide.

The Final Collapse

When the evidence and arguments which should determine how people behave are ignored or cannot be acted upon, then one must be convinced that world systems are quickly coming to chaotic conditions. When the world can no longer mobilize the courage or the resources to fight well-recognized threats, then it has lost its moral fibre. The Romans were well aware of the political internal threats and the barbarian external forces, but they could not mobilize to meet those threats. It is becoming quite evident that western technological society is now having to cope with the same threats to basic structures. Even though the threats are well recognized, carefully researched and described, nothing effective is being done. For example, for years it has been evident that violence on television promotes violence among children and adults. Still the television puts out increasingly violent programs. Why?— "That's what people want."

Bound to Lose

There are three issues on which it is quite clear that Christians, no matter how hard they fight, are going to lose:

(1) *Abortion* - It is apparent that pro-lifers can win all the arguments but are losing the political and legal battles. They correctly argue: (a) that abortion is not therapeutic; (b) it is not a woman's right, as it contravenes both the husband's right to have the child and a fetus's right to life; (c) it is no longer necessary for psychiatric or medical health; (d) it cannot be justified for unwanted or abnormal fetuses for they are also human and enjoy life; (e) it is not an adequate type of population control. Abortion is done for convenience, while it is increasingly apparent that children are an inconvenience. Abortions increase as the despair of the nations regarding their own future deepens. Why should one invest one's life in caring for and educating children when there is little assurance that they can survive and less that they can be happy?

The only country to deny legalized "liberal" abortions is West Germany. Everywhere else, despite letters, demonstrations, arguments and research, abortions increase.

(2) *Lawlessness* - Increasingly severe crimes, increasing number of criminals, and the decreasing effectiveness of the law indicate that whole population areas are becoming ungovernable. The reasons appear to be twofold: (a) Increasing anonymity. When people live one above the other in apartment complexes, they cannot communicate. It then becomes possible to rationalize not being involved in somebody else's disaster because they are known not as a person but as a face in a crowd. (b) Passivity. Millions are entertained many hours by watching man's inhumanity to man. They do so while they sit back, passively reacting to terrible aggressions and injustice. Watching television, they are sufficiently excited by their passive participation in terrifying aggression and gross injustices to alleviate the boredom of mechanical existences. This learned response of watching while violence is done to others has been generalized to real-life situations. All the efforts of Christians to uphold law and order fail when countered by "I don't want to get involved."

(3) *Abnormal sex* - It has become the current hedonistic philosophy that the body is the source of all pleasure. The emphasis is on tactile pleasure, particularly genital. Unfortunately, orgasmic sensations are short-lived. Since life's purpose has become genital pleasure, more frequent and more intense stimulation and excitement is demanded. There is a vicious cycle of stimulation, gratification, satiation, and boredom, with no end in sight to the amount of stimulation that is going to be required. When sufficient stimulation can no longer be obtained to prevent their boredom, there is

complaint of depression. The media attempts to keep up with the demand by producing more bizarre kinds of stimulation. Live and recorded scenes of anal intercourse and sadomasochistic relationships are becoming increasingly frequent. The protests against pornography have little impact compared to the powerful media-backed lobbies against any kind of restraint.

The Kingdom of God

Christians have made progress in some areas of major moral issues: education, slavery, government have changed because of brave Christians. Yet Christ said, "the poor we will always have with us." This seems to indicate that we should not expect that the world can be made perfect. Christ's kingdom is not of this world. If it was, he would have sent his legions to fight for justice. A Christian's position is that we must work toward the solution of the problem as if it could be solved, realizing that, if solved, it would soon be replaced by another. Where there is progress, then we can be very thankful. If there is no great change, we should not be surprised. Derogatory discrimination seems to be an inherent part of man's inhumanity to man. Tyranny and injustice will continue but we battle for our own good.

For the Christian, the process is more important than the product. The choir rehearsal is where the real action is, not the Sunday presentation. God is most interested in what we are becoming. He wants us to be like himself because, if we are, there will be no doubt how the course of the world history would go.

There are many issues on which Christians have an opportunity to speak. They have the confidence of knowing that what is morally right is also scientifically correct. They have the responsibility of speaking to critical dilemmas in such a way that the witness is to the grace of God in their own lives. Thus, while fighting moral issues, the Christian's main goal is to portray God's love. Though he seeks a social solution to problems, his main interest is the individual.

The Real Issues

Some Christians have felt that their most important task was to win the battles for rights, equalities, freedoms. But their insistence on winning has characteristically killed individual people. On the way to rescue Jerusalem from the infidels, they slaughtered and plundered. The ends never justified the means. When Christ told Peter to put away his sword, it was the end of Christians taking up arms to defend either themselves or their most important possession.

The real issue for the Christian is to speak both to the moral dilemma and to the person simultaneously. He must be prepared to lose the issue in hopes of winning a person. Christ ably demonstrated that, even when it was not possible to set up his kingdom on earth because of man's lack of faith, it was possible to be victorious. He was able to establish then the spiritual kingdom in which the individual God-man relationship was the most important issue.

The Christian speaks to the issue by persuasion and by example. He should seek to initiate policies and to support people who attempt to establish righteousness in the world. Christians should have no fear of getting into politics themselves. By acting boldly, the Christian can show the importance of the issue.

A group of Christian physicians and nurses, present at abortions (particularly hysterotomies), could attempt to resuscitate. They would clearly demonstrate their determination to give life to every human. Eventually, they would have the joy of a live child. Apathetic millions might then give attention to the real issues.

On the issue of television violence, Christians could have a real impact by boycotting any programs that showed violence. They should bring to the public's attention the conclusive evidence of the detrimental effects of television violence. This may be by conducting public debates or even demonstrating in front of television studios.

In speaking to the person, the Christian must be able to speak to where the person feels his individual hurt and anxiety. We must never forget that everybody has some point at which he can be contacted. In any interpersonal relationship, it should be quite apparent that there is a commitment to a continuing relationship. People do not like to feel used or related to only as objects of evangelism.

Speaking to the individual about abortion, it must be quite clear that the Christian does not approve of abortion but that he will continue to care for the person even though they elect to have an abortion. The Christian physician should be able to tell the pregnant mother, if she does not wish to keep the child, that he will find the baby a home.

In speaking of the lawless individual, the Christian should be able to demonstrate that, although he disapproves strongly of the behaviour, he can see that the person has a need and will respond to that. He will help the person face his guilt and make restitution.

For those who are involved in abnormal sexual behaviour, Christians should be able to demonstrate Christ's love can heal people and restore in them a desire for truly interpersonal heterosexual involvement. Christ can heal people though the healing will leave scars. Christian families must show loving heterosexual relationships. Christian couples must convey that since their heterosex involves two whole people, it is therefore more fulfilling.

Conclusion

Christians have always maintained that unless a grain of wheat falls into the ground, it dies and remains alone. They are well aware of the fact that death and new life are interconnected. Unfortunately, Christians increasingly fear the loss of their body because they have insufficient faith in their eternal existence. We are susceptible to the media which tells us that we too should have the "good life." We retreat from challenges and even when we attempt to meet them, we aren't very brave. Christians must work hard to correct the major moral dilemmas of our time. But, in doing so, we must speak both to the individual and to the issue. When attacked, we must maintain the stance of those who are sure of their existence. Knowing that all we do for Christ can never lose its value, we are able to fight a losing battle victoriously.

The Divine Game of Pinzatski

Murray Pura

Vol. XXIV, No. 4 (December 1988):8-10

A curious and entertaining game was played by Ellen Pinzatski and her husband. They only played it once a year and then only when they were camped far out in the mountains by a silent turquoise lake they had named Infrequent. The game consisted of one of them pointing out a natural object, say a moss-swaddled cedar stump or a high and voluminous cloud formation, and the other stating, to the best of their ability, what characteristic of God was expressed in that object. The idea for the game had arisen from Paul's statement in Romans, "Since the creation of the world God's invisible qualities, that is, his eternal power and divine nature, have been clearly seen, being understood from what has been made." No sort of score was kept, and there were no rules, except that the person interpreting the natural object had to be able to explain to the other, if it was not patently obvious, how they had come to see a particular aspect of God's being manifested in the stump or cloud or grazing elk. The game would go on for hours, days, weeks, as long as the two of them were able to stay in their tent by the lakeside. Once they had retired—both worked and they had no children—there was, of course, much more time for the game. They never tired of it.

I first heard about the game when I was chatting with Arthur, Ellen's husband, after a church study group on the nature of God. Arthur explained how Ellen and he played the game by Lake Infrequent every year, toyed with his teacup as we talked about God's various characteristics, and finally asserted, "Abstractions are a poor second cousin to analogies. Analogies always get you closer to the truth. Never rely on an abstraction if you can get an analogy."

This coming from a professor of mathematics and physics! I asked him why he felt this was so. "Because abstractions establish distance, cool, logical, objective distance," he answered. "Analogies get you in close so you can smell the sweat. They're warm-blooded, make you feel something. That's why the Bible is loaded with them when it gets down to talking about God."

I mentioned the theory that the Bible was loaded with metaphors and analogies because it was addressed primarily to an uneducated and naive peasant population. Arthur snorted. "If you believe that," he told me, "you'll believe anything."

Perhaps it was this encounter that led to the Pinzatski's invitation to join them on a camping trip that August. I was purportedly an Old Testament scholar, at least Princeton had said so, and they may have felt I needed a good dose of the analogical to set my lecture notes straight. I took them up on the invitation, if for no other reason than to get out of the city for a week. I threw a few pair of jeans into a dufflebag, a bottle of insect repellent and a canteen. They had been quite firm about doing all the cooking. "Think of it as spending a week at our house," said Ellen. "Would you bring over your own plate and fork?"

The drive out to Lake Infrequent was long, about nine or ten hours. Part of the highway was out through pale desert, but the lake was situated high above on a plateau, a good hour down a potholed dirt track that shook my teeth. The four-person tent was erected; Ellen got a fire going, and Arthur started wrapping corn cobs in aluminum foil. I had just brought several containers of water up from the lake when Ellen said in a clear voice: "Ash."

Arthur looked up from his cornhusking. "Ash," he repeated. "I can't believe we've never talked about that one before."

I set the water down. The pair of them were oblivious to me. Arthur took his time, rolled a few more cobs of corn into tight foil bundles. Finally, he said, "The purity of God."

"How so?" demanded Ellen, raking white coals to another area of the fire so they could be used for cooking purposes.

"Because God also uses fire to burn what is unholy."

"But God also uses fire to burn what is holy, such as a sacrifice, or he uses fire in order to make something holy," retorted Ellen.

"All right," mumbled Arthur, bringing a bowl of wrapped corn cobs over to the fire and placing them on the coals. "But whatever God uses the fire for, ash symbolizes something that has been consumed because the purity of God required it."

While they were eating the meal, Arthur pointed to the ground in front of him as he was chewing. "What would you say about that, Ellen?" Ten or twelve ants were staggering off under bits of corn that had fallen in the dirt.

Ellen laughed. "I think we've come close to something like this before, but okay, I'll go with it. To me, these ants express God's desire to use what is apparently weak and puny to do those tasks which are most difficult and arduous. God is rarely the show-off. Most of the time he likes to work at the big things quietly, operating from a person we'd least expect his power to be present in. I think it also has to do with God's innate pleasure in surprises. It may also have something to do with his sense of humour."

"Good," commented Arthur, sipping at his tin mug of coffee, "good."

When we were washing the plates down by the lake and the sun set in a line of bright green, Ellen asked, "And this particular sunset?"

"This particular sunset," responded Arthur using a bit of sand to clean grease off his plate, "expresses the peacefulness of God, that inner tranquility represented by his use of the colour green in the creation of pastures and meadows and forests. In fact, green is the dominant colour found both on dry land and under the sea, indicating God's preference for it and suggesting that a great deal of his character is bound into a correct understanding of that colour and all its shades."

I could not believe the Pinzatskis took the game so seriously and I told Arthur this as the two of us were putting out the fire. Sparks glittered at our feet like a distant galaxy. Arthur poked a large orange coal with his stick. "Who is to say," he asked me, "which is the proper way of approaching God and the universe? As a child or with a pretense to sophistication?"

The game got underway again the next morning after breakfast while we were hiking along the lakeshore. Arthur mentioned the trout basking in the sunlit shadows. Ellen said it had to do with God's pleasure in creating freshwater creatures who enjoyed a lazy moment as much as any human did. In the afternoon, when we reached an alpine meadow that was solid yellow with flowers, Arthur said it had to do with God's extravagance, what he called, "the appropriate slaughter of the fatted calf at the appointed season." On another meadow that was windswept and barren of colour, when Arthur's hand inadvertently revealed a tiny, hidden flower of a purple tint, Ellen declared it had to do with God's frugality. I laughed.

"So a balance is struck," I said.

"Of course," Arthur responded soberly. "God is all balances struck."

By the third day, I was ready for the city. It was not that the game was the only thing that was being verbalized. Far from it. Arthur discussed his work in the field of physics quite freely and Ellen was not adverse to debating the finer points of Shakespeare and James Joyce. But I began to feel as if I were starting to see the world as they did and this was a disturbing sensation. Ellen would point at something and I would come up with an answer faster than Arthur, though I never vocalized it, and I knew I was really in trouble when I began to mull over whether my interpretation of the natural object was closer to the truth about God than Arthur's or Ellen's.

On the fourth day, I was considering various excuses or ploys I might use in order to get them to return to the city a few days early. I could always tell them I needed to revise some of my lecture notes because of our camping trip and that I needed to do this before classes began the following Tuesday. We were hiking high on a ridge of boulders and dead grey trees and I had decided to spring this excuse on them the moment we stopped for lunch when an immense shadow passed over my face and an incredibly violent beating of wings filled my head. I thought of death, ducked my head, threw myself down on the ground.

"A golden eagle!" cried Ellen. "My God!"

I lifted my head and the bird was there, dark and light and fiercely beaked, moving like a scythe across the sun's arc. Arthur was the first to yell "golden eagle!"

It was obvious that they had never come across a golden eagle in the wild before. Ellen, gaping after the bird, did not respond. I got to my knees, watched the enormous bird drop towards a white mountain, and I spoke, answering Arthur.

"Freedom," I said. "God's freedom to be God without a single chain, a single restraint. His utter liberty to be the wild God."

The three of us stared after the eagle until it was too small. Then we looked at one another, smiled and continued our hike. I said nothing about going back to the city at lunch. A line had been crossed. I would now play the game along with Ellen and Arthur.

The next three days were a brilliant collage. Nothing was inanimate anymore, but neither did anything exist in terms of its own spirit as an animist would have it. Every rock and tree and bird became a flicker of God's fingers, a certain tilt of his head, a play of light and darkness in his eyes. Doors to God were springing open throughout the entire cosmos and I gazed as a child gazes at his first thunderstorm. I peered at God through flames, through water, glimpsed him in the visage of a doe. His laughter rang out of the throats of birds; his shout was in the waterfall; I heard him whistling to himself as a wind scoured the cliffs and deadfall. At night, I did not sleep under stars but under God.

This was not the only camping trip I took with Ellen and Arthur. Over the next six years, I joined them each August for a week by Lake Infrequent. I actually did revise my lecture notes, not once but four or five times. And our three imaginations became virtually inseparable.

The final night we ever camped together, Arthur and I put out the fire once more. Sparks whirled as Arthur stirred with his stick.

"Man is born to trouble," he quoted from Job, "as the sparks fly upwards."

"Meaning what about God?" I challenged him.

He did not hesitate. "Meaning God is not soft. If he thinks a person needs to go through something in order to carve more glory out of him or her, he'll do it. He might weep, but he'll do it."

Four months later, Arthur was diagnosed with cancer of the lung, the liver, and the stomach. They opened him, took a look, and stitched him back up again. They gave him maybe half a year. When I saw him at church after the diagnosis, he had lost weight but not his wit. He pointed at his chest and asked me, "What does this say about God?"

I shook my head, kept my lips in a straight line. Arthur laughed.

"The resurrection of the body," he answered. "God is not interested in phantoms. That's why the earth is an earth of substance. Heaven will be the same. The Incarnation, my friend, the Incarnation. He's committed himself."

Arthur was not the kind to take a lot of drugs or to end his days between four white walls. "When this cancer releases me," he said, "it will not do so in the presence of what is fashioned by man. I will go into the mountains and let it kill me before the face of God."

He and Ellen threw a banquet of salads and roasts and wines for all their friends one clear evening in July and the next morning the two of them left for an extended camping trip in the vicinity of Lake Infrequent. Ellen returned alone one month later, notified the authorities, then came to see me.

"He took the canoe while I was asleep," she said. He didn't leave any note. I thought he might come back. I waited two weeks."

She paused and looked down at the rug, at her slender brown fingers. "I know now what he meant the afternoon before when he mentioned something about only God knowing where the body of Moses was."

As far as I know, Ellen did not stop playing the game. I know I did not. Nor did either of us stop camping by Lake Infrequent, though we never went there together.

One August night, I had just pitched my tent when there was a remarkable display of shooting stars, a true firefall. I got into my sleeping bag and lay outside of the tent and watched the sky for hours. I caught myself imagining how Arthur might have interpreted a shooting star in terms of God's personality. Then I had the sensation that he was right beside me, playing the game, answering my challenge, only I was not able to make out his words. The sensation did not frighten me, but it did keep me awake half the night wondering if Arthur knew all the correct interpretations now, or whether, in light of his different perspective on God, he had to start all over playing a game that could never end.

The God Who Mixes His Metaphors

Luci Shaw

Vol. XXIII, No. 4 (December 1987):2-4

Close to two years ago, my husband of thirty-three years, who was also my best friend, died of lung cancer. During all my coping and grieving and searching and reorientation in the days that followed, an incident occurred which cleared my thinking and flooded my imagination. It condensed itself into this brief parable, which begins with some phrases from Isaiah 61:

The spirit of the Lord is on me to comfort
all who mourn, and provide for those
who grieve...beauty instead of ashes, the
oil of gladness instead of mourning, and
a garment of praise instead of a spirit of despair.

Soon after Harold died, my good friend Bernie Bosch and his sons took down the old, dead oak tree that stood in our front yard. The spring before it had never leafed out at all, and we had known it must be topped, scarred as it was by lightning so that it was rotting at its core. It was much too close to the house to be safe. Bernie had waited until the ground was frozen hard so that the crash of its enormous bulk wouldn't damage the lawn too much.

It was a huge job, and after the screaming power saws were silent and the tree was dismembered, all the wood had to be split and trucked away (that was the deal—he cut the tree down in exchange for the wood), and the mass of debris piled on top of the stump and ignited. The white hot blaze burned for days, and even after the flames had died down, a thin tendril of smoke still threaded the air above the site. The fire ate away most of the stump and the roots deep below the surface so that a week later all that was left was a black-rimmed saucer of ashes, like a wound in the sod.

It was then that I realized why the felling of the tree occupied my thoughts so consistently and with such a sense of significance. It was because I was the frozen sod with the deep wound, and Harold was my tree who was simply...gone. Vanished. How unreal that seemed that his roots that had for over thirty years penetrated deep into my life, that had anchored us, joined us so solidly and securely, were being eroded by the fire of decay. The space above ground that for so long had been filled with his vertical strength and solidity and shape was empty; air had rushed in where, before, the towering trunk had outbranched to leaves.

Now I lie in wait for the tissue of earth and the skin of sod— the beauty of green instead of the grey ashes of a spent fire—to fill in and heal over the naked scar. And it will. It will.

But the oak tree stands strong and straight and thriving and leafy in my memory, and no one can cut it down.

Somehow, in my thinking about Harold, and his life and its meaning to me, and the shape of our relationship, and the looming desolation of his loss, I need something more than an abstract truth to latch on to. It's not enough for me to make a general statement: "Harold's gone. How I miss him! Somehow I must come to terms with life without him." I find I need a *picture*, something so real in my imagination that I can derive sense impressions from it, and building from those I can perhaps draw significance from this image—the oak tree and the sod.

A metaphor, because of its reality and force in one arena of life, can carry over its meaning into another arena. The oak tree was real and strong, and its loss gave meaning to my own experience of losing a husband. The hole in the sod was ragged and deep, but knowing how grass grows gave me hope for my own healing.

Though most of us are not aware of it, *we think in pictures*. Our imaginations are like screens on which are projected a series of colour slides.

Dorothy Sayers, in her book *The Mind of the Maker*, states categorically that "we have no way to think, except in pictures."

Yet there is a school of thought among theologians and philosophers which tries to get at truth without use of metaphors. Carl Henry, for instance, tells us that "truth is only rational-verbal." The logic goes something like this: "Small and strong is beautiful. We're looking for some statement that ends all discussion, a concise proposition that is so immensely powerful that it condenses thought into 'pure truth'."

I am not a scientist, but my doctor son, John, who was a chemistry major in college, contributed the following scientific information: In the world of chemistry the process of purification involves condensation. That is, if some substance has been dissolved in water, and all we want is the original substance, we can isolate it again by heating the solution to boiling point and evaporating the water.

Unfortunately, this doesn't always work. There are substances which, when mixed with water, or any solvent, forms solutions called *azeotropes* which cannot be separated by boiling; they are chemically bound.

My point is that there seem to be at least two kinds of truth. One kind can be condensed out from all other additives and be made pure and potent, with the simple elegance of a formula, like Einstein's $E = MC^2$. It can be called "propositional thinking." Another kind— an "azeotropic" truth, if we can call it that—is bound to imagery. It involves "metaphorical" thinking. An obvious example of this bonding of truth to metaphor occurs in paradox, where two contradictory statements are both shown to be true.

Think, for instance, of two biblical images for Christ—the *Lamb* and the *Lion*. Startlingly contradictory pictures rise in our imaginations when we hear these words. For all of us, Lamb means small, innocent, helpless, naive, submissive, white-fleeced, a follower, the victim of the biblical rituals of sacrifice. Lion, by contrast, suggests adjectives such as huge, golden-maned, dangerous, powerful, untamed, dominant, aggressive, a leader and victor by very nature. Both of these contradictory images add to our understanding of Christ and his infinite capabilities. We cannot sum up our Lord in our proposition, one theological statement. And think of all the other pictures Christ gives us of himself—Word, Grapevine, Cornerstone, Pioneer, Door to the sheepfold, Shepherd, Rock foundation, Bridegroom, Morning Star, Wine, Water, Bread, and on and on.

It is paradoxical for Isaiah to use oaks as a metaphor for humans, as he does in Isaiah 61:3: "They shall be called oaks of righteousness, the planting of the Lord," and elsewhere to describe them as grass, in Isaiah 40:6-8: "All men are like grass, and their glory is like the flowers of the field. The grass is cut down and withers and the flowers fall, but the word of our God stands forever."

It is paradoxical for me to think of my husband in terms of the toughness and height and strength and durability of an oak tree, and yet affirm that he also partook of grass's tenderness, and transience, and vulnerability. Yet both are true. Because I want you to know this truth at an emotional as well as a rational level, let me show you two poems that illustrate the dual nature of the truth about humans.

The meaning of oaks

> It is light that tugs,
> that teaches each
> acorn to defy the pull
> down, to interrupt
> horizontal space.
> And falling, filtering
> through the leaves
> it is rain that rises,
> then, like a spring
> at a sapling's heart.
> It is wind that trains,
> toughens the wood.
> It is time that spreads
> the grain in rings—
> dark ripples in a
> slow pond.
>
> The oaks learn slowly,
> well, twisting
> up, around and out,
> finding the
> new directions of
> the old pattern branded
> in each branch,
> compacting, a wood
> dense enough for men
> to craft into a crib
> for a new born, a cross
> for pain, a table
> for bread and wine, a door
> for day light.
>   (from *The Sighting*, ©1981, Luci Shaw)

That's an oak. Here's grass:
....**but the word of our God will stand
forever** (Isaiah 40:6-8)

> All flesh is grass
> and I can feel myself growing

an inch an hour in the dark,
ornamented with a lyric dew
fine as glass beads, my edges
thin as green hair.

All flesh
and there are seventeen kinds
of us in this one corner of the
hayfield, along with clover,
oxalis, chicory, Wild Wilber—
close enough cousins for a
succulent hay.
Early mornings
we all smell of rain
enough to drown the microscopic
hoppers and lubricate snails
along their glistening paths:
a fine, wet fragrance, but not
so sweet as this evening, after
the noon scythe.
No longer,
now, are the windows of air
hung with our lace, embroidered
with bees. Laid low, we raise
a new incense, and under the brief
stubble, our roots grieve.
(from *Postcard from the Shore,* ©1985, Luci Shaw)

Mixed metaphors? God doesn't always obey our literary rules. In the Bible he expands our imaginative thinking with a multiplicity of metaphors—images that work.

We need that multiplicity. We need to know that God can minister to us, both in strength and in weakness, and that he can use both our vigour and our vulnerability in his service. It's the principle of the Wounded Healer, of strength made perfect in weakness.

I don't want to leave you hanging. Let me read you my journal entry for a spring day not very long ago:

I started this new morning with a fast, two-mile walk. The air is silky with breath from the south. A chickadee whistles her spring song 'Phoe-be' over and over. The air is perfectly still so that the calls and songs of robins and phoebes and mourning doves form a web of clear sound all around me as I walk, sound not muffled or blown away by the strong winds that gusted earlier this week. The grass, tinged on the sunny slopes with green, glitters in the thawing frost. The morning is intoxicatingly fresh. What exhilaration! The idea of "being dead to sin yet alive to God" grows consciously in my mind. The edges of the turf, the sun-warmed banks and sheltered spots, are brightening with green and colour—spears of grass and scillas pushing up through the pale straw.

I am greening too. My winter of bereavement and depression is melting. There are traces of fresh growth, of beauty instead of the ashes of mourning. The wounded rawness of earth is being healed, grown over by the tender new skin of sod.

I read from the Song of Solomon this morning, and for the first time I really *knew* what it meant—that the empty space of my life is being filled by God, who has said he will be my Husband:

My lover spoke and said to me:
"Arise, my dear one, my beautiful one,
    and come with me.
See, the winter is past; the rains are over
and gone.
Flowers appear on the earth.
The season of singing has come.
The sound of birdsong is heard in our land."

And then this verse of George Herbert's was sent to me by a friend. It could have written specifically for me last year, after the dying of not only my husband but my 99-year-old mother- in-law, my life-long friend and mentor Clyde Kilby, my encourager Joe Bayly, and Hugh Franklin, husband of my sister in Christ, Madeleine L'Engle.

And now in age I bud again —
After so many deaths I live and write.
I once more smell the dew and rain
and relish versing: O, my only Light —
It cannot be
That I am (s)he
On whom thy Tempests fell all night!

Relating Human Personhood to the Health Sciences: An Old Testament Perspective

Bruce Waltke

Vol. XXV, No. 3 (September 1989):2-10

Introduction

"The most powerful of all spiritual forces," wrote Emil Brunner, "is man's view of himself, the way in which he understands his nature and his destiny; indeed it is the one force which determines all the others which influence human life."[1]

Apart from divine revelation mankind is incapable of knowing itself and tends to reduce itself and its gods to the level of animals as the histories of religion (cf. Romans 1:21-22) and philosophy show. In the thinking of many, mankind at best is the glorious pinnacle of the animal kingdom. For others, he is less. Gilbert, doubtless with Sullivan's approval, said, "Man is Nature's sole mistake," and Robert Louis Stevenson thought of man as a devil weakly fettered by some generous beliefs. For B.F. Skinner mankind has moved beyond dignity. It began to lose its dignity when it lost its address in the Copernican revolution; it debased itself when it embraced the theory that it accidently originated in primordial mud; and its last claim to dignity is now threatened by artificial intelligence. When the pessimistic philosopher Schopenhauer, sitting on a park bench, hair all disheveled, was asked by a park custodian who he was, he replied: "I would to God I knew!"

To know itself and to reclaim its true dignity and destiny mankind needs to return to the Bible, a revelation from its Maker. In this paper the writer aims to understand from an Old Testament perspective the nature and destiny of mankind and the implications of that understanding for both modern biomedical technology and patient care. Theologians in their quest to define humanity have rightly looked to the laconic revelation that mankind is created in God's image (Genesis 1:26-27). In this paper the writer will exegete that crucial test with particular attention to the meaning of "image of God," then discuss the extent of the *imago Dei* with particular reference to the unborn and malformed, and finally its implications for biomedical technology and patient care.

Definition of Image of God

The inspired literary artist who recounted the origins of terrestrial and celestial beings (Genesis 1:1-2:3) distinguished and elevated the creation of mankind[2] in 1:26-28 above the rest of creation in several ways. The narrative about mankind's creation does not differ in structure from the creation narratives of other beings. God's command effecting mankind's creation, "Let us make mankind in our image," (v.26a) is followed by the explanatory report:

And so God created man in his own image,

in the image of God he created him;

male and female he created them (v.27).

But it does differ in tempo. The account slows down to the balanced rhythm of Hebrew poetry, the first poem in the Bible. With the creation of mankind as the last of God's creative acts the creation reaches its grand climax. The unique resolve of God, "Let us make mankind," represents God as participating more intimately and intensively in mankind's creation than in any other. The word "make" (Hebrew *asah*), which often has humans as its subject, is clarified in v.27 by the more restricted term, "created" (Hebrew *bara*), which has only God as its subject and is uniquely repeated three times in that one verse. Finally, and above all, the distinguishing characteristic of mankind is that it is created in the "image" (Hebrew *tselem*), according to the "likeness" (Hebrew *demuth*), of God.

The two terms, "image" and "likeness," do not refer to two aspects of mankind as many earlier scholastic writers thought. The better texts[3] do not add the conjunction "and" between them, but understand the second term as a reinforcing, explanatory appositive. Elsewhere, apart from 5:3 (see below), they occur in isolation with no intended difference in meaning (cf. 5:l; 9:6). Of these two terms "image" is the more important because it alone is emphatically repeated twice in the very solemn report (1:27); similarly in the very important verse, 9:6.

Although the antecedent of the pronoun "us" is unstated, P. D. Miller[4] validates his interpretation that it refers to God and his angelic court by noting, among other things, that the use of the plural pronoun with reference to God is reserved for those passages where the human world impinges on the divine world (3:22; ll:7; Isaiah 6:1-8) and by David's poetic reflection on Genesis 1:26: "You made mankind a little lower than angels" (Psalm 8:5; Hebrews 2:7). Wenham[5] calls attention to Job 38:4, 7: "When I laid the foundation of the earth, all the sons of God shouted for joy" (cf. Luke 2:13-14). Mankind has a closer relationship to heaven and divine beings than to earth and animals, even though it originated out of the earth (Genesis 2:7). Elmer Martens says: "If one were to imagine a scale of 1 to 10 with living creatures such [as] beast at 1 and God at 10, then, so high is the writer's estimate of man, one should have to put at 8 or 9'. [6] Though dwarfed by the enormity of the cosmos, mankind alone is the *imago Dei,* a concept so important and profound that it has rightly attracted numerous studies by exegetes and theologians.[7]

The word "image" is used sixteen times in Hebrew and eight times in Aramaic (Daniel 2, 3 of statues).[8] Four times it is used of mankind in God's image, once of Seth in Adam's image (Genesis 5:3), once of a human figure painted on a wall (Ezekiel 23:14), thrice of the golden copies of the mice and swellings that afflicted the Philistines (1 Samuel 6:4, 5, ll), and seven times of idols. These uses strongly suggest that mankind is an earthly, representative copy of God. In Oriental myths gods also make men in their likeness, and in ancient Egypt the Pharaoh was regarded as "the image of God living on earth."[9]

The fourteen uses of the "image" outside of Genesis and the representations of God in the Pentateuch as having human form validate the opinion of many recent exegetes and theologians that Moses did not intend to exclude man's glyptic form from the notion, "image of God." Although other biblical writers stress God's incorporeality, and in that light corporeality would be excluded from the notion of "image of God," in Genesis God walks and talks with mankind (2:l6f.; 3:8ff.; 4.6ff.; 5:24; etc.). In this narrative Moses lays the foundation for his later stories about encounters on earth between heavenly beings and mankind.

The statement "in the image of God" represents God himself as having form, even as Seth is in the image of Adam (Genesis 5:3).[10] This anthropomorphic presentation of God is entirely consistent with the rest of the account. God calls the cosmos and terrestrial life into existence with his voice, or according to the Psalmist's reflection, "by the breath of his mouth" (Psalm 33:6). God brings the cosmos under his dominion by labelling them with Hebrew words, *Yom*, "Day," *Laylah*, "Night," *Shamayim*, "Heaven" and *Erets*, "Earth." E. J. Young rightly comments: "It is certainly true that God did not speak with physical organs of speech nor did he utter words in the Hebrew language."[11] Although ontologically God is spirit, he often assumes a human form. In contrast to the rest of Israel, who saw no form [Hebrew *temunah*] (Deuteronomy 4:12,15), Moses saw his form [same word] and spoke with him face to face (Numbers 12:6). In an even more intimate revelation he saw God's back (Exodus 33:23).

In summary, the Pentateuch offers no reason to take image in any other way than in its normal significance. The distinction between the material and immaterial aspects of mankind have their place in theological discussion, but that distinction is out of place in Genesis 1:26-28. Mankind as a physical-spiritual unity is the image of God. This creature is uniquely God's image in its erect posture and, above all, in its spiritual nature. In Dryden's paraphrase:

Thus, while the mute Creation downward bend
Their Sight, and to their Earthy Mother tend,
Man looks aloft; and with erected Eyes,
Beholds his own Hereditary Skies.[12]

Clines clarifies the meaning "image of God" from images of gods in the Ancient Near East. Citing the study by Bernhardt, he notes that "the primary function of the image was to be the dwelling-place of spirit or fluid which derived from the being whose image it was."[13] So also in the second account of creation, adumbrating the creation of mankind, the LORD God breathes into Adam's nostrils the breath of life so that he possesses the very life of God (2:7).

From the solemn declaration, "So God created mankind in his own image, in the image of God he created it; male and female he created them," (1:27) one could infer with Barth and others that sexuality, and implicitly fellowship between persons, are definitive, essential features of the *imago Dei*. These features, however, are accidental, not substantial. Adam's son, Seth, without qualification is said to be begotten "in Adam's likeness, according to his image," and the same is true, the reader should assume, of Adam's other sons and daughters (5:3-4).

Genesis assumes the specific features of the *imago Dei*. Philosophers and theologians try to spell them out in terms of the assumed "moreness" that distinguishes humans from animals. Many define it in terms of the ability of humans to reason; some point to mankind's artistic and musical achievements and/or to the fact that it buries its dead with flowers. The Bible emphasizes man's rational ability to communicate, moral consciousness, and eternal destiny, lifting it above the rest of creation and uniquely linking it with heaven.

Possessing the life of heaven and belonging to the same order as divine beings with unique notions of rationality and morality, mankind, both male and female, is capable of knowing and of communing with its Maker (cf. 2:16-18; 3:8-18; 4:10-16; 5:24), and of being tempted by divine beings (cf. 3:1-6) or of being ministered to by them (16:7ff.; 21:17ff.; 28:12). In contrast to animals, which merely respond to external stimuli in gratifying their drives and appetites (cf. Psalm 49:8, 20; 73:21f.) and which are without moral responsibility as voluntary agents, mankind understands God's words and laws (Genesis 2:16-17; 3:2-3), fears his threats (3:7-8), trusts his promises (3:14-2; 4:1), and praises him for his sublime attributes and works (The Book of Psalms). As Karl Barth expressed it, mankind is a being whom God addresses as Thou and makes answerable as I. Men and women fulfill their dignity when they hear God's word, speak with him in prayer, and obey him in service.

Yet mankind is an image, not the original, even as a painting is a far cry from the subject portrayed. God is transcendent and heavenly, mankind is temporal and earthly; God is spiritual, imperishable, glorious, and powerful, mankind is not, though in Christ men and women can become more like God (1 Corinthians 15:42-44); God is non-sexual, mankind is sexually differentiated; God is Creator, man is creature. Mankind is not an exact duplicate of God, any more than idols were facsimiles of the gods, but rather an adequate and faithful representation of him. The psalmist asks:

Does he who implanted the ear not hear?
Does he who formed the eye not see? (94:10).

Extension of Image

Genesis explicitly teaches that all descendants of Adam, in spite of the Fall, are in the image of God. The inspired writer implies this truth by linking the creation of mankind with the birth of Seth, who was born after the murder of Abel and so unquestionably after the Fall (Genesis 4:25). After recapitulating the original creation, "When God created mankind, he made it in the likeness of God; he created them male and female," he links the next generation with the original *imago Dei*, by repeating "likeness and image": "Adam had a son in his own likeness, in his own image; and he named him Seth" (5:1-3). In keeping with the style of Hebrew literature, which often links texts by chiasms, the author links Genesis 5:3 with 1:26 by reversing the words, "image" and "likeness."

The Bible consistently affirms the unity of the human species, all of that species having descended from common parents and so participating in the *imago Dei* (Acts 17:26). Like the other species, mankind's essential feature, the image of God, is immutable and can be propagated indefinitely. To be sure there are many and great varieties within the species with regard to race, nationality, economy, sexuality, function, capability, and other physical and spiritual factors. Nevertheless, all humans descend from Adam and Eve and possess the essential and immutable feature of being in God's image and are blessed with the capability of indefinite propagation (Genesis 9:6).

Rich and poor have this in common:
The LORD is the Maker of them all (Proverbs 22:2).

Though recognizing that humans pass through many stages from gestation to death, the Bible assumes that the *imago Dei* is always present. When the genealogies record that so-and-so begat so-and-so, no precise differentiation between conception and birth is intended. In another paper the writer attempted to define the image of God more precisely as clay personally fashioned by God and possessing a moral-spiritual nature and to demonstrate that these minimal features were present in the stage of humanity between gestation and birth.[14] He validated his argument by David's poem, to be sung by all mankind (Psalm 51: superscription), that he was a spiritual being between the time of conception and parturition from the womb (Psalm 51:7-8). Following Edwin Dalglish's doctoral dissertation, the writer drew the conclusion that at that stage of its being mankind is both sinful and yet possessing conscience. In the Old Testament only mankind can be the subject of these predicates, and in this case they are comments about the unborn.

God teaches children to trust him at their mother's breast (Psalm 22:10).

At the other end of the passage, when heart and flesh fail, the faithful find God to be the strength of their heart and their portion forever (Psalm 73:26). The psalmist, whose days vanish like smoke, whose bones burn like glowing embers, whose heart is blighted and withered like grass, who because of his loud groaning is reduced to skin and bones, and who is like a desert owl among the ruins, expresses his true nature and dignity by praying earnestly to God for deliverance (Psalm 102:3-6).

In addition to mankind being an immutable species capable of indefinite propagation from a common parent, God personally fashions each one in the womb. In a transparent metaphor Job represents the human situation:

Your hands shaped me and made me.
Will you now turn and destroy me?
Remember that you moulded me like clay.
Will you now turn me to dust again?
Did you not pour me out like milk
and curdle me like cheese,
clothe me with skin and flesh
and knit me together with bones and sinews?
You gave me life and showed me kindness,
and in your providence watched over me.
(Job 10:8-12)

It would be highly mischievous to pit the theological statement about the Ultimate Cause of mankind's origin by an inspired poet and theologian, "You created my inmost being; you knit me together in my mother's womb" (Psalm 139:13), against a scientific statement about the immediate cause of its origins by a geneticist. It would also be mischievous to distinguish the unborn as a developing human being from a developed person in order to deprive the former of the rights and privileges of the latter. The Bible does not validate such a distinction. In these passages, and others, the inspired poet represents himself in the period of gestation as an answerable I before the sovereign Thou.

God shapes every human, including the malformed. When Moses complained that he was slow of speech and tongue, the Lord rebuked him by asking: "Who gave mankind its mouth? Who makes it deaf or dumb? Who gives it sight or makes it blind?" He then answers his own questions: "Is it not I, the LORD?" (Exodus 4:10f.). Furthermore, the Bible contains no thought that some malformed creatures of woman's womb are less than human or that the *imago Dei* is relative to some standard of normalcy. All are the image of God and entitled to love and impartial justice.

Moreover, God sustains life and refreshes the earth with each new generation:

These all look to you
to give them their food at the proper time.
When you give it to them,
they gather it up;
when you open your hand,
they are satisfied with good things.
When you hide your face,
  they are terrified;
when you take away their breath,
  they die and return to the dust.
When you send your Spirit,

they are created,
and you renew the face of the earth.
(Psalm 104:27-30)
At the end of man's and woman's passage on earth, God reserves the right to take innocent life. In Job's famous words:
Naked I came from my mother's womb,
and naked I will depart.
The LORD gave and the LORD has taken away;
may the name of the LORD be praised.
(Job 1:21)
The psalmist concurs: "My times are in your hands" (Psalm 31:15). In the giving of life, God passes it along through mankind's own hands, but he reserves for himself alone the right to take innocent life.

In summary, though mankind is differentiated in many ways, born and unborn, healthy and malformed, the life of each member possesses the nature, value, and dignity of being the *imago Dei*.

Implications of Image for Biomedical Technology

Moses links God's resolve "Let us make mankind in our image, in our likeness" with his resolve that men and women have dominion over all terrestrial life: "and let them rule over the fish of the sea and the birds of the air, over the livestock, over all the earth, and over all the creatures that move along the ground" (Genesis 1:26b). As verse 27 is an explanatory report about the making of mankind's nature in God's image, so verse 29 is an explanatory report about mankind's destiny: "God blessed them and said to them, 'Be fruitful and increase in number; fill the earth and subdue it. Rule over the fish of the sea and the birds of the air and over every living creature that moves on the ground.' " God's blessing (that is, filling man and woman with the potential for life and victory) is accomplished through the divine imperatives expressing his will.[15]

Clines[16] documented that in the ancient Near East virtually only the king is reckoned as an image of god. For example, one document dated to about 675 B.C. says: "A [free] man is as the shadow of god, the slave is as the shadow of a [free] man; but the king, he is like unto the [very] image of God." In Genesis, however, the right to rule is democratized. Martens[17] recalls a remark by C. S. Lewis at the coronation of Queen Elizabeth in 1953 that "the pressing of that huge, heavy crown on that small, young head was a symbol of the situation of all men. God has called humanity to be his vice-regent and high priest on earth." Martens went on to say, "Human beings are persons of dignity because of their affinity with God and persons of responsibility because of their role in relation to creatures." One must take care, however, not to define man's nature by fulfilling this function.

Man began to fulfill his mandate in the naming of the animals (Genesis 2:19). As God expressed his dominion over the cosmic spheres of man's life supportive systems of air, water, and land by naming them (1:5, 8, 10), so now mankind, "crowned with glory and honour" (Psalm 8:5), takes up the task by naming the terrestrial objects. Von Rad comments:

> Language had bestowed upon it [language] the dignity of creative faculty, by means of which man coped with the task of reducing the world around him to conceptual order. So understood, its primary function is not to serve men's need to communicate with one another, but to enable them to comprehend objects and separate them into natural divisions.[18]

Solomon furthered the task by naming the flora and fauna of his realm and coining proverbs of man's social experiences: "He spoke three thousand proverbs...He spoke of plant life...He also spoke of animals and birds..." (1 Kings 3:32-33). Earlier the Sumerians had categorized and systematically arranged their whole world of objects and experiences. In this way, as Fohrer explains, "[they] sought to master the world by means of the order of names."[19]

Biomedical researchers by naming the parts of the body, resulting from their observations, analyses, and systematic classifications of its parts, bring it under dominion. By this mandate the holy God intended mankind to bring the earth under its dominion in conformity with his sublime character, including his justice and mercy. The mandate cannot be used as license for unbridled experimentation such as the Nazis inflicted on the Jews.

Medical research is a part of this mandate. Throughout the ancient Near East sickness was traced back to the influence of the divine, especially a demonic, power. In Israel, however, it is traced back to the LORD. Also, ancient Near Eastern peoples were well aware that wounds, injuries, and fractures had natural causes and were subject to medical treatment. The Code of Hammurabi contains a whole list of medical prescriptions in paragraphs 215-225. In 2 Kings 20:5-8 the LORD promises to heal Hezekiah, and Isaiah immediately prescribes a fig poultice. There is also a very modest start toward something like hygiene in Leviticus 13-15 and Deuteronomy 28:27f., though this was not their primary purpose as Mary Douglas[20] has shown. The rules given to the priest for deciding the virulence of skin diseases (Leviticus 13:18f, 31; 14:3ff.) suggest that such a diagnosis is the beginning of medical treatment.

Balsam appears chiefly as a means of healing (Jeremiah 8:22; 46:ll; 51:8).

In summary, the Hebrews showed no hesitancy to apply medical treatment to their maladies, but they never divorced these "natural" means from the Lord's activities. In 2 Chronicles l6:l2 Asa, King of Judah, is reproached because in his sickness he did not seek help from the Lord but from a physician. Likewise, in the final analysis, the diagnosis of an infection in the Levitical Code does not lie with the priest but with God. Deuteronomy 32:9 encapsulates the Old Testament view: "I put to death and I bring to life, I have wounded and will heal, and no one can deliver from my hand."

Biomedical research has an added honour and responsibility because the divine will that mankind subdue and rule terrestrial life is combined with God's other command, "Be fruitful and multiply." The genealogies and the Table of Nations (Genesis 10) bear silent witness to the blessing. In contrast to pagan thought and modern thinking, the Old Testament regards life an unqualified good (Genesis 9:l, 7). Pagan myths, and even the Trojan war as recovered by Kikawada and Quinn [21] from an ancient commentator in *The Il-iad*, look for a divine solution for the problem of overpopulation. The epic *Atrahasis*, against which background Genesis l-ll is possibly composed, represented the Flood as the gods' final answer for controlling human population. Genesis polemically contradicts this view. Kikawada and Quinn write:

> When we turn to the Hebrews, we find population also important— but in exactly the opposite sense. The Hebrew God, far from punishing man for population growth, is rather ordering him, 'Be fruitful and multiply, and fill the earth.' This command, so long familiar to us, is in its cultural context utterly startling, as unexpected as the monotheism. Frymer—Kensky suggests that this command to fertility represents 'an explicit and probably conscious rejection of the idea that the cause of the flood was overpopulation and the overpopulation is a serious problem.' A command, which now seems a common place to us, was argumentative, almost polemical, in its original context. [22]

Genesis answers the problem of overpopulation by calling on man to spread out over the face of the earth. Man's refusal to spread out, motivated by impious thinking (cf. Genesis ll:4) and/or by intractable political realities, results in overcrowded cities and lands, and so cheapens life and calls into question its goodness. The Old Testament, however, consistently regards children as a gift and a reward. Modern man regards too many as a curse, or at best as a qualified good. This is partially due to mankind's selfishness, immorality, and love of city living, which take the place of loving God, and serving him, and looking for his heavenly city. Because of unnegotiable political lines that separate states, Christians may have to accept that a more loving act than bringing others to sit at the banquet table of life is to protect those already at the table from starvation. (By the figure, "starvation," the writer intends more than food deficiency.) But Christian parents need to take heed not to use this reasoning as a rationalization for birth control that in truth is motivated by self-love.

While the Bible robustly affirms science and technology, especially as it furthers life, it condemns impiety and injustice. Research must be conducted in the love of God and love of man, and in the cause of life and justice.

Mankind's technology "backfires" on it because mankind is in rebellion against God. For a profound insight into the nature of sin one needs to reflect upon the story of the tree or knowledge of good and evil (Genesis 2:16-17). One begins to understand this story only when it is realized that the fruit of the forbidden tree is good. By eating it mankind became more like God. After the representatives of mankind had eaten it, God announced to his angelic court: "Mankind has become as one of us, Knowing good and evil." What is wrong with becoming more godlike? more angelic? more heavenly? with enhancing the image of God? *It is mankind's illicit, autonomous reach in unbelief for something good.* Mankind's technology reflects God's blessing on men and women and makes mankind even more like God, capable of furthering and hampering life, but, when the good tree of science and technology is seized in unbelief, it alienates men and women from God and from one another. That is why the Old Testament never separated medical practice from prayer and dependence on God. Secular mankind through science and technology is paradoxically becoming ever more like divine beings in knowledge and at the same time becoming ever more lonely in its social connections on both the vertical and horizontal axes.

When researchers act autonomously and think of themselves as being restricted only by the limits of their power, they impiously sin against God and unjustly damage their neighbour. In-vitro fertilization, cloning, and the recombinant DNA can be called good only to the extent that it unqualifiedly furthers life and is just to others. Recall that it was argued above that the image of God extends to the impregnated egg. To the extent that biomedical research kills the life of others and unduly jeopardizes human life, thereby violating the command, "You shall not take innocent life" (Exodus 20:13), it is evil. Only in cases of two evils, as in the case of war, does the Old Testament tolerate the notion that one must choose the lesser of two evils. Genetic engineering is good when it functions to advantage the life of some without disadvantaging the life of other viable human embryos, or when it functions in a moral context of being the lesser of two evils, but in no case can it be regarded as morally neutral. The exegetical and theological conclusion that the image of God extends to the embryo logically entails that the fetal person is entitled to the same rights and protection as the adult on the operating table.

Some have tried to justify killing of the unborn on the basis of death sentences exacted in the Mosaic Law for some sexual crimes. For example, persons guilty of incest were to be put to death, entailing the death of a possibly unwanted pregnancy (Leviticus 20:11, 12, 14). That sort of argument cannot stand under close scrutiny. It cannot be sustained consistently with modern tastes; it is facile; and it is unjust. The death sentence was exacted on both the man and woman in the case of consenting adulterers but only on the man in the case of rape (Deuteronomy 22:22-27). Possibly one could argue for castration in the case of rape but certainly not for abortion. Second, one must first determine the purpose of the penalties for sexual offences before attempting to imply their use in other situations. For example, the Bible exacts no penalty for harlotry but does demand death for the daughter who was promiscuous in her father's house (22:20-21). The writer does not aim to explain these laws but to note the difficulty of extrapolating principles without first understanding their original intention. Finally, to apply the death sentence to the innocent unborn and not to the offenders themselves would be unconscionable. It is beyond the scope of this paper to debate the merits of reconstructing society according to the Mosaic penalties for sex crimes.

In summary, mankind's destiny to rule the creation is restricted by the Law of God to love him and so his image.

Implications of Image for Patient Care

An implication of the understanding of the *imago Dei* as including man's physical form is of utmost importance. As Clines says, "the value of the body is strikingly affirmed."[23] Man's body as part of the image of God links heaven and earth. As we have seen, David drew the conclusion that man is only a little lower than heavenly beings (Psalm 8:5). When a doctor or physician treats a patient he or she is treating a heavenly being.

The Bible closely ties the image of God with its Maker; to affect one

is to affect the other. For example, the sage said:
He who oppresses the poor shows contempt for
their Maker,
but whoever is kind to the needy honours God.
(Proverbs 14:31)
The New Testament makes a similar association: "With the tongue
we praise our Lord and Father, and with it we curse men, who have
been made in God's likeness. Out of the same mouth come praise
and cursing. My brothers, this should not be" (James 3:9-10).

Because of this connection, doctors and physicians, who uniquely
influence the life, death, and well-being of the *imago Dei*, enjoy at one
and the same time the highest honour and the gravest responsibility.

The doctrine of the *imago Dei* not only invests the medical
profession with a glorious dignity, honour, and responsibility, it also
protects the life of every human against abuse by impious doctors
and physicians. After the Flood, God draws the implication from the
doctrine of the *imago Dei* that innocent blood must be avenged with
the ultimate penalty.
Whoever sheds the blood of man, by man shall
his blood be shed; for in the image of God has
God made man.   (Genesis 9:6)
Faithless doctors and physicians, who take the life of the unborn
through abortion or of the elderly, weak, and infirm through
euthanasia, assault and affront the Creator. The Old Testament,
placing the highest value on human blood because the life of God is
representatively in it (Leviticus 17:11), clearly and repeatedly teaches
that the shedding of innocent blood must be avenged (Numbers
35:33). If man does not avenge it, then God will (Genesis 4:10;
Deuteronomy 19:11-13; 22:8; 32:43; 2 Samuel 4:11; 1 Kings 2:32; etc.). In
the light of current practices, thank God for the sprinkled blood of
Jesus that speaks a better word than the blood of Abel, for the former
cries out for forgiveness whereas the latter cries out to be avenged
(Hebrew 12:24).

The Bible also teaches that aid should be extended to all in need.
For example, the sage coined the truth:
Rescue those being led away to death;
hold back those staggering toward slaughter.
If you say, "But we knew nothing about this,"
does not he who weighs the heart perceive it?
Does not he who guards your life know it?
Will he not repay each person according to what
he has done?   (Proverbs 24:11-12)
In the light of this responsibility, Christians in the medical

profession, need to ask themselves: "Is it right America's cities are surfeited with doctors and physicians, while rural areas stagger toward death without them?" They also need to relate their billing practices to the needs of their patients.

> He who despises his neighbour sins, but
> blessed is he who is kind to the needy. (14:21)

The Bible sanctions in principle the use of drugs to ease the pain of the suffering and warns against their abuse by those that are well. King Lemuel's mother verbalized the principle, using the specific medications of wine and beer:

> It is not for kings, O Lemuel—
>   not for kings to drink wine,
>   nor for rulers to crave beer,
> lest they drink and forget what the law decrees,
>   and deprive all the oppressed of their rights.
> Give beer to those who are perishing,
>   wine to those who are in anguish;
> let them drink and forget their poverty
>   and remember their misery no more. (31:4-7)

Conclusion

In summary, Christian researchers, doctors, and physicians need to measure their practices by the Golden Rule: "Therefore in everything, do to others as you would have them do to you, for this sums up the Law and the Prophets" (Matthew 7:12). The rule extends to "everything" (e.g., in-vitro fertilization, cloning, recombinant DNA, abortion, euthanasia) and to all mankind,[24] including unborn and malformed, rich and poor, foreign and native. The rule is given to Christ's disciples, who are neither demented nor deranged, and so capable of making sound judgments. It is heavenly; this is God's will in heaven, and his son calls upon his disciples to pray for its execution on earth (Matthew 6:9-10).

The linking of the rule with prayer is that which distinguishes it in our Lord's teaching. As is well known, negative equivalents of the Golden Rule are found in other religions and philosophies (Tobit, Hillel, Isocrates, Philo, the Stoics, and Kant). But none linked it with prayer. By introducing this saying, summarizing the Bible's teaching on ethics, with the logical particle, "therefore" (Greek, *oun*), our Lord binds the rule with the preceding command to pray. "Ask and it will be given you; seek and you will find; knock and the door will be opened to you. For everyone who asks receives; he who seeks finds; and to him who knocks, the door will be opened. Which of you, if his sons asks for bread, will give him a stone? Or if he asks for a fish, will give him a snake? If you, then, though you are evil, know how to give good gifts to your children, how much more will your Father in heaven give good gifts [Greek *agatha*] to those who ask him." "Good gifts" refers to that which is morally good, and the parallel passage in the Synoptics replaces "good gifts" with "Holy Spirit" (cf. Luke ll:1-13). Only through iterative prayer and the Holy Spirit can any Christian fulfill this supernatural ideal that is so readily portable to every situation.

Let all of us pray, earnestly petitioning God to restore piety and justice to medical practices. This is not a bromide with which to conclude a paper, but a sincere call to turn our darkening night into increasing light through the Spirit and prayer.

This paper was presented to a symposium of the Christian Medical Society and the American Scientific Association in Wenham, Massachusetts in June, 1988 and was the basis of a lecture given at Regent College in July, 1989.

Endnotes

1. Emil Brunner, "The Christian Understanding of Man" in *The Christian Understanding of Man*, ed. by T.E. Jessop (Allen Ltds., 1938) 146.

2. The writer represents the Hebrew collective *'adam*, which never occurs as a plural, by the English collective "mankind." In 2:4ff Adam [Hebrew *ha'adam*] refers to the male of the species. Though the writer usually follows NIV, he occasionally translates independently.

3. Only the Samaritan Pentateuch, which elsewhere, tends to add the conjunction "and," inserts it here.

4. P.D. Miller, Jr., Genesis 1-11: *Studies in Structure and Theme* (Sheffield: Journal for the Study of the Old Testament, 1978).

5. Gordon J. Wenham, *Genesis 1-15*, Vol. 1: *Word Biblical Commentary* (Waco: Words Books, 1987) 27-28.

6. Elmer Martens, *God's Design* (Grand Rapids: Baker Book House, 1981), 164.

7. For a survey of the history of the study and its meaning D. J. A. Clines, "The Image of God," *Tyndale Bulletin*, 19 (1968) 53-103.

8. A homonym in Hebrew means "shadow," "something shadowy" (Psalm 39:6; 73:20).

9. Gerhard von Rad, *Genesis* (Philadelphia: Westminster Press, 1961) 58.

10. Clines, p.75 wants to translate "as [i.e., in the capacity of] the image of God" but the parallel passage of Genesis 5:3 excludes his

exceptional interpretation. Adam begets a son not as his likeness but "in his likeness, according to his image." Furthermore, Clines can find no precise analogy in the Hebrew language to validate his translation. See also, Mettinger, *ZAW* 86 (1974) 406 and Sawyer, *JTS* 25 (1974) 421.

11. Edward J. Young, *Studies in Genesis One* (Philadelphia: Presbyterian and Reformed, 1973).

12. Cited by Clines, p. 57. Clines wants to make out that Calvin had a similar view. Calvin, however, faults Osiander for "extending the image of God promiscuously to the body as well as to the soul" (*Institutes*, 1. 15, 3).

13. Clines, 81.

14. Bruce K. Waltke, "Reflections from the Old Testament on Abortion," reprinted in *Journal of the Christian Medical Society,* 19/1 (1988) 24-28.

15. Claus Westermann, *Creation,* translated by John J. Scullion, S.J. (Philadelphia: Fortress Press, 1974) p. 42.

16. Clines, 83ff.

17. Martens, p. 164.

18. Gerhard von Rad, *Old Testament Theology,* 1 (New York and Evanston: Harper and Row, 1962) 158.

19. G. Fohrer, "Sophia," in *Theological Dictionary of the New Testament,* VII (Grand Rapids: Eerdmans, 1975) 478.

20. Mary Tew Douglas, Purity and Danger: *An Analysis of Concepts of Pollution and Taboo* (London: Routledge and Kegan Paul, 1966).

21. Isaac M. Kikawada and Arthur Quinn, *Before Abraham* Was (Nashville: Abingdon Press, 1985) 37.

22. Kikawada and Quinn, 38f.

23. Clines, p. 86.

24. "Others" renders the Greek word, *anthropos,* a collective for mankind.

'Art as Creation' or 'Art as Work'?

Loren Wilkinson

Vol. XIX, No. 1 (March 1983):23-28

Most Christians would agree that the arts are important—if not because they are activities good in themselves, at least because they are powerful means for the praise and worship of God. However, although Christians across the centuries have valued well-shaped artifacts of tone or stone or story, not till quite recently has there been any systematic attempt to think about the arts in a Christian framework. In recent years, however, thinkers from within two Christian traditions have laid the foundation for what might be called a "theology of art."

The first tradition is much broader than the second: it consists of all those branches of Christendom—Catholic, Orthodox, Anglican, Lutheran—which have taken the sacrament of the Lord's Supper to be more than just a sign or a reminder, but rather as a symbol, in which the bread and wine in some way participate in the reality to which they point. Thus we will call that tradition "Sacramentalist" (without meaning to imply either that all within this tradition hold the particular view of the nature of the arts outlined here, or that *any* within it maintain that the arts are themselves sacraments). Within this Sacramentalist tradition, the most eloquent voice has been that of Dorothy L. Sayers in her book, *The Mind of the Maker.*

The second tradition is that of Reformed Calvinism, particularly in those theologians and philosophers descending from Abraham Kuyper. This tradition generally places much less emphasis on the symbolic value of the sacraments, but elevates the stewardly task of the human in creation. We will call the ideas about art in this tradition "the Reformed aesthetic." The best spokesman for this view is Nicholas Wolterstorff, in his recent work *Art in Action.*

Unfortunately, these two positions do not merely differ; in some important ways, they disagree: the Sacramentalist view leaves out much which the Reformed position takes to be essential, and Reformed thinkers take offense at the main premise of the Sacramentalist position. This essay represents an attempt to articulate the differences between these two views, and to suggest a synthesis that points to a Christian understanding not only of the arts, but of human action generally. For the arts are, profoundly, a paradigm for human activity.

The Sacramentalist Aesthetic: Art as Creation

The central idea of Sacramentalist aesthetics is that the "image of God" in man can best be understood as a creative image: a finite replica of divine creativity. This is Sayers' premise in *The Mind of the Maker*. Though she acknowledges there the ambiguity surrounding the concept "image of God," she argues that if we take seriously the passage in which the phrase "image of God" appears, we can draw only one conclusion: "the characteristic common to God and man is apparently....the desire and ability to make things" (*The Mind of the Maker*, p.34).

Several other twentieth-century Christian thinkers have put the matter similarly. J.R.R. Tolkien, for example, in a letter written in defense of fantasy to C.S. Lewis shortly before Lewis' conversion, puts the premise in verse form. "Although now long estranged," writes Tolkien, "man is not wholly lost nor wholly changed." He is still "Man, Sub-Creator," and thus has both the right and the ability to build his own secondary worlds. So Tolkien concludes that "Used or misused.... That right has not decayed: We make still by the law in which we're made" ("On Fairy Stories," in C.S. Lewis, ed., *Essays Presented to Charles Williams*, p.72). From this basic analogy between divine creation and human art, three conclusions can be drawn.

1. **Human creativity is its own justification.** The concept of man as "sub-creator" making "secondary worlds" both supports and is supported by the modern assumption of the "autonomy" of the work of art. But some Christians have seen in this autonomy of art a further hint of the Creator. Thus David Jones, a Catholic Welsh poet writing on "Art and Sacrament" argues that "Art is the sole intransitive activity of man....it is the intransitivity and gratuitousness in man's art that is the sign of man's uniqueness" (Nathan Scott, ed., *The New Orpheus*, p.27). Jones' meaning is clear: works of human art share with the whole created world the fact that they are made not from necessity, but out of the free will of the

creator. Thus they are related, through the fact that man, the free creator, is made in the image of the Creator God of the Universe.

2. Human creativity, like the God it images, is triune. From this assumption of a basic connection between divine and human creativity comes a more elaborate idea, which though it is developed with most precision in Sayers' work, can be seen quite clearly by a look at popular language used in connection with the arts.

The words, "create," "creator," "creation" and "creative" have all been claimed first for aesthetic discussion and then vulgarized almost to the point of nonsense—so today we have "creative writing," "creative clothing," "creative cookery" and "creative divorce." Creativity has come to be understood as a common human trait that can best be grasped by applying to it a word formerly used only of God. The same thing has happened to the words "incarnate" or "embody." Images are described as the "incarnation" of a writer's ideas: artists are criticized for insufficiently "embodying" or "fleshing out" their vision. Finally, a set of terms drawing on the idea of "spirit" are frequently used of works of art: since Greek times, artists are said to be "inspired"; language of "inspiration" is popularly used to describe the impetus for new ideas. And works of art are said to "inspire" feelings or responses in their audience.

The Trinitarian shape of these three concepts is difficult to ignore. Denis de Rougemont points it out cautiously in these words:

> I say again, these three verbs are used improperly, and deserve the greatest severity on the part of the theologians. But the exorbitant misuse itself suggests a possibility of faithful and sober usage. The three everyday verbs that I have just cited—to create, to incarnate, to inspire—irresistibly evoke the attributes of the Holy Trinity ("Religion and the Mission of the Artist", in Nathan Scott, ed., *The New Orpheus*, p.70).

This Trinitarian pattern to artistic activity provides the structure of *The Mind of the Maker*, that work of Christian aesthetics that has probably exerted the greatest influence on evangelical thinking about the arts. She sets forth what later becomes the thesis of that book in the concluding speech of *The Zeal of Thy House*, a play about a medieval architect:

> For every act of creation is threefold, an earthly trinity to match the heavenly. First, there is the Creative Idea, passionless, timeless, beholding the whole work complete at once, the end in the beginning: and this is the image of the

Father. Second, there is the Creative Energy, begotten of that idea, working in time from the beginning to the end, with sweat and passion, being incarnate in the bonds of matter: and this is the image of the Word. Third, there is the Creative Power, the meaning of the work and its response in the lively soul: and this is the image of the indwelling Spirit. And these three are one, each equally in itself the whole work, whereof none can exist without other: and this is the image of the Trinity (cited in *The Mind of the Maker*, p.47).

Whatever one's judgment of the final worth of Sayers' analogy, it is nevertheless the case that the kind of dynamic interrelationship among idea, embodiment, and response that Sayers points out is remarkably parallel to theological speculations about the Trinity. More important, perhaps, is the fact that the experience of artistic activity which Sayers here describes, and which is familiar, in at least some form, to every human being, provides a way of understanding the Trinity which is probably more helpful in illustrating that mystery than a centuries-long list of cloudy examples. Particularly useful are the parallels that Sayers draws between various heresies in understanding the Trinity, and various similar kinds of "heresies" in art. For example, the temptation to docetism—the attempt to preserve the purity of God by denying the inescapable materiality of the Incarnation—is matched, in countless works of bad art, by artists who prefer to preserve the purity of an abstract idea, apart from the messy and exhausting struggle with embodiment. On the other hand, the parallel with the Arian heresy is also a helpful analogy for those so concerned with the "humanity" of the work, i.e., its sensuous surface or formal coherence, that they deny its necessary connection with the "father" of a controlling idea. Indeed, so useful as a parallel is this trinitarian analogy that Denis de Rougemont goes so far as to say that "Christian meditation will find in the vocabulary and dialectical arguments employed for nearly twenty years by trinitarian theologians the whole of a theory which introduces us better than any other to the human mysteries of the act of art ("Religion and the Mission of the Artist," *The New Orpheus*, p.72).

3. The works of human art are "Incarnations." Not surprisingly, the central idea in this understanding that human creativity is an expression of the image of God is that works of art are embodiments or images from the artists, that is, they are words "made flesh." Eric Gill, the versatile English Catholic calligrapher, sculptor, and illustrator, declares this incarnational centre to his aesthetic in these words:

What is a work of art? A word made flesh. That is the truth, in the clearest sense of the text. A word, that emanates from the mind. Made flesh: a thing, a thing seen, a thing known, the immeasurable translated into terms of the measurable. From the highest to the lowest, that is the substance of works of art ("The Priesthood of Craftsmanship," in Robert Goldwater and Marco Treves, eds., *Artists on Art*, p.45).

The main foundation of the Sacramentalist aesthetic, then, is the basic assumption that artistic activity can best be understood as creativity. From this implicit analogy between the Creator and the artist, thinkers like Sayers draw three conclusions: 1) a work of art, like creation itself, needs no justification beyond the will of the creator to make it; 2) artistic activity, in its basic form, images the triune nature of the divine image in man; and 3) all works of art are in some sense "incarnations": words made flesh.

The Reformed Aesthetic: The Artist as Steward

The Reformed aesthetic is developed both positively, out of solid Calvinist thinking about the place of humans in creation, and negatively, out of a critique of the Sacramentalist view—or at least of heresies that the Reformed thinkers regard as being dangerously close to the Sacramentalist view. Since the Reformed critique is usually the obverse of a positive point in the Reformed position, we can well begin this brief survey of Reformed aesthetics by looking at its negative side: the critique of Sacramentalist view of the arts.

I. **Thinking of humans as "Creators" leads to sinful pride.** The major Reformed criticism of Sacramentalist aesthetics is set forth most clearly by Wolterstorff in *Art in Action*. It amounts to a recognition of one of the "covert blasphemies" that (as Seerveld warns us in his *Rainbows for a Fallen World*) lie implicit in the artist-Creator analogy. That danger is the temptation to pride that words like "create," "creator" and "creative" represent when they are applied to human activity.

Some historical background is necessary if we are to fully appreciate Wolterstorff's criticism. Although the use of the word "create" in reference to human activity can be traced back at least to the Renaissance, the idea was not developed with any thoroughness till the late eighteenth century. Then it entered European thought in a major way as a part of that vast, complex, and still-current movement of mind and spirit loosely called "Romanticism."

The most explicit linking of divine with human creativity in the English Romantic poets occurs in Samuel Taylor Coleridge's definition of the "Primary Imagination." He calls it "the repetition in the finite mind of the eternal act of creation in the infinite 'I AM'." That is, the mind in the very act of perceiving is understood to be creating—or at least participating in the creation of—the world that it perceives. That many of the Romantics considered this newly-discovered power to be divine is evident in the religious awe with which other writers, especially Wordsworth, regarded it.

Perhaps the most vivid expression of this idea that human imagination is actually identical with the creative mind of God is in William Blake's powerful illustrations of the book of Job. In the first of that series of twenty-one plates Job is sitting, with his children, under a tree reading a book. In the background is a Gothic cathedral, and a setting sun. On the tree hang musical instruments, symbolic of the imagination that Job is not using. Job's trials serve to make him aware of his imagination: when he learns that his sin has been a failure to imagine, he is restored to greater wealth. Thus the last plate of the series shows Job and his family again under the tree. But now they are standing; the book, symbolizing the "letter of the law" has vanished; instead they are all playing the instruments and singing—that is, using the imagination. The sun is rising, and no church is visible.

The message is clear enough. But the most dramatic statement is more subtle. In many of the plates, God and Job appear together, God above and Job below. And the faces of the two are unmistakably identical. God the Creator and Job the creator are potentially one: when Job recognizes this, God is no longer outside of him. Instead, God and Job become one: the fully incarnate, divine-human maker. And this, says Blake, is what awaits all who open the eyes of their imagination.

Wolterstorff argues that the concept of the artist as creator has these dangerous Romantic roots, even in its Christian form in the work of Sacramentalists like Sayers. In his words, "The basic image of the artist underlying modern Western art is that of the artist as a center of consciousness who challenges God by seeking to create as God creates" (p.56).

Thus the first main Reformed criticism of the Sacramentalist aesthetic is that any comparison of the human artist with the divine Creator is likely to invite pride and rebellion: for though God creates freely, human creation must be either in obedience to God, or in disobedience. And the more the artist attains to the ideal of free, untrammelled creativity, the more likely he is to be disobedient to God.

2. When understood as "creation," human art is "anti-Creational." A second Reformed critique of the sacramentalist position grows out of another aspect of this fear that seeing human creativity in terms of *divine* creativity will lead to a rebellious attitude that can tolerate no limitation. One limitation for the human artist is, of course, the will of God. But another limitation is the sheer fact of being in a "primary creation." A radical understanding of the artist as creator is therefore likely to lead to a kind of anti-Creational stance, and an urge to escape from Creation. The anti-Creational direction of this attitude is reflected in words that Wolterstorff quotes from Virginia Woolf. When asked whether or not art should copy nature she replied, "Art is not a copy of the real world. One of the damn things is enough." Implicit therefore in the idea of artist as creator, says Wolterstorff, is this dangerous idea that the human maker has no responsibility to God's Creation, but only an artist-centred passion for making his own worlds. And those worlds must, in a sense, shoulder nature aside in order to find a place to stand. Human creation thus is seen not as stewardship, but as a competition with divine Creation.

So much for the Reformed critique of the Sacramentalist aesthetic. We turn now to a consideration of the positive alternative that Reformed thinkers offer as a theological explanation for the activity of the arts.

1. The arts as responsibility to God. Reformed aesthetics rest on two connected theological foundations, which represent the positive side of the two main criticisms of Sacramentalist aesthetics. The first of these is a warning against a Romantic tendency in sacramentalism towards a sinful elevation of the human maker. And, from Kuyper on, Reformed thinkers on the arts are insistent that the basis for the arts lies in a divine command. That command is not to *create*: it is rather to *work* in Creation: to subdue and have dominion. This command is the basis for that distinctively Reformed concept, the "cultural mandate." And any mandate is a command, which implies both a master with authority, and a servant who obeys. Thus the first foundation of Reformed aesthetics is a recognition of our responsibility to God.

2. The arts as responsibility to Creation. The second foundation of the Reformed position is the obverse of the criticism that the "creative" human artist is likely to be in competition with God's creation. Because Christians are related *upward*, in loving obedience to God, they are related *outward* as well, into the world of Creation.

This outward relationship is, of course, the working dimension of the "cultural mandate." The Christian's redemption through Christ leads to a renewed relationship with the Creation.

This is Wolterstorff's thesis in what is perhaps the most important chapter of his book: "The Artist as Responsible Servant." Says Wolterstorff, "The image appropriate to subduing—to ordering nature for the benefit of man—is that of *gardening*. Man's vocation is to be the world's gardener." And the arts are a prime example of this "gardening" of Creation. Wolterstorff again:

> It is not difficult to see how man's vocation of master, of subduer, of humanizer of the world, of one who imposes order for the sake of benefiting mankind or honoring God, applies to the artist. The artist takes an amorphous pile of bits of colored glass and orders them upon the wall of the basilica so that the liturgy can take place in the splendor of flickering colored light and in the presence of the invoked saints. He takes a blob of clay and orders it into a pot of benefit and delight... *(Art in Action*, p.77).

And so on. Wolterstorff moves through many of the arts, showing how each is not so much a new creation as it is an elevation of unformed Creation into a higher possibility: a kind of gardening of Creation, till it blossoms into what that Creation can most fully be. So he concludes this description of the stewardly artist: "The artist, when he brings forth order for human benefit or divine honor, shares in man's vocation to master and subdue the earth."

The Reformed aesthetic, stemming from a strong sense of obedience to God and responsibility to act caringly in the world, rooted in the theological profundity of Calvinism, and in the godly activism of Abraham Kuyper, is a rich contribution to contemporary theological articulation of the nature of the arts. Particularly in Wolterstorff's book, the Reformed concept of art as work shows itself to be a remarkably effective tool for laying bare our understanding of the arts.

Towards a Synthesis

We can grant the force and helpfulness of the Reformed criticisms without discarding some important insights of the Sacramentalist aesthetic. The Reformed warnings about the dangers of a "heaven-storming" sinfulness are certainly justified. Christians cannot undertake any activity apart from their relationship to God: all actions must be done as "unto the Lord." Likewise the Reformed emphasis on our human task in God's Creation is a necessary reminder that we are made to exercise responsible stewardship for

Creation, not to be in competition with both God and his world.

But these reminders seem to provide grounds not so much for rejecting the Sacramentalist view of art as they do a framework for rethinking and strengthening that view. For in at least one important way, the Reformed position needs something like the Sacramentalist understanding in order to provide an adequate theological foundation for the arts. (Space does not permit the discussion of an even more basic way in which the Reformed aesthetic requires a Sacramentalist insight: that is in the very nature of language itself. Here Seerveld follows Kuyper in arguing that analogical or symbolic thought about God is always suspect. Kuyper asserts that "the more Religion develops itself into spiritual maturity, the more it will extricate itself from art's bandages, because art always remains incapable of expressing the very essence of Religion." But in so eliminating the validity of analogical, metaphorical, or symbolic thinking, Kuyper strikes at the root of the most basic of arts, language itself. For it is always necessary to express something distant and not well known in terms of what is close at hand, and better known. Strictly speaking, this illusion of a non-symbolic, non-allegorical speech is rooted more in Zwingli's view of the sacraments than in Calvin's.)

That essential Sacramentalist idea is in the affirmation of what seems to some a blasphemously close link between the work of God and the work of man. While we must not lose sight of the Reformed warning, that such thinking can cause man to forget his utter dependence on God, we must nevertheless recognize that this picture of God sharing with man his power over creation is a biblical one.

For Sayers' point about the image of God is well-taken: whatever else it might mean, the most obvious fact about God in Genesis 1 is his transcendent creativity. To be in God's image means that man represents his Creator in the world, with a delegated dominion over it that could hardly be expressed in stronger terms than the Hebrew verbs translated "subdue" and "have dominion." God's willingness to share in at least the sustaining of Creation is evident when God brings the animals before Adam "to see what he would call them." To name a thing is not only to exert power over it; it is also to recognize its true nature—even to shape and release that true nature, to direct it into what it could not become without the namer. We see God often naming people in this way. Abram, for example, becomes Abraham, and so reveals his destiny as father *of a multitude*. This kind of naming is involved in Eden. And, significantly, God does not do it; he brings the creatures to Adam, and lets him do it.

God waits to see what man will do. And "whatever the man called a living creature, that was its name." This is not creating from nothing by word, as we have seen God do at the beginning. But it is nevertheless a kind of creative power, over Creation, by means of words. In it, God invites man to participate with him in shaping the world.

Some have argued at this point that even if God did in Eden extend to Adam the invitation to exercise his own creative response to God's Creation, that possibility has been wiped out by man's disobedience and fall. Yet the Psalmist, writing out of a deep sense both of human finitude and of human wickedness, recognizes the same transcendent human power over the rest of Creation that is described in Genesis 1 and 2. In Psalm 8, in what is almost a recapitulation of that Edenic scene in which man names the animals, the Psalmist wonders that God has given man such potential for greatness, exclaiming, "thou hast made him a little less than God." Certainly the infinitely greater works of God—the starry heavens with which the Psalm opens—keep that exclamation of man's greatness in perspective. But when the Septuagint writers translated this Psalm into Greek, they chose to translate the *elohim* with the more modest " angels." And it is in this form that the Psalm enters the epistle to the Hebrews.

Nevertheless, something important is being said in this Old Testament declaration of man as being made "a little lower than God." And the brief quotation and discussion of Psalm 8 in Hebrews is extremely important for answering that question of whether or not God's activity in creation can in any way be understood as a model or pattern for man's. For the writer of that great epistle presents Jesus as "appointed heir of all things..... through whom he [God] made the universe." Thus Jesus is clearly portrayed here as Creator. Yet he is linked in the discussion of Psalm 8 with Adam as well. After recounting the Psalmist's cry that "thou hast put all things under his [man's] feet," he observes that all things are not yet so subjected. Whether through failure, or incompleteness, the mandate given man at Creation has not been carried out. But, despite this failure, whereas the first Adam failed in his task, the last Adam, Christ, completes it: "We do see him who has been made for a little while lower than the angels, namely Jesus, crowned with glory and honor . . . ." It would appear, then, that at least at this one point, the analogy between man and God is acceptable. God completes in Christ what man began, and failed, to complete. It is perhaps only a profound coincidence that the resurrected Jesus was first seen in a garden, and mistaken for a gardener. But the "yet" in verse 8—"we do not yet see all things subjected to him"—suggests that we may indeed participate in Christ's gardening at Creation, a promise hinted at in the declaration in verse 10 that Christ will "bring many sons to glory."

There is just a suggestion here that Christians are invited, through the work of Christ, into a relationship with Creation in which they will be restored to the true human place, "a little lower than the angels." But that hint is made much more explicit in Romans 8:18ff, in which Creation is pictured as waiting for "the revealing of the sons of God." The unmistakable import of this passage is that man, through Christ, has not only a redemptive, but a creative role to play in the "ministry of reconciliation" with God's Creation.

The idea that man is, actually or potentially, a creature called to creativity is a very dangerous one, as the Reformed thinkers have pointed out. It is particularly prone to the Promethean heresy of the Romantics. That heresy grasps something enormously important about the potential stature of man in the image of God. Nevertheless, this understanding of man as "sub-creator" can only be held along with a continual recognition that we are called by God, both in Creation, and in our redemption, to sacrificial, obedient service. We are given enormous powers—powers appropriate to the delegated representatives, in his Creation, of the Creator Lord of the Universe. But every power is to be used for the sake of others: other persons, certainly, but also the mute "other" of primary Creation, which the human arts can so eloquently *selve* (to use a phrase of Gerard Manley Hopkins). Our human gifts, creative or not, are to be crucified, laid aside, not grasped at.

This idea is not stated often enough within the confident affirmations of the Sacramentalist aesthetic. Thus that view requires the Reformed reminder of sinfulness. But so also does the Reformed position need the Sacramentalist reminder of the stature to which, in Christ, we are restored. If the people of God can be shaped by both insights into the nature of the arts, perhaps they will be able yet to fulfil the promise given to Abraham: that those within whom the image of God has been made new will "rebuild the ancient ruins, and will raise up the age- old foundations" and become, through the Godly use of all the arts, "The Repairer of Broken Walls, Restorer of Streets in Which to Dwell."

What Meals and Books Have to Do With Each Other

Mary Ruth Wilkinson

Vol. XXIII, No. 3 (September 1987):2-6

"A bookseller," said Grandfather, "is the link between mind and mind, the feeder of the hungry, very often the binder up of wounds. There he sits, your bookseller, surrounded by a thousand minds all done up neatly in cardboard cases; beautiful minds, courageous minds, strong minds, wise minds, all sorts and conditions. And there come into him other minds, hungry for beauty, for knowledge, for truth, for love, and to the best of his ability he satisfies them all... In my experience when people once begin to read they go on because they must. Yes. They find it widens life. We're all greedy for life, you know, and our short span of existence can't give us all that we hunger for, the time is too short and our capacity not large enough. But in books we experience all life vicariously."
— Elizabeth Goudge, *A City of Bells.*

When I was growing up, the Christian-home counterpart of the essential *Joy of Cooking* was a cookbook called *Food for the Body —Food for the Soul.* In it, pithy Christianity in the form of Bible passages, sermonettes (with a "From My Kitchen Window" view of the world), stories with a *very* definite message, and recipes for Christian character ("seven cups of love, one pint of forgiveness, a pinch of honesty") alternated with an excellent collection of basic food recipes. Our copy had a greenish cover with a black spiral binding— just thinking about it calls up a complex of memories. They centre on my Scottish grandmother who used every meal as an opportunity for getting the lessons of life very clearly in focus. She would rehearse, with considerable knowledge, both international and neighbourhood news—from the deceit of the Russians right down to the latest woman who had painted her lips "bloody"; and each evil she would then pierce with a straight and sharp (with chapter and verse) biblical sword.

From our perspective we may marvel that such a digestive mix to meals in a Christian home did not kill off both body and soul. From the longshot view of the world, however, the perspectives of both the cookbook and my grandmother were absolutely right. The wisdom of the cookbook was its recognition that just as the body needs its own biscuits and gravy, so the soul or mind needs to be fed *its* own nutritious mix or (as we say) food for thought. And the wisdom of my grandmother was that the *mealtime* is a natural focal point for communication. Indeed, her sharp, incisive mind and tongue prompted lengthy heated discussions, despite the attempts of my gentle grandfather (the Head of the House; this was, after all, a Brethren family) to cool things down with an occasional lament of "Now Emily ..." (His relish for heat at the table was strictly in the food-for-the-body line: mustard and horseradish. The latter he was required to keep under the table.)

The cookbook, my grandmother, and all of us human beings have taken the most animal-like, gut-driven action of each day—eating—and transformed it into the highest celebration of our humanity: our ability to interact with other minds. At this mealtime crux of body and soul we get close to a crux of earth and heaven. For the deeper implication of both the cookbook and my grandmother's attitude is that two sorts of nourishment meet when human beings *eat* together. The use of the meal—of the eating of food to nourish human bodies—is meaningless if the soul has not had its proper meal. Just as biscuits and gravy must be taken and digested in order for us to grow strong bodies, so the food for the soul must be eaten and digested in order for us to communicate well with each other.

Now, we can all list our favourite foods for the body. Our family's is "creamed something" (chicken, tuna, tofu...) "over something" (biscuits, rice, bulgar wheat...). Food for the soul, however, is much more elusive and often, unfortunately, not nearly as rigorously calculated and controlled. In speaking of the minds of young children, Jane Yolen, a writer of modern fairy tales, catalogues the various "foods" that build a personal mythology—what we could call the "bones of the mind ":

Take one small child and throw into the bubbling pot of its mind all that it sees and hears: TV, superheroes and superstars, cartoons, mother's and father's opinions, the teacher's assertions, the misrepresentations of its peers. What comes out is a semi-coherent mythology that the child carries into adulthood. I believe that a child—and an adult—needs a mythology.

Many of us would hasten to add the salt of sermons and Bible reading to Yolen's bubbling pot. But whether we are children *or* adults, all that we put into that pot of our minds gets digested, or (as Yolen puts it) "comes out" as a mythology. Certainly we need to exercise at least as much care in checking out the vitamins and calories of the nutrients we put into our souls as we do those we put into our bodies.

And so, in an age which has been called the TV generation, which has been criticized for being image-oriented and nurtured on the "plug-in drug," which has been warned that it is in danger of losing its own soul to the maw of superficial mass culture, we would do well to analyze carefully a food which, in verbal form, is as old as the soul and yet is the most threatened ingredient in the bubbling pot of the mind. That ingredient is literature. Perhaps the most significant "eating" our souls do is the reading of good books. Just as we take great care, when planning meals, to look at the value and effects of (say) oatmeal in the whole eating process, so we need to examine the effects of a diet of literature.

When we eat a meal we are doing something awfully mundane. We eat pretty much the same old foods on the same old dishes and often enough with the same old people. And yet rarely does a meal seem mundane. We know that hamburger, like us, can have a thousand faces; these bowls and pots are really a potsherd record of our family's history; and we take joy (most of the time) in yet another meal with these same old people. And so it is with reading. We have the same old letters, the same old words, and all too often the same old plots. Without our minds there to interpret the data of our eyes, the whole mass would be a meaningless jumble. So just the bare reading of those squiggles and lines in good books is a wonderfully imaginative activity.

Our reading—our re-creation of those letters into words and those words into a plot—is, however, only a beginning. Each word we read carries (much like our dishes) memories and reminders of the history of the human family. Each word we read hangs in a balance between objective dictionary definition and subjective nuance: with our experience, we tip the scales. Phrases like "Once upon a time" and "big bad wolf" arouse emotional responses that go strong and deep. And each word we read has its own taste and texture—the alliterated "w's" and "l's" rolling along our tongue in "... weeds in wheels, shoot long and lovely a lush" or the snowy night's feathery softness in "The woods are lovely, dark and deep."

Edward Fenton, a translator of children's books, points out that God was not called the Word for nothing. Words, he says, have an infinite potential of meaning that makes the job of a translator very difficult: "We may have the facts, perhaps, but not the phosphorescence." Just as a writer uses words imaginatively to create meaning and nuance, so that particular phosphorescence intended by the author is seen by the reader from his own angle of vision at the moment of his own life in which he is reading. That is why, in going back to a good book after many years, we often find it to be quite a different book from the one we read long ago.

But the imaginative activity of reading a book goes far beyond the richness of the words. Here a comparison with the visual media (television or movie) is helpful. When we *watch* a story (like E. M. Forster's *A Passage to India*) translated into a movie, we *see* what happens; we see the characters. We see in their faces and gestures and we hear in their tone of voice the actor's and the director's and the screen-writer's interpretations of the story. In fact we see the whole story through the grid of other people's points of view on what is really happening. Not only do they flatten the ambience in a story to one line of meaning, but they may even be completely wrong. And yet research has shown that once we *see* the events of a book through someone else's eyes we will find great difficulty in finding our own internal vision again.

When we read a story, on the other hand, our minds supply highly personalized imaginative data of the two most vital senses, sight and sound. The fairy godmother in "Cinderella" which our mind's eye conjures up is a marvelous combination of homey grandmotherliness and fairy glory. So *any* picture of her, whether by Walt Disney or Arthur Rackham, is an immense disappointment, both because it is never quite true to *our* fairy godmother and because we can never go back through that picture on the page or in the movie to what is, for us, the *real* fairy godmother. Our heavenly vision has been murdered.

Reading is, therefore, far more than just seeing meaning in words. As we turn the pages of print, our minds are busy manufacturing elaborate details for our eyes to see and our ears to hear—and our noses to smell, our tongues to taste, and our bodies to feel. In reading, the whole imaginative activity of our minds becomes geometrically magnified. Of course some might worry that such an intensely personal world-creation might lead to a dangerously solipsistic narcissism. We create our worlds in our image. At the heart of this worry is a truth that helps us grasp what a profound experience reading can be. In a way, reading comes close to dreaming. Our subconscious can choose that very configuration of truth—can create that very shape from the world of words—which matches the fairies and dragons, the green pastures and dark tunnels, of our subliminal world. This match of story world and inner world explains the importance both of fairy tales—and of Jesus' parables. On those spare bones of story we drape the clutter and tatter of our fears and longings—the paucity of detail in fairy tales allows our minds plenty of latitude for shaping the archetypal figures of wolf, grandmother and woodsman—and of course we *all* are Little Red Riding Hood.

And so, in the end, we live happily—or at least happier—ever after: we have carried the burdens of our souls safely through to the good ending of the story. Any story in literature is like the fairy tales in that, with our imagination, we remake (or digest) the story into the image of our own experience and hopes and fears, and thereby go through a catharsis. This catharsis may lead to healing or it may lead to hurt—but any story in which we imaginatively dwell with all our senses *will* be a catharsis.

In spite of the thoroughly personal nature of reading as a food for the soul, it does *not*, however, lead to a self-centred solipsistic narcissism precisely because at heart, reading is a profoundly Christian experience. In Philippians, Paul reminds us of the central teaching of Christian life:

> Your attitude should be the same as that of Christ Jesus: who, being in very nature God, did *not* consider equality with God something to be grasped, but made himself nothing, taking the very nature of a servant, being made in human likeness.

In one sense, as we read a book we are all, like God, looking down from some high exalted place into the world of the story. Through the eyes of Charles Dickens we see the world of *David Copperfield*: gentle Dora, sturdy Agnes, 'umble Uriah, cocky Steerforth, and those whiny Micawber kids. But as the story progresses we take in the nature of David and vicariously we go with him through the events of his world. In the end we have immersed ourselves in the likeness of another being to a degree that we rarely could or would in the real world. What is more, we have vicariously lived through the death of parents, a childhood of torture and insecurity, fickle friends, the death of a wife, and two marriages. We have, in fiction if not in fact,

lived quite a hard life in which we have learned many lessons, not
the least of which (for our own day) is the goodness that can come
from enduring a bad marriage.

In every book we read we are new people going through new
experiences. Precisely because these characters of fiction are faceless
and factually unreal, we can in ourselves give flesh and blood to their
being. In so doing we lay aside our "selfish ambition" and "vain
conceit," and we take up the cross of their pain, the burden of their
care. Kornei Chukovsky, the father of children's literature in Russia,
discusses the importance of stories to children; what he says rings
true to the experience of all of us:

> The goal of storytellers...consists in fostering in the child
> compassion and humaneness—this miraculous ability of
> man to be disturbed by another being's misfortunes, to feel
> joy about another being's happiness, to experience another's
> fate as one's own.

Part of the wonder of literature in helping us experience another's
fate as our own is the diversity it can span. In Rosemary Sutcliff's
Sword at Sunset we can cut across history and suffer through the
intrigues of the Round Table with King Arthur. In Francois Mauriac's
Viper's Tangle we can become an old man looking back over the
choices of life and realizing what big and tragic turns resulted from
misunderstanding his wife. In Joy Kogawa's *Obasan* we share the
uprootedness of Japanese-Canadians in World War II.

And so as we read books, as we digest this feast for the soul, we
realise that we have not made our world in our image; rather, our
experience of all these worlds has remade *us*. Bertholt Brecht once
said that the principle of Hell is "Eat or be eaten"; the principle of
Heaven is "eat *and* be eaten." Our digestion of literature as food for
the soul is profoundly Christian in that, as we eat this food for the
soul and digest it to strengthen our hearts and minds, all these books
end up somehow eating away at us, biting off our selfishness, our
misunderstanding, our prejudice. Eventually (if we allow ourselves
to read the greatest story of the world) we may in a great communion
of body and soul so eat Christ's body and drink Christ's blood that we
may be "eaten"—or transformed—into his image.

What results from all this eating and digesting of a good book as
food for the soul? When we eat food for the body our digestive
system transmutes the biscuits and gravy into physical energy for
digging gardens and playing hockey. Perhaps the richest result of
the food of literature is a spiritual energy for deeply relational
interaction—and now we're back to the dinner table. Around the
table, whether the meal be a family supper or just an impromptu

"cuppa" with a friend, our communication becomes a workout for the soul. Here it is that we use the sturdy bones and strong muscles of our soul to have communication that becomes in itself food for the soul. And just as a Scottish grandmother helps to steer the conversation in a straight course toward the Kingdom of God, so our reading of good books can guide us toward the "what" to talk about.

Literature also helps us work through the weary chatter of our conversation toward meaning and patterns. Certainly the rain (perhaps the greatest source of small talk in Vancouver) and the daffodils on the front lawn and the cuddly comfort of our dog are worth talking about, but as human beings we always yearn for more. And so, often we discover that the "what" of even rain, daffodils, and the dog can be wellworn pathways to the "why" "how" and "wherefore" questions of the soul—pathways cleared and tended and even bordered by literature: pathways that somehow, if followed to their end, often lead to God.

Not only does literature give content and direction to our interaction, it also helps us understand the others around the table. Because we have lived other's lives in books, we can live other's lives in a mealtime. Around the table we see not only our family and friends, but, having richly eaten and digested the lives of many others, we can through the flesh and blood of their experience see (for example) in this young son of ours a "Toad" of *The Wind in the Willows*, who may have to go off caravaning before he appreciates the value of a more sturdy stability; in this daughter we see an Anne of Green Gables who must test the strength of her own wings before she settles down; and in this dear husband we recognize a Sam Gamgee from *The Lord of the Rings* who gives us a sense of the comforts of home wherever we are. And so, in ourselves and in each other, we recognize the thousand faces of the other souls of *story*. When we talk around the table we respond not just to son or daughter or husband but to the complex and diverse mix of those many storied selves in these persons who are talking to us with their mouths full and gesticulating with their forks and struggling to say what they want to say.

At this point in the meal, or the conversation—we come back to words, the basic ingredient of that culinary concoction of the soul that is literature. For, if in our reading we do nothing else, we have digested words, we have tasted their subtle flavours of nuance and meaning and, vicariously, in the likeness of others, we have learned the real ingredients—the hidden anger, the bold and merry face of desperation and the tight control of fear—in that conversational stew that we serve up to each other at our meals. We have also learned the words with which to spice and season what we say to each other, so that not only will the words of our mouths richly express the thoughts of our minds but they will also be words well-chosen for the emotional and mental palates of those who hear us speak. From our experience in literature, from being in the likeness of another, we can begin to conjecture the right recipe of love, forgiveness, honesty, kindness, and even maybe harshness that will make our words fit food for another's soul.

So in the *meal* we have both food for the body and food for the soul. Here eating and reading come together. Our reading of good books involves us in a wonderfully imaginative activity that stretches our minds by the sheer infinite variety in that smorgasbord of the world's words. Our reading of these words becomes in turn a profoundly Christian experience as we vicariously digest the joys and sorrows of another's life and make them our own. This food for the soul which we have digested is then transformed into the muscles and strength for deeply relational interaction with others. And yet, literature does more than all that. It gives us a perspective which helps us see each meal as more than just a meal.

Our discussion of eating meals and reading books and communicating with others can, however, seem a crushing burden. Why can't we just eat? Well, we're not just animals, that's why. Each meal, each conversation, each word we say is (to adopt a metaphor from Frederick Buechner) a letter in the *Alphabet of Grace*. The good of Buechner's metaphor is that—as he reminds us—the alphabet of grace is full of gutturals. Our reading helps us to see that all the gutturals, the harsh words, the noisy chaotic meals—and even the silent sullen ones—are parts of a greater glory that is the plot of our own story. Buechner uses the imagery of music to describe the makings of a work of art in a meal:

> Here with butter on my chin and egg on my tie, I forget myself in the recitative of my children, the arias of myself and my wife, the patter songs and yammering quintets. It need not always happen that way in a family, but this morning we are lucky, all of us caught up together in the comic opera of being at breakfast and being with each other and being ourselves and alive. We are noisy and talk with our mouths full. We are far from always considerate of each other. Some of us cry and some of us thump the table for a little silence, a little respect. But instead of standing each in the wings of his own face awaiting the cue to enter and sing some bravura passage, we are caught up together in a common cacophony.

And yet, Buechner's breakfast, our meals—and our lives—only *seem* cacophony. Behind all the confusion, a providential choreography is at work, making of the cacophony a symphony, of the gutturals a book of life.

The sacrament of communion helps us accept the imbalance in all our meals and conversations. We do not come perfect to the meal of God. We are never perfect in our communication with God or with our family and friends while we eat this meal. We may, if only of our God has come to us in this bread and this wine. The meal reminds us that food for the body and food for the soul come together at the dinner table of our God and at the dinner tables of our homes.

Evening is here
The Board is spread
Thanks be to God
Who gives us Bread.

Renewal: An Antidote for Entropy

Walter C. Wright, Jr.

Vol. XXIV, No. 4 (December 1988):2-5

In the current literature of organizational life, management and leadership, two key concepts are entropy and renewal. Renewal, I believe, looks at the process that is evoked by the images of "rooted" and "built up," which are biblical metaphors for growth.

I would like to focus on three thoughts: entropy is the antithesis of growth; renewal is the antidote for entropy; and community is the enabler of renewal.

I would like to take off from the Song in Isaiah 40:27-31, particularly verse 31. In this section of Isaiah, the author is writing as if the Babylonian exile is about over. In chapter 40, he offers a song of praise, describing first the majesty of God, followed by these verses focusing on the goodness of God, who will renew his people and give them strength, if they will "hope in the Lord"—if they will grasp on to the vision of God's promise to them.

> Why do you say, O Jacob,
>   and complain, O Israel,
> "My way is hidden from the Lord;
>   my cause is disregarded by my God?"
> Do you not know?
>   Have you not heard?
> The Lord is the everlasting God,
>   the Creator of the ends of the earth.
> He will not grow tired or weary,
>   and his understanding no one can fathom.
> He gives strength to the weary,
>   and increases the power of the weak.

Even youths grow tired and weary,
and young men stumble and fall;
but those who hope in the Lord
will renew their strength.
They will soar on wings like eagles,
they will run and not grow weary
they will walk and not be faint.

Entropy is the antithesis of growth.

Entropy as an organizational concept is a derivative of the Second Law of Thermodynamics. Basically, it says that all organized systems will move toward chaos unless energy is brought into the system to reestablish order. In other words, everything that is organized will break down or run down unless it is maintained. Everything moves toward disorder, unless you intentionally intervene to reestablish order. Have you looked in your closet lately? or perhaps the top of your desk or your back yard?

In organizational life, there are signs of entropy. Max DePree, chairman of Herman Miller, Inc. a *Fortune 500* manufacturer of office systems, lists several signs in his recent book, *Leadership is an Art*. We need to watch for these signs as we enter the next era of Regent College. Here is a partial list:

1. A tendency toward superficiality
2. Tension among key people
3. No time for celebration and ritual
4. Thinking that rewards and goals are the same things
5. No longer telling the stories of the past
6. Avoidance of complexity and ambiguity
7. Problem makers outnumber problem solvers
8. Seeking to control rather than liberate
9. Pressures of today pushing aside concern for vision and risk
10. When rules, manuals and ratios replace contribution, spirit, excellence and joy
11. When we rely on structures rather than people.

These are some of the signs of entropy in organizations.

But what about entropy in personal life? Have you looked in the mirror lately? You may not notice much difference yet, but keep looking. Entropy is occurring whether you like it or not! The question most of us have to deal with is: "Are you going to speed up the process of physical entropy or tend to your diet and exercise?" For people in academia and in ministry, I think this is an occupational hazard. There is so much to do, and so much is done at a desk or over meals, that the body can go unattended and we become accessories to entropy. I don't need to say more about this...check yourself out in the next window or mirror you pass.

A more serious concern, though, is our relationships. Relationships, when neglected, fall into the same disrepair as organizations. They lack vitality and meaning; they tend toward superficiality; tension increases; celebration, spirit, and joy are missing. Relationships need time and careful nurturing or they will not last.

At a Time Management workshop that I was leading in San Diego, a young woman raised her hand and noted that her fiancé was a seminarian, and was too busy studying to spend much time with her now. She wanted to know if it would improve when they were out in ministry.

Unfortunately, I had to tell her, no. The patterns and priorities for the use of your time are being set now. The demand upon your time will only get worse in the future. If her fiancé has no time for her now, he will have less time for her in the future. This is a particularly strong concern for me. I have worked in theological schools now for twenty years and I am very saddened by the number of marriages that do not survive. Graduate schools are notoriously hard on marriages, but in the theological schools it can be worse, because we are busy about "the Lord's business." Personally, I believe that if God has called you to marry, you have been given a priority field of ministry. Failure to nurture that relationship causes me to question your call to ministry. Take the time to be with, talk to and listen to your spouse. It's probably more important than anything else we ask you to do.

And finally, the spiritual life. This too is a relationship that must be nurtured. When we get too busy to spend time with God, to engage him in Scripture and in prayer, to allow the Spirit of God to work through us in ministry to others, we lose our vitality, our sense of purpose, our very identity. I am talking here about the thinking, reflective and communing side of our relationship with God, that personal interaction and commitment that empowers our life. Again, I have watched too many persons, lay people and clergy, who are so busy about the work of the ministry that they have lost the breath of the Spirit. God is faithful and unchanging but spiritual entropy can enter an untended door on our side of the relationship.

Entropy is the antithesis of growth. If we do not intentionally intervene, we will watch our organizations, our physical condition, our relationships and our spiritual development erode and even die.

So, what do we do about it? This brings us to the second point.

Renewal is an antidote for entropy

In the current research on organizational life, renewal is seen as
the antidote for entropy. Renewal comes from the infusion of new
energy at crucial points to reduce the forces of entropy. In the
literature on leadership and organizational life, three key ingredients
for renewal are identified: a vision of excellence, a commitment to
service, and the courage to break habits.

a) A vision of excellence
When I consult with an organization, the first thing I ask is:
"What is your vision of excellence?" What would it look like if you
were operating at your best? What is important to you and how is
this evident in the way you do things? With a clear vision of where
the organization wants to be, the process of developing a plan to get
there is much easier. The same is true on the personal level. When
you think about your life before God, your physical existence, your
personal relationships, your spiritual development, what is your
vision for excellence? Who do you want to be before God? What is
important to you? What does this look like when it is lived? In other
words, to use the words of Isaiah 40:31, what is your "hope in the
Lord?" What would your life look like if you laid hold of the
promises of God?

Every organization has a different statement of vision. Each
person's vision will also be different. I would ask an organization to
go through the painful process of writing out their statement of
vision, articulating their belief about themselves in words—words to
which they are willing to be held accountable. This is the first step
toward organizational renewal. As an organization rallies around its
vision, new energy is directed into its life.

I would suggest that you do the same assignment. Take the time
to try to express your personal vision of excellence before God in
words. Write it down. Share it with someone you trust. The very
process of articulating and communicating your vision is the first
step toward renewal. This becomes the standard by which you
measure all that you do in life.

Now I can imagine a few wrinkled brows here. Some might think
it improper to use this crass management technique in regard to the
spiritual life. I disagree! What do you want your spiritual life to look
like? Do you want to be a man or woman of God? What does this
mean? What would it look like if you were living your life in the
power of the Spirit of God, as you believe that God wants you to? We
worship a God who is Lord of our lives. What difference does that

make in your life? Write that out. The more detail the better.

The problem with many of us is that we have a vague feeling of discontent. We think we ought to be better than we are but we are not exactly sure how, and perhaps not sure we want to know. Articulating and communicating a vision requires us to take a stand and then to strive to live up to it.

Let's look at the second ingredient in organizational life.

b) A commitment to service

Organizations have learned that renewal comes when they focus on the intended results of their efforts rather than on the products they offer or the structures they have built. The current literature calls for an intense focus on the customer—a commitment to provide service to the customer, not to the organization.

If we apply this to Regent College, we would continually be asking how everything we do has an impact on the students' ability to understand and integrate their faith and live a life of active ministry. Achieving that result is more important than any building, course, curriculum, tradition or administrative model.

Now, does this ingredient for renewal have anything to say about personal renewal? I think so. I believe that it calls for a shift in focus from ourselves to our service to others. If our vision for excellence focuses on what *we* can achieve, what *we* can collect, what *we* need to feel good about life, renewal will always be just out of reach. Renewal comes when we focus our vision on what we can contribute, what we would like to accomplish in the lives of others. In other words, how we can serve and minister.

In a very real sense, we find personal renewal when we invest in the nurture and renewal in another person. Visions of excellence usually come alive when they are incarnated in application to others.

But there is a third ingredient, and this is the hard one.

c) Have the courage to break habits

Organizations, like people, form habits—traditions that are very difficult to change. It requires motivation, desire, and will to break habits. Usually in organizations (and people) it takes a crisis to provide the motivation.

But effective organizational leaders can encourage habit breaking by holding up a mirror, letting the organization see the reality of what it is doing—by listening to people, collecting ideas and evaluations and by questioning everything.

But, who holds up the mirror for individuals? That is where the community comes in!

Community is the enabler of renewal

In the world of organizational life this takes the form of participative management and team building. The leadership literature today stresses the importance of an organizational style that involves people, that builds them into a team or community. A leadership style is commended that provides structures that give meaning to people's work and creates ownership of the organizational outcomes; that treats people as valuable contributors to the institutional life and organizational mission and gives them freedom to take risks and grow; that encourages people to talk to people and question everything in the organization.

What is ironic is that you often find this incarnated better in secular corporations than in our Christian organizations.

When it comes to enabling the renewal of persons in their professional, personal and spiritual lives, I believe community becomes incarnate in other individuals. The community as such does not foster renewal. Rather, individual persons form intimate, caring relationships that provide a safe environment to take a risk, to test your wings, to live your vision, to break old habits.

This community relationship is captured well in a video cartoon that I use in a leadership course I teach. The cartoon picks up one theme from Isaiah 40. Let me share the story line:

As the cartoon starts out, we are taken to the high crags of a mountain top where we see a fluffy, scruffy little eaglet peering over the edge of its nest trying to get up the courage to fly. A full grown eagle descends to the nest and encourages the eaglet to try. The little eaglet takes one serious look over the edge, noticing in terror the ground far below the nest, and scurries to the back of the nest, hiding under its wings. Patiently but sternly, the eagle marches the eaglet out to the edge of the cliff and demonstrates how to use its wings, encouraging the fluffy little bird to take the risk. The little eaglet puffs up its tiny chest and jumps off the cliff, with wings flapping wildly, scattering baby fluff feathers. As we watch it plummeting toward the ground, it is evident that the little eaglet is completely out of control. As the eaglet plunges toward certain doom, the eagle above swoops down and scoops up the little bird on its back, communicating that everything is okay, and modelling how to use its wings.

When the little eaglet is deposited safely on the cliff again, the eagle encourages it to try once more. Again, the eaglet awkwardly jumps off the edge with wings flapping wildly, scattering baby fluff feathers. Again, the eaglet plunges out of control toward the ground.But this time, it begins to flap its wings, slow its fall and, finally, to fly, at first recklessly like a new teenage driver, and then more regally as befitting an eagle.

As the little eaglet stretches its wings and climbs into the sky, the cartoon shows the little bird evolving into a full grown eagle, gracefully gliding over the mountain tops, diving into the valleys, and soaring again into the heights. As it does, it spots a fluffy, scruffy little eaglet peering over the edge of its nest trying to get up the courage to test its wings. As the cartoon ends, the newly-grown eagle swoops down beside the little eaglet and begins to encourage it as it was encouraged.

This is the essence of community!

So, I leave you with three questions: What are the signs of entropy in your life, your relationships, your walk with God? What is your vision for excellence before God today? For whom are you the safe wings of community, enabling and empowering their renewal.

Our theme here is growth: being rooted and built up in Christ. "Rooted in Christ" images the energy drawn up by the Christian from our union with Christ. It is the source of energy that restrains the process of entropy in our spiritual development. "Built up" images the community structures and forces for renewal that are ours as members of the Body of Christ. Both are metaphors for the renewing spiritual power provided by our union with the risen Christ, the energy that inhibits entropy and stimulates renewal, the energy that finds its expression in the relationships of the Christian community.

Place your vision before God, risk the spreading of your wings to pursue the vision of excellence that you have set for yourself before God. And keep one eye open for other fluffy, scruffy eaglets who need you.

References

Max DePree, *Leadership is an Art*, Michigan State University Press, 1987.

John W. Gardner, *Renewing: The Leader's Creative Task*, Independent Sector, 1988.

Robert H. Waterman, Jr., *The Renewal Factor*, Bantam Books, 1987.

Contributors

Carl E. Armerding is Professor of Old Testament at Regent College and served as the College's Principal from 1978 to 1988.

Klaus Bockmuehl was Professor of Theology and Ethics at Regent College from 1979 to 1989 and served as Editor of *Crux* for four years. He died in June, 1989.

Jonathan Chao is an adjunct faculty member of Regent College. He also serves as Director of the Chinese Church Research Centre in Hong Kong, and is the President of Christ's College in Taipei, Taiwan.

William J. Dumbrell is currently the Vice-Principal of Moore Theological College in Sydney, Australia. He taught at Regent College in 1982-83 and from 1985-88 served as Academic Dean, in addition to teaching in both Old and New Testament studies.

Gordon D. Fee is Professor of New Testament at Regent College.

W. Ward Gasque has taught New Testament at Regent College since its founding and has served as the book review editor for *Crux*. He was recently appointed Provost of Eastern Baptist College in St. David's, Pennsylvania, and will continue his relationship with Regent College as an adjunct faculty member.

Julie Lane Gay is an alumna of Regent College who lives in Vancouver and currently serves in the Development Department of the College.

James M. Houston was the founding Principal of Regent College and now serves as Professor of Spiritual Theology at the College. He was the editor of *Crux* between 1979 and 1985.

Donald M. Lewis is Associate Professor of Church History at Regent College. He has been editor of *Crux* since 1989.

Preston Manning is a management consultant based in Edmonton, Alberta and is a former member of Regent College's Board of Governors. He is also the leader of a recently formed national political party.

Linda Mercadante is an alumna of Regent College. She earned her doctorate in theology from Princeton Theological Seminary and is an ordained minister in the Presbyterian Church of the United States of America. She is Associate Professor of Theology at the Methodist Theological School, located in Delaware, Ohio.

Philip G. Ney is a psychiatrist who teaches at the University of Victoria in Victoria, British Columbia and is a long-time friend of Regent College.

James I. Packer is a well-known author and is the Sangwoo Youtong Chee Professor of Theology at Regent College.

Murray Pura is a Regent College alumnus who serves as a pastor of a Baptist Church in Comox, British Columbia. He is also an author; in 1988 he published his first novel, *Mizzly Fitch*.

Luci Shaw is the President of Harold Shaw Publishers in Wheaton, Illinois. She also serves as a Writer-in-Residence at Regent College for six months of each year.

Bruce Waltke is Professor of Old Testament at Westminster Theological Seminary in Philadelphia. He taught at Regent College from 1976 to 1985 and is an adjunct member of the Regent College faculty.

Loren Wilkinson is Professor of Inter-Disciplinary Studies at Regent College.

Mary Ruth Wilkinson is a sessional lecturer at Regent College with a special interest in children's literature.

Walter C. Wright Jr. is President of Regent College. He has a special interest in the application of Christian principles to organizational management.